Thomas E. Willey, associate professor of history at McMaster University, has degrees from Butler University (B.A., 1959), and Yale University (M.A., and Ph.D., 1965). He has published in several scholarly journals.

BACK
TO
KANT

The Revival of Kantianism in German Social and
Historical Thought, 1860–1914

BACK TO KANT

The Revival of Kantianism
in German Social and Historical Thought,
1860–1914

Thomas E. Willey

McMaster University

Wayne State University Press

Detroit, 1978

Copyright © 1978 by Wayne State University Press,
Detroit, Michigan 48202. All rights are reserved.
No part of this book may be reproduced without formal permission.

Library of Congress Cataloging in Publication Data

Willey, Thomas E   1934–
  Back to Kant.

  Bibliography: p.
  Includes index.
  1. Neo-Kantianism. 2. Philosophers—Germany—
Biography. I. Title.
B3192.W54   142'.3   77-29215
ISBN 0-8143-1590-9

To Françoise

It is certainly true that
modern philosophy, insofar
as it is at all critical,
consists of a series of
footnotes on Kant.

W. Urban

Contents

Preface

The last quarter of the nineteenth century has been seen variously as a time of increasing cultural pessimism or as a generation of optimistic materialism. Both descriptions ring true, depending on what segment of the European public one is describing: the avant-garde intellectuals or the comfortable middle classes. Yet students of this period are aware that there was an impending spiritual crisis, a progressive erosion of confidence in the general tenets of liberalism bequeathed to modern civilization by the Enlightenment. The vitalism of Nietzsche and the libido theory of Freud were only two of the more dramatic symptoms of the imminent replacement of rational, technological man by psychological, instinctual man, at least in the minds of a growing number of philosophers, social thinkers, and imaginative writers.

Although the cult of scientific positivism and faith in unlimited human development through political reform and technical innovation were by no means dead, the Crystal Palace was crumbling and Underground Man, first announced by Dostoevsky in the 1860s, was struggling to the surface, asserting his willfulness and refusing to agree that two and two make four. But there was an important countertendency—the revival of idealism, especially in the neo-Kantian current of that revival. The neo-Kantian movement was naturally of German provenance, but it eventually affected all European cultures to some extent from England to Russia. The aims of neo-idealism were to reassert the role of human consciousness in the historical process, to establish a methodology for humanistic studies different from that of the physical sciences, and to defend the efficacy of moral striving in the political arena against the claims of economic determinism. Neo-idealists as diverse in doctrines as Hermann Cohen in Germany, Jean Jaurès in France, and T.H. Green in England were trying to rescue rational and moral man from the impending shipwreck of classical liberalism. They were, in fact, trying to bring liberalism and socialism into line with the new realities of mass industrial society in the closing decades of the century. In practical terms they wanted to overcome the antipathy of the liberal middle classes toward enfranchisement of labor and toward

9

social welfare through state interference. The socialists among them hoped to steer the working-class movement away from revolutionary Marxism and in the direction of democratic socialism, or social reform through the ballot and parliamentary debate.

Owing to the comparative weakness of the German Reichstag under Bismarck's constitution, the neo-Kantians achieved very little in Germany, where their movement was academically the strongest. Indeed, they would have to wait for the military defeat of 1918 for the attainment of most of their practical goals. But failure is no reason to neglect their efforts or to assume with the advantage of hindsight that they were doomed from the start. The vigor of social democracy in the Federal Republic today is in some measure indirectly owed to their contribution, and in their own time they greatly enriched the discussion of significant historical and social issues confronting the new German empire. The subject of neo-Kantianism, to which this essay is devoted, illustrates the complexity of the German past and suggests that the notion of a straight march from Sedan to Stalingrad, or from Nietzsche to Hitler, is the kind of reductionism which has bedeviled the interpretation of German history for most of our century. There is no legitimate place for Procrustes' bed in the historian's workshop.

Acknowledgments

A project in the making as long as this one acquires a great burden of personal and professional debts. The first and greatest is to my family, whose encouragement and forbearance have been unfaltering—especially to my wife to whom the book is dedicated. She typed several earlier versions of the manuscript, but her countless gifts of confidence and affection were much more important.

It was the late Professor Hajo Holborn of Yale University, then doyen of German historians in America, who originally called my attention to Heinrich Rickert and the neo-Kantians. Professor Holborn was my supervisor when this essay began as a doctoral thesis in 1962. He shared with me not only his great knowledge but his delightful sense of humor, warning me at one point that some of my ponderous footnotes were becoming too "Germanic." I must also thank three other Yale mentors for introducing me to the pleasures and elusions of intellectual history: Franklin Le Van Baumer, and Leonard Krieger, now of the University of Chicago. And finally, the late and unforgettable Lewis Perry Curtis, who combined tough standards, kindness, and rare wit in his memorable seminar.

The friendships that have sustained me through nearly twelve years of further research and revision are too numerous to mention, but·I am compelled to single out the following: David J. Russo, fellow graduate student and now colleague; the late Richard Cauger, boon companion and frequent fellow traveler to Indiana University; William J. Brazill of Wayne State University, whose advice has been crucial in many areas; John Campbell, Harvey Levenstein, R.H. Johnston, Alan Cassels, and C.M. Johnston of McMaster University, those extraordinary morale builders who contributed laughter and helped me to keep many matters in perspective. The latter, C.M. Johnston, his wife Lorna and entire clan, including Mr. and Mrs. John Kempf, have helped make Canada an irresistible second homeland for my family. I must also express appreciation to my colleague Jiri Fabsic, who translated the Fischer-Liebmann correspondence from very obscure German handwriting.

11

A Faculty fellowship granted by the President and Trustees of Butler University in Indianapolis allowed me reduced teaching duties and made possible an earlier revision of this essay. The Arts Research Committee of McMaster University provided three generous grants deriving from Canada Council funds, which supported summer research trips to the British Museum, and to the libraries and archives of the universities of Freiburg and Heidelberg. I should like to thank the personnel of those institutions for their assistance and counsel.

Special bouquets go to Sheena Gorman and Jean Radigan of the department of history at McMaster University. Both their typing services and their unfailing good humor were instrumental in bringing the manuscript through its final phases. Also, there must be a word of gratitude to Professor and Mrs. F.N. Shrive for their friendship, and to Professor David Damas for that and for keeping me reminded that deadlines are not to be taken lightly. Finally, I owe thanks to Marguerite C. Wallace, editor, Wayne State University Press, for her experience and expertise.

1

The Political and
Intellectual Setting

Liberal Philosophy and Politics in the Burgher Century

If sixteenth-century burgher civilization can be called a German invention, then it would be no great exaggeration to say that nineteenth-century civilization was in large measure the invention of German burghers.[1] Germany, with its highly successful institutionalization of scientific activity, came to lead the world in what Alfred North Whitehead called the distinctive achievement of the century—the invention of invention itself. The nineteenth century was, indeed, the age of the German bourgeoisie.[2] Without overlooking what was accomplished elsewhere, for example, in Britain from Darwin to Rutherford, it can be fairly said that the era of scholarship beginning with Ranke's historical seminar and culminating in the new physics of Einstein, Planck, and Heisenberg was an age of genius. And this dramatic revolution in physics was accompanied by equally startling developments in other areas, most notably psychology and music. The most dynamic ideology of modern times, exceeded only by nationalism as a historical force and solvent, was revolutionary socialism, another German invention. The coup de grace came from Friedrich Nietzsche, another German from the middle class, who made a devastating assault on modern Christianity.

13

In the nineteenth century Germany experienced a secular Great Awakening of bourgeois talent, a surge of creativity that generated baffling and often contradictory tendencies. It could surely be called Wagnerian with its superabundance of energy, its reaching for the infinite, for the cosmic perspective, while at the same time penetrating the Orphean realm of myth and psyche. And it was Wagnerian also in its tendency toward excess and its lapses into vulgarity. Yet, the same generation which celebrated Sadowa and Sedan and flocked to Bayreuth produced the Kantian revival with its critique of Hegelian metaphysics and its insistence on rational limits and moral values. It also witnessed the ambiguous phenomenon of Nietzsche, without doubt the most radical heir of German humanistic individualism and the most uncompromising critic of national hubris as exemplified by his one-time idol, Wagner. But they both belonged to the future also: in Nietzsche's existential transvaluation of all values and in Wagner's dissonances in *Tristan* we can discern aspects of twentieth-century modernist culture. The intriguing paradox is that German *Kultur*, steeped in nostalgia for preindustrial times and deeply immersed in reverence for its own classical heritage, probably more than any other European culture caused the dissolution of traditional science and art.

The German bourgeoisie was just as successful in economics as in scholarship and art. Although Germany challenged the industrial leaders only after 1871, the conditions for "take-off' were appearing during the Restoration. The Customs Union, the mechanization of textiles and mining, the application of chemistry to agriculture, the development of internal transport, and the creation of credit facilities were well underway by 1848.[3] The revolutions of 1848 marked a new stage in the political consciousness of the middle class; but 1848 also revealed a lack of revolutionary realism and a myopic social vision on the part of the middle-class rebels. The largely self-serving economic program of the bourgeois liberals at Frankfurt deprived them of mass support and destroyed the spontaneous revolutionary front of early spring.

It has been persuasively argued that the social philosophy of pre-1848 liberalism in Germany was not a narrow Manchester ideology. There were social liberals who favored a degree of state regulation of working conditions so that Germany might avoid the abuses of early industrialism experienced in England.[4] Besides, German social thought in the tradition of Fichte, Hegel, and Friedrich List expressed a positive idea of the state. Even the natural-law heritage, going back to Pufendorf in the seventeenth century, was statist, unlike the English Lockean. tradition with its contention that freedom requires minimum government from the state. German liberalism, which evolved within a framework of princely and bureaucratic absolutism, should harbor no particular aversion to social welfare. The conversion of the National Liberal party between 1879 and 1889 from free trade and laissez-faire to protectionism and social welfare would seem to confirm that prognosis. After 1889, only the left-wing liberals, the Progressives, and their offshoots, stuck to laissez-faire and free trade. Nonetheless, the bourgeois liberals of 1848-49 stood very close to their Smithian relatives in England: "Despite their occasional efforts to end industrial abuses the liberals refused to meddle in the practice of laissez faire legalized by the [Prussian] decrees of September 7, 1811, and January 17, 1848."[5] The liberals at Frankfurt clearly showed their intentions in the economic committee's report on the industrial code. "Liberalism was a more zealous champion of the factory and the bank than conservatism in its heyday had dared to be."[6] This social rift between liberalism and labor was, according to Hamerow, the main reason for the failure of the liberal revolutions and deepened in the 1860s when Germany's modern political parties began to form roughly on class lines. This development was of great concern to a group of neo-Kantian philosophers at the University of Marburg who attempted to close the ideological gap with a new kind of social liberalism based on the ethics of Kant.

The liberals of 1848 were also hampered by their support of monarchy, the very institution they were trying to reform and capture for the national cause. As O'Boyle has pointed out, the liberals were not aiming for exclusive power but for partnership with the monarchical state.[7] The cultural, political, and social tenets of the liberal creed were designed to justify middle-class recognition by and participation in government, but social prejudice militated against success. This prejudice, greatly aggravated by elemental fear and growing class hatred during the revolution itself, was also reinforced by the Weltanschauung of German humanism. The humanistic tradition was built on the ideal of personal *Bildung* or moral and aesthetic cultivation through classical education. But the opportunity for *Bildung* was well beyond the reach of the lower classes; it was also irrelevant to their needs and interests. The combined effect of classical humanism and ethical idealism later created a two-edged attitude on the part of the educated middle class which not only isolated it from the lower classes but after 1848 gradually estranged it from its former allies of the commercial and industrial bourgeoisie. The legacy of German classicism, originally created in the late Enlightenment as the cultural expression of a bourgeois revolt against aristocratic privilege, princely absolutism, and the slavish imitation of French culture, narrowed slowly until it became the moral and aesthetic defense of a privileged but increasingly beleaguered caste.[8]

Thus Theodor Fontane exaggerated the apparent openness and freshness of middle-class culture when he wrote: "A new power has established itself: the intelligent bourgeoisie, its face turned away from the medieval, and toward progress. Free from tradition and prejudice, it lives for the sake of *this* world and sees happiness in property and in the celebration of the secular."[9] The middle class was not, as Fontane thought, free from prejudice, and soon developed quasi-feudal attitudes of its own. But it was the standard bearer in intellectual life and, up to a certain point, in politics as well. The closing decades of the nineteenth century seemed to confirm Hegel's dictum that the requisite of national development is a strong middle class.[10]

The elitist implications of cultural humanism encouraged many liberal burghers to assume that they were the exclusive agents of progress and universal rights.[11] Their notion of who constituted the active citizenry was no more democratic than was the French Constitution of 1791 or the English Reform Bill of 1832. Citizenship required the possession of *Bildung und Besitz*—education and property—qualifications which allegedly fitted the middle class for its cultural and political mission. The Rhenish businessman David Hansemann expressed this attitude when he said: "A true majority consists of those who have property, culture and knowledge, and have the interests of the nation at heart."[12] The liberal movement in Germany remained essentially anti-democratic to the end of the century, for it ignored the lesson it might have learned from the solid popular support it received during the constitutional struggle with Bismarck from 1862 to 1866.[13] But whether for cultural or economic reasons, or for genuine fear of democratic Caesarism or mobocracy, the German bourgeoisie was only reluctantly brought into the age of democracy by way of defeat and revolution in 1918–19.

Thus the rapid ascent of the German middle class in the nineteenth century was not an unqualified triumph because the burghers deprived themselves of what could have been their most powerful weapon. When some of the liberal leaders (Weber and Friedrich Naumann, for instance) finally got on the democratic bandwagon in the 1890s, they were already outflanked on both sides by the socialist and Catholic parties. Consequently, while the middle class was acquiring property, culture, and knowledge to a remarkable degree, its drive for political influence commensurate with its wealth and education was faltering. The prosperous and literate bourgeoisie failed to attain the form of government and the extent of power it sought in the abortive revolutions of 1848 and later was able to influence the policies of Bismarck only when its ideals and interests happened to coincide with those of the Prussified state. Bismarck realized that middle-class wealth and talent were indispensable to a strong Germany, but he successfully thwarted the efforts of the liberal politicians to make their class the principal partner of the state through representative institutions accountable to the middle-class political parties.[14] He was able by his impressive triumphs in foreign affairs and his deeply divisive manipulation of social tensions at home, to defeat the liberals in their struggle for true parliamentary government and civic freedom. Often many liberals were themselves unwilling to accomodate sectarian minorities and unprivileged social classes; they even cooperated with Bismarck in such nonliberal programs as the *Kulturkampf* and the banning of organized socialism. These persecutions revealed the limits of middle-class liberalism and forecast the fragmentation of German politics in the twentieth century. In retrospect, the problem was that the middle class feared its old rival, German Catholicism, as well as its new antagonist, the industrial proletariat, more than it resented the abridgment of its own ideals.

It is generally believed that Bismarck defeated not only the Austrians at Königgrätz but the liberals as well. Lacking civil courage during Bismarck's four years of unconstitutional rule, then dazzled by the brilliant victories of the Prussian army, the liberals rendered ecstatic homage to blood and iron, indemnified the Prussian minister president, and thereby traded liberty for unity and national power. What the liberals had sought for decades to achieve with their own resources was accomplished in a few weeks by the authoritarian state with its order, its army, and its discipline.[15] The expression "Now one should accept the accomplished fact" ("Jetzt müsse man sich mit der vollendeten Tatsache abfinden"—according to Ziekursch, a slogan of the victorious hour) was by most accounts a fitting epitaph for German liberalism. But the genuflection of the liberals before the altar of Prussianism appears the more compromising in the light of later history than in 1866. The German liberals were no different from other Western European liberals in accepting what they considered the necessary employment of force to attain legitimate national objectives. And, after all, the victory was over clerical, reactionary Austria. The tragedy was in the timing, for it was the peculiar misfortune of German liberalism that it yielded to the imperatives of power in the midst of its struggle with the principal wielders of that power, the monarchy and the aristocracy.

To continue the internal fight after Königgrätz would have not only repudiated the astounding successes which were being greeted almost universally by all classes in Prussia but would have also disavowed one of the cardinal goals of liberalism itself—German nationhood. For other Western European liberals, the dilemma of liberty and power did not present itself so starkly, for to them national unity was a reality of long standing. It is questionable whether in the German predicament (and in the larger context of nineteenth-century nationalism) the liberals could perceive an alternative. To the liberal of 1866 it was half-a-loaf or nothing, but he could look ahead to the prospect of a genuine parliamentary and lawful state which he could now begin to develop within the new nation created on the field of battle. That this evolution did not take place was as much the fault of the defensive social philosophy of German liberalism as it was of its much-criticized nationalistic *trahison des clercs*.[16] The Prussian state with its army was both the victor at Königgrätz and the only protection against social revolution.

But left-wing liberalism did not vanish after the indemnity vote of September 3, 1866. The Progressives lost ground in the elections of 1867 for the Diet of the Confederation, but they elected eighty-seven deputies, and their leader Eugen Richter continued vigorously to oppose Bismarck's policies.[17] The left-wing liberal factions attained a new electoral peak in 1881 when they managed to return 105 deputies and became the second largest party. Thereafter, their fortunes varied, and they generally remained smaller than the National Liberals. In 1890, they enjoyed another brief resurgence and again outpolled the National Liberals. After that, down to the last prewar federal election in 1912, they ran closely behind their right-liberal opponents, electing forty-two deputies in 1912 to forty-five for the National Liberals. The progressive factions, contrary to the conventional view, were by no means dead after 1866. Beginning in the 1890s, the left wing of the German liberal movement began gingerly to shift away from laissez-faire individualism and to consider at least a tactical alliance with the socialists against Junkerdom, autocracy, and big business. Occasional second-ballot cooperation in the 1890s culminated in the election of 1912, when the socialists became the largest party in the Reichstag with help from their left-wing liberal allies. But this conversion came too late. The Progressives had waited too long to abandon their Samuel Smiles philosophy and their antidemocratic sentiments. The right-wing liberals, however, had broken away in 1867 to support Bismarck's constitution and to establish themselves formally as the National Liberal party. But the die-hard Progressives remained in opposition.

Unfortunately the Progressive party was limited from its very inception in 1861 by its rejection of political democracy. The Progressives wanted a constitutional nation-state, not a democratic republic. Many of the early Progressives were also prominent members of the *Nationalverein,* established in 1859 to promote German unity and constitutionality under the aegis of Prussia. Hermann Schulze-Delitzsch, a charter member of both organizations, referred to the founding committee of the Progressive party as the "Executive of the *Nationalverein.*"[18] The dues were so costly that laborers were originally excluded from it, and when they were offered only honorary membership without voting privileges, Ferdinand Lassalle was vindicated in his view that cooperation with the bourgeois politicians was futile. In 1863, he formed the *Allgemeine Deutsche Abeiterverein,* an avowedly proletarian organization which looked to the Prussian state rather than to the liberal movement for its salvation.[19] Lassalle believed that acquisition of power through the democratic ballot was imperative; thus the breach between the Lassalle movement and the Progressives was inevitable, given the latter's refusal to include universal manhood suffrage in their platform.

The basic problem was that many Progressives feared democracy and blamed it for the "anarchy" of 1848. When the inveterate democrat Johann Jacoby used the term *democratic party* (*demokratische Partei*) in an article prepared for the *Danziger Zeitung,* its Progressive editor altered the expression to read, *secular Progressive party* (*freisinnige Fortschrittspartei*), and excused himself on the grounds that "in Danzig even dedicated opponents of the ministry have a horror of the word Democracy."[20] Yet to be effective, the middle-class opposition to Bismarck needed to win mass support by promising the ballot and social reform. Here is precisely where German liberalism erred. This failure encouraged the tendency of major parties to form along class lines and gave credibility to the Marxist view that the barrier between bourgeoisie and proletariat was insuperable. A few, such as Leopold Sonnemann, Ludwig Büchner, Ludwig Eckhardt, and the neo-Kantian F.A. Lange who represented the left, or democratic, wing of Progressivism tried to prevent the class split by supporting counterorganizations like August Bebel's *Verband Deutscher Arbeitervereine,* and the South German *Volkspartei* (anti-Prussian, democratic, and federalist).[21] Their strategy was to unite labor with democratic elements of the middle class in common opposition to social injustice and the Prussian hegemony. In the middle sixties, the socialists Bebel and Wilhelm Liebknecht wanted an alliance with the bourgeois democrats and were willing to overlook the theoretical differences between socialism and middle-class democracy.[22] But most of the petty bourgeois democrats clung to the doctrine of *Selbst-hilfe*, and their continued neglect of social issues into the late sixties gradually destroyed their credibility with the socialist leaders.

Bebel had as little success in collaborating with the democrats as Lassalle's union had in trying to woo a significant number of workers. The course followed by the anti-Lassalle socialists eventually took them to Eisenach in 1869, where they founded the German Socialist Workers' party. Their program was democratic and moderately Marxian, with a profession of affiliation with the Socialist International that, in effect, terminated the alliance with bourgeois democracy.[23]

Admittedly this breach would have been difficult to prevent, and the dilemma faced by the liberals has usually been underestimated. The decision of the *Nationalverein* to take no position on suffrage and to include no workers among them was dictated by their concern of frightening away moderate bourgeois support, for fear of the *Rote Gefahr* still haunted the propertied classes. It would also have required Delphic wisdom to construct a program of social reform that would have appealed to a heterogeneous working class in a state of transition from handicraft to industry.[24] The preindustrial workers wanted preservation and extension of the guild privileges which had been partially restored after 1848; the industrial workers were still weak and only beginning to organize in the 1860s. Moreover, the corporative and hierarchical economy favored by the guildsmen had long been the basis of autocracy and conservatism, which the liberals wanted to undermine. The liberals could not go back to an illiberal paternalism any more than they could at that time go forward into the new social liberalism of the 1880s, which was predicated upon the rapid expansion of the industrial labor force and the abandonment of doctrinaire individualism by the National Liberal party for political and economic expediency. Even then the left-wing liberals remained trapped for a decade in rigid ideas and fears which doomed them to parliamentary impotence in a purely oppositional role.

But after the failure of petty bourgeois democracy in the 1860s and the left-wing liberal, labor rift in 1869, there were still prominent middle-class intellectuals who knew that the Reich democratic franchise and the Reichstag itself were frauds—merely window dressing for an empire dominated by Prussia, the Junker aristocracy, and the new plutocracy. They also knew that the liberal vision of a German lawful state was a chimera so long as this coalition of powerful interests manipulated by Bismarck was able to deny the urban masses their rightful weight on the political and social scales. And some of these progressive intellectuals also recognized that the puffed-up cultural chauvinism born of the *Gründerzeit* was a dangerous substitute for the eighteenth-century bequest of cosmopolitan liberalism; they, therefore, stressed the importance of Germany's cultural ties with the West. Those influenced by neo-Kantian theories hoped that Kant's philosophy could be used to build bridges between social classes and between Germany and Europe, as well as provide new epistemologies for science and history.

The Political and Social Implications of Neo-Kantian Thought

The ideas and attitudes of those intellectual liberals who were associated with the revival of Kant's philosophy formed one of the main threads of German thought in the second half of the century.[25] The neo-Kantian movement was the work of middle-class professors, a few of whom took an active interest in politics and social reform. Neo-Kantianism emerged in the late 1850s and early 1860s, achieved academic supremacy in the 1890s, and rapidly lost its academic preeminence (but not its entire following) after 1914. The neo-Kantians did not manage to redeem German liberalism. They were impeded not only by an unpropitious political environment but also by serious limitations of their own. Yet neo-Kantianism did give liberal thought a needed fillip just when it seemed that the ideals of 1848 were dead. The application of Kant's ethics to social questions offered an opportunity to remedy the most serious deficiency of German liberalism—its narrowness and its inability to develop a broad social philosophy reaching beyond the confines of the professional, academic, and propertied middle class.

The social philosophy of Lange and the Marburg neo-Kantians did not convert many liberal and socialist politicians, but its effects did reach beyond the universities. Not only were academicians of national stature such as Weber and Troeltsch influenced in varying degree by neo-Kantian doctrines but mavericks in the Social Democratic party as well, most notably Eduard Bernstein and Kurt Eisner.[26] Neo-Kantianism created an alliance of political sympathy between a handful of left-wing liberals and a number of socialist intellectuals who were dissatisfied with doctrinaire Marxism. It was a promising alliance, prefiguring in part the Weimar Coalition, and potentially capable of closing the chasm of mistrust between liberalism and social democracy.[27] Unfortunately, the alliance was tentative and weak. And it is doubtful whether, short of revolution, a liberal-labor combination would have been able to defeat the industrial-agrarian interests in the Reichstag. The chances for peacefully legislating imperial Germany into an industrial democracy seem in retrospect very remote indeed. But some modest degree of integration of the middle and laboring classes through democracy and social reform could have been achieved before 1914 only by the joint efforts of the two principal industrial classes, each willing to use the resources of the other and to abandon its own sterile preachments. There were some gestures in this direction: The dissenting vote against the anti-socialist law in 1878; the "socialists of the chair" and their recognition of labor's problems; Naumann's national socialism; second-ballot cooperation at the polls, most successfully in 1912; and the continuing but fruitless campaign against the three-class voting system in Prussia.[28] Perhaps most promising was the tentative rapprochement between left-wing liberals and Eduard Bernstein's revisionists beginning under the changed conditions of the 1890s. The Marburg neo-Kantians sought to provide a theoretical touchstone for such pragmatic cooperation. That they did not succeed is no reason for the historian to write off their efforts as insignificant. By evaluating the strengths and weaknesses of neo-Kantian social philosophy, it can be seen that there was much more on the spectrum of German politics than red and black. Nothing more quickly dispels the notion that the Second Reich was an era exclusively of *völkisch* neo-romanticism, ambivalent social democracy, and state-worshiping liberalism than a study of neo-Kantianism, for here is revealed the complexity, the richness, and—unhappily—the unrealized possibilities of German intellectual life before World War I.

Although the neo-Kantians did not succeed in uniting liberalism and socialism, neo-Kantian speculation on the logic of the humanities encouraged a reappraisal of historical method. As a consequence, the philosophical problems raised by German historicism were faced anew. The ensuing discussion of values and objectivity in historical judgment influenced such leading figures of the Wilhelmine intelligentsia as Weber, Troeltsch, and Meinecke, and helped produce a new concept of history, distinct from that of the physical sciences.

The most enduring achievement of neo-Kantianism was in the logic of the *Geisteswissenschaften*. But the neo-Kantian theory of historical knowledge developed by the Baden or Heidelberg school of Wilhelm Windelband and Heinrich Rickert had definite cultural and political implications. Their theory of value is the key to the politics of Baden neo-Kantianism, just as Kantian ethics is the key to the politics of Marburg neo-Kantianism. The word value in neo-Kantian literature often leads to confusion because it has several meanings. In the historical methodology of Windelband and Rickert, value means a subjective criterion of selection, or a category of historical thought. Values are also taken to signify the actual products (*Güter*) of cultural history. Then again value can mean an unconditioned standard of what "ought to be," a transcendent value unaffected by the time-bound judgment of the historian.[29] Behind this often perplexing discussion of values lay the fundamental questions of neo-Kantianism: How to find appropriate but distinct methodologies for the physical and humanistic sciences, how to overcome the relativistic implications of historicism, and how to establish human autonomy against the claims of scientific determinism.

Just as a eudaemonistic value theory predisposed the Benthamites in England toward a utilitarian view of politics and society, so the fundamentally Kantian value theory of the intellectual liberals in Germany shaped their social and political beliefs. The key to Kant's value theory in relation to society is his contention that the purpose of social existence is not happiness or useful citizenship (though he did not rule out these utilitarian values as natural and desirable) but the freedom of the individual to enhance his moral worth under laws hypothetically of his own making. Historically, man civilizes himself in this manner in order to make himself first worthy of happiness in a republic of laws. In contrast to the felicific calculating of the Benthamites to determine how to make most men happy, the neo-Kantians wanted to create social conditions conducive to making some men good and protecting the personal autonomy of all. The eudaemonism of utilitarian ethics was repugnant to them because it sought the lowest common denominator among men instead of the highest ("given an equal amount of pleasure, pushpin is as good as poetry") and based the social good on transitory notions of happiness. This qualitative social ethics of neo-Kantianism, built on Kant's doctrine that the only absolutely good thing is a good will, was truly in the spirit of the elitist humanism of *Bildungsliberalismus* already described. But it did not preclude expansion into a democratic ethics as in the case of Marburg neo-Kantianism.

Undoubtedly, the neo-Kantians were also affected by the problems facing their own social class. According to Karl Mannheim, one of the postulates of post-Hegelian sociology is that the "history of the human mind expresses the consecutive tensions and reconciliations of groups."[30] Without accepting this formula literally, I believe the neo-Kantians expressed the tentative and unsuccessful efforts of a segment of the upper bourgeoisie to make peace with the proletariat and to retain an attitude of cultural community with the West. Mannheim has also suggested some useful criteria for the study of intellectual groups: The social background of the intellectuals themselves, their particular associations, and their functions in the larger society.[31] These questions will be asked of the neo-Kantians; therefore, something will be said about the personal background of each before describing his ideas. But first, early neo-Kantianism must be placed in its historical situation.

The Divergence of Philosophy from Politics and Science

Perhaps only in the barren interval between the death of Leibniz and Kant's inaugural dissertation had German philosophy seemed more sterile than in the 1850s. The philosophical scene at mid-century has been compared to a battlefield strewn with corpses and debris.[32] Idealism, the strongest of German traditions, seemed in full retreat. It had taken deep root in the soil of German mysticism, Protestantism, and pietism, but was transformed by Kant into a secular ethics for the middle class, and his Copernican Revolution, announced in the *Critique of Pure Reason*, brought German epistemology into the age of Newtonian science. But then Fichte and Hegel transmogrified the Kantian legacy from critical into absolute idealism, resolving its dualities in abstruse and ultimately monistic concepts. After Hegel died in 1831, his followers argued over, among many other matters, the rationality of the real. This was a crucial debate. It led to the young Hegelian conversion of Hegel's metaphysics into the secular humanism of Feuerbach and the radical application of the dialectic to social history by Marx and Engels. But idealism was temporarily in decline.[33] Dramatic developments in science and politics hastened this, and caused the rise of materialism. Rapid advances in nineteenth-century science made Hegel's metaphysics and the "scientific" theories of *Naturphilosophie* seem quaintly inadequate; and a growing awareness of the disparity between philosophical aspirations and political realities after the unsuccessful revolutions of 1848 eroded faith in the progress of reason.[34]

Early in the second quarter of the century, German science began to show the first signs of its later greatness. In the German universities, until the late 1820s, a hybrid *Naturphilosophie* had been taught which, as Dampier says, "deduced its conclusions from doubtful philosophic theories instead of obtaining them by the patient study of phenomena."[35] In 1826, Liebig, who had studied under Guy-Lussac in Paris, founded his laboratory at Giessen. One year later, the lectures of Alexander von Humboldt in Berlin raised empirical science, as Alfred Dove put it, "to the spiritual throne of the time."[36] During the same quarter century, Robert Mayer, Christian Gauss, and Hermann Helmholtz brought further prestige to German science in physics, pure mathematics, and optics. The old idealist philosophy of nature (one of whose proponents had defined the diamond as quartz which has achieved self-consciousness) could no longer be taken seriously by the rising generation of tough-minded, empirical scientists.[37] The indifferent response to Schelling's inaugural lecture at the University of Berlin, November 15, 1841, was mute testimony to the decline of speculative philosophy. (Schelling's Berlin lectures of 1841 were heard by Kierkegaard, Bakunin, Engels, and Burckhardt, and thus his anti-Hegelianism contributed to the rising crescendo of criticism directed at Hegel's metaphysics by the Young Hegelians and others who were going beyond Hegel or rejecting him altogether as a negative and abstract philosopher. The diverse anti-Hegelians of the 1840s, including Schopenhauer, cleared the way for the Kantian revival later.)[38]

The methods of the natural sciences, of physics, chemistry, and especially physiology soon became paradigmatic for the historical sciences. By the middle of the century empiricism was so firmly ensconced that it became virtually a metaphysical cult. The uncritical worship of empirical method produced a crude philosophical materialism which briefly became the Weltanschauung of the age. The materialists believed that "matter, with its primary properties and their relations as revealed by science, are the ultimate realities, and that human bodies are mechanisms, though perhaps occasionally controlled . . . by minds."[39] Crude materialism was sometimes capable of even greater absurdities than *Naturphilosophie*. Jakob Moleschott explained mental activity by using the physical analogy that the brain secretes thoughts just as the liver secretes bile.[40] In *Energy and Matter* (1855), Ludwig Büchner reduced consciousness to molecular configurations. His bestseller went through nineteen editions by 1898. Only Ernst Haeckel achieved comparable success in the genre of popular scientific literature; his *World Riddle* (1899) reached seven editions within two years of publication. By 1926, it had been translated into twenty-five languages, and 400,000 copies were in print.[41] Popular materialism and Haeckel's monism continued to grip the public mind long after scientists had rejected the gross simplifications of Büchner and his successors.

The naive scientism of the 1850s—which added little to the eighteenth-century materialism of Condillac, La Mettrie, and Holbach—eventually had a constructive influence, for it concerned more sophisticated scientists like Helmholtz and Liebig so that they began to reexamine the relation between science and philosophy and to question the foundations of scientific knowledge. This process of reappraisal led them back to Kant.[42] Kant seemed the appropriate authority for one in search of an epistemology attuned to modern science. Helmholtz, first of the scientists to advocate Kant's epistemology, deplored the increasing separation between science and philosophy, for which he blamed the Hegelians. He believed that, in Kant's time, science and philosophy had been in harmony and that "Kant's philosophy rested on exactly the same grounds as the physical sciences."[43] The crucial test of any philosophy are the facts of nature, but it was here, Helmholtz thought, "that Hegel's philosophy utterly broke down."[44] Materialism was faulty for the same reason.

There were other prominent scientists who did not share Helmholtz's aversion to materialism. The chief advocates of materialism—Karl Vogt, H.C. Czolbe, Büchner, Jakob Moleschott, and their followers—brought the so-called materialism conflict into the open during the scientific convention held at Göttingen in September 1854. At this time the scientific community was deeply divided over the philosophical issues raised by the materialists. The Göttingen debate brought epistemological issues to the foreground and quite naturally encouraged the subsequent return to Kant's critical standpoint. In addition, as a sensitive religious question was involved, the "struggle for the soul," Kant's dualism was attractive to the defenders of Christian doctrine because it preserved an "unknowable" noumenal domain for the regulative ideas of God, freedom, and immortality transcending physical laws. Men of a scientific disposition could have at the same time both their faith and their science, because Kant's theory of knowledge gave full justice to the phenomenal domain governed by the mechanical principle of causality. Kant's dualism was, to many German thinkers, an appealing compromise in an age of transition from Christian belief to a wholly naturalistic view of the universe. To the extent that Kant had demolished the claims of metaphysics without denying the ultimate truths of religion, he also appealed to the skeptical temper of a generation disenchanted with speculative philosophy and enamored of physical science but not yet ready to jettison its transcendental beliefs altogether.

The materialists were coming under fire not only for their physiological and mechanistic theories but also for the political and religious implications of their ideas. Many were critics of the Prussian regime; they considered themselves free thinkers and champions of political liberty.[45] Karl Vogt, for example, was an outspoken radical democrat in the Frankfurt parliament of 1848.[46] The materialists were also thought to be enemies of religion, for they seemed to be repudiating such important articles of Christian orthodoxy as the independent existence of the soul. It soon became difficult for professed materialists to hold jobs. Büchner was dismissed from Tübingen and Moleschott from Heidelberg. David Friedrich Strauss, author of the controversial *Life of Jesus* (1835), suffered similar difficulties. Strauss was an errant Hegelian who used the critical method of the Tübingen *Stift* to reduce the life of Christ from history to myth. Later, his *The Old Faith and the New* (1872) became the vade mecum of positivism and a literary monument to the middle-class worship of science. This successful but banal book provoked Nietzsche's famous attack on the Philistines in *David Strauss the Confessor and Author*. In spite of Nietzsche's occasional japes at Kant, his scathing indictment of Strauss's shallow materialism was an expression of the same mood that fostered the neo-Kantian critique of positivism and encouraged the return to Kant's anti-eudaemonistic ethics. The distance between the moral humanism of the neo-Kantians and Nietzsche's heroic ethics was great indeed, but they shared in common the incipient crisis in values and the search for ethical ideals beyond the accommodating bourgeois values of the era represented by Strauss. Nietzsche's anarchic cultural individualism was at bottom no more than an extreme expression of the moral *Bildungsideal* which the neo-Kantians were trying to revive in a spirit appropriate to modern industrial society. Straussian optimism rested on assumptions equally repulsive to Nietzsche and the neo-Kantians, because both belonged to the German tradition which saw the autonomous and self-developing personality as the nodal point of the moral universe.[47]

Strauss's *Life of Jesus* helped aggravate the breaking up of Hegelianism into left and right wings. It was Strauss, in fact, who first applied the misleading dichotomy *left and right* to the fissiparous Hegelian school. The collapse of Hegel's imposing synthesis, therefore, was brought on not only by the criticisms of eminent scientists like Helmholtz but also by dissension among the Hegelians themselves. Picking up the revolutionary implications of the dialectic, the left-wingers began to move along the entire range of radical politics, from socialism to anarchism. The right-wingers, or conservative Hegelians, stressed the identity of reality with reason and championed religious orthodoxy. They were execrated by their opponents, in some cases unfairly, as defenders of the political reaction and as mandarins of Prussian absolutism.[48] When Marx and Engels appropriated the dialectic and gave it social and economic substance in place of Mind or Spirit, Hegelianism was inverted and the philosophical assumptions of pre-March historical metaphysics were profoundly challenged. Political developments further attenuated the optimistic premises of absolute idealism.

Through the 1830s and 1840s, the actual course of politics in Germany and Western Europe seemed increasingly to belie Hegelian confidence in the historical immanence of reason. After the ineffective social rumblings in Germany that followed the July Revolution in France, the supposed congruency of Hegel's immanent reason with political evolution appeared unconvincing if not totally false. Then Hegel's philosophy of state, with its emphasis on the progressive character of Prussian institutions, was given the coup de grace in 1849 when the Hohenzollern king declined to place himself at the head of liberal revolution. In the years before these thwarted upheavals, Hegel's philosophy had seemed to suit perfectly the "situation of people who were deeply convinced of the power of reason over reality, but wanted to be persuaded that progress toward freedom was possible within an authoritarian political order."[49] Long before 1848, the intellectuals were beginning to defect from Hegelianism and to embrace a more radical liberalism based on modern science or on the Saint-Simonian philosophy imported from France by the Young Germans.[50] Hegelianism was assailed from conservative quarters as well, when the obscurantist regime of Frederick William IV brought Schelling and Friedrich Julius Stahl to Berlin to "trample the dangerous dragon's seeds" planted by Hegel's philosophy, which the Prussian conservatives believed was inherently revolutionary. After the furor over Bruno Bauer's seemingly heterodox *Critique of the Synoptic Gospels,* the Hegelians were permitted to lecture only on aesthetics.[51] The restrictive policies of the Prussian government, from censorship to the summary dismissal of radical professors, further alienated the intellectuals both from Prussian politics and from Hegel, who by then was being posthumously demythologized by the left Hegelians. So oppressive was the atmosphere that Heine did not feel safe from Prussian spies even in his Paris exile.[52]

Although the alleged correspondence between idea and reality was being challenged before the 1848 revolutions, it was the failure of reason to triumph in 1848 that brought final discredit to Hegel's rational logos.[53] The trust of the liberals in the power of principle suffered, as Pflanze says, "a terrible blow from which it never fully recovered."[54] Pre-March liberalism died. It was replaced in the 1850s by an idealism of resignation, by the flight from politics, or in some cases, by tough-minded realism and eventual accomodation to the primacy of power over principle.[55] It was as inevitable as any intellectual response can be that the convergence of empirical science, industrial progress, and political disillusionment would provoke the repudiation of a speculative philosophy seemingly so out of joint with changing times. Both as a theory of knowledge and a philosophy of history, Hegelian idealism had been peculiarly appropriate to the period of its ascendancy, but the conditions of its success had been wholly altered by the 1850s. A hostile critique by the liberal literary historian Rudolf Haym, *Hegel und seine Zeit,* which appeared in 1857, was symptomatic of the new anti-Hegelian spirit.[56] Hegel still had a few staunch defenders like Karl Rosenkranz, but his philosophy had lost its sway over the German mind.[57]

No formulation of Hegel was more vehemently fought by the new generation of critics than his generally misunderstood statement in the *Philosophy of Right* that the rational is real and everything real is rational.[58] This doctrine, more than any other, laid Hegel open to attack and made him sound like the voice of reaction, the soul of the status quo. His attitude toward the contemporary Prussian state, however distorted by his enemies, only seemed to confirm his ultraconservative reputation. This was the Hegel—in many ways a straw man—who drew the fire of Haym and soon thereafter of the neo-Kantians. Yet Hegel's dialectical idealism, whatever the errors of its detractors, was a departure from the traditions of Western rationalism and natural law. In Hegelianism the immutable canons of reason are dissolved in the dialectical process. In the crucible of Hegel's dialectic, universal notions of justice and right are reduced to passing and incomplete manifestations of the world spirit. Therefore, until the world spirit achieves its end in freedom, all principles of reason and right conduct can be only temporary and imperfect. Dialectical philosophy ends in relativism and the impermanence of values. The neo-Kantians were hostile to Hegel because his dialectics threatened the very universality of values they hoped to secure. The "anarchy of convictions,"[59] in Dilthey's expression, was more than an academic question. The nineteenth century was an age of radical change. Science, industry, and nation building were releasing titanic energies that would consume their creators unless contained within rational and ethical bounds. Material power was assuming colossal proportions with little moral guidance. This was especially true of Wilhelmine Germany, when the appearance of giant cartels dangerously coincided with imperialism and the erratic diplomacy of Bismarck's successors.

To some of Hegel's critics, the dialectic not only undermined values but excluded the possibility of freedom, too. It has become one of the weary truisms of German history that from Tauler and the mystics, through Luther down to Hegel, the Germans have contented them-

selves with inner, spiritual freedom while accepting the demands of
authoritarian government for absolute obedience—"Quiet is the first
duty of citizenship" ("Ruhe ist die erste Bürgerpflicht."). German idealism generally places "freedom of thought before freedom of action,
morality before political justice, the inner life before the social life of
man."[60] The philosophy of Hegel belongs to this tradition in both its
personification of the state as the embodiment of objective spirit and in
its monism, which is difficult to reconcile with real freedom. As Schnabel points out, "Freedom and multiplicity of the historical world could
never be understood from the standpoint of monism. Hegel recur-
rently considered and studied the individual and particular . . . he admired Caesar and Napoleon, he deemed states and peoples as individual entities . . . but the philosopher's first interest was the *Weltvernunft,*
which follows its course with an inner necessity while the freedom of
the will remains problematic."[61]

It was logical, then, for the critics of Hegel's panlogism to invoke
Kant. The idea of freedom was at the heart of Kant's practical philosophy, and indeed was the principal theme in his entire system of
thought.[62] Yet Kant's resolution of the antinomy of freedom and necessity has been given poor marks. The phenomenal domain of mechanical causality in nature seems inconsonant with the external freedom
that true moral action requires. Kant also allegedly failed to clear up, as
Leonard Krieger has argued, the confusion between political and moral freedom. Because of these ambiguities, Kant has been used by some
to provide "a moral basis for political obedience [and by] some to fur-
nish a moral basis for political liberty."[63]

Kant, Freedom, and the Law of Nature

Since the argument here is that the Kant revival was in large part
meant to counteract relativism and to enlarge the narrow liberalism of
Bildung und Besitz, a summary of Kantian fundamentals is in order. A
discussion of Kant's ethics and politics is especially obligatory at this
point because some commentators have seen Kant as an author of
paralyzing dualities, a demolisher of natural law, and an advocate of
docile obedience.[64] That these are among the problems in the Kantian
legacy cannot be gainsaid, but there are others who have found different implications in Kant's philosophy.

The usual treatment accorded Kant by Western historians is to stress
the ambivalence of his liberalism, for example: "The schizoid nature of
German liberalism was apparent in the thought of its founder, Imman-

uel Kant. His belief in human equality, the dignity of man, the supremacy of law, and the theoretical right of popular sovereignty brought the
German political tradition temporarily much closer to that of Western
Europe. His rigorous ethics of duty, nevertheless, had an unfortunate
effect in conjunction with his insistence on the practical necessity of
authoritarian government. It reinforced the Prussian tradition of obedience to authority."[65] Kant's philosophy "funnelled" the traditional
German association of liberty and the absolute state into the nineteenth
century.[66] An earlier view, expressed by a young philosopher otherwise
well-disposed toward Kant, is that he applied his political ethics only to
the leaders of the state and all others had no choice but to submit
themselves to authoritarian judgment. Therefore, in political matters,
"no field was left open to independent moral activity."[67] Yet some of
the intellectual liberals found in Kant the rudiments of social democracy, and used his ethics not to enjoin mindless obedience but to attack
Wilhelmine authoritarianism. The application of Kant's philosophy to
late nineteenth-century social and political problems—and indeed its
use as a weapon against the Prussian authoritarian state—indicate that
Kant's influence has not been limited to the reinforcing of obedience to
authority. But there are important and admittedly plausible criticisms
of the Kantian legacy which must be considered before it can be understood how Kant could become the prophet of democracy, socialism,
and humanity to certain members of the Wilhelmine intelligentsia.

The main tenet of Kant's moral philosophy is the primacy and autonomy of conscience. The essential point of his ethics is that obligation
derives neither from the empirical nature of man nor from the circumstances in which he is placed. Obligation must be sought "' *a priori* solely
in the concepts of pure reason."[68] Kant posits a universal community of
self-legislating wills: "The material contents of our actions . . . have
different origins. But when I concern myself with these contents, a
mere relative obligation gives rise to an absolute obligation through my
consensus with an intelligible universal law. This consensus is the consensus of a rational being with himself and other rational beings."[69]
Therefore, the moral autonomy of persons, the sanctum sanctorum of
individual dignity which no external authority may invade, is no more
the source of a purely inner, supersensible freedom than it is the basis
of, as Leo Strauss implies, an asocial individualism.[70] Rather, it is the
moral autonomy of the self-legislating will that associates the individual
with a universal rational order: "[Man] is only bound to act in accordance with his own will, which is, however, designed by nature to be a
will giving universal laws."[71] Here, in the doctrine of moral autonomy,

the neo-Kantian democrats and socialists found the ethical fulcrum of their politics. Karl Vorländer, a prominent Kantian socialist and historian of philosophy, characterized the Kantian position existentially: "The world itself, compared to the ultimate value of persons, is without purpose and worth because the continuation of the world has value only insofar as the rational beings in it are able to attain the ultimate purpose of their existence."[72] The moral personality, in Vorländer's phrase, is the freedom of a rational being under moral laws.[73]

The incompatibility of this doctrine with any form of tyranny is obvious. According to Kant, the highest aim of mankind was to create and maintain a civil society under laws, but as one of Kant's modern interpreters explains, "we must not employ evil as a means, for . . . as we are rational beings and therefore moral beings, all planning, all striving for power is subject to the standard of the ethical imperative. Kant's philosophy goes counter to the totalizations that began with the systems of German idealism and led by way of Marxism to the practice of total knowledge and total planning." [74] Viewed from the perspective of moral autonomy, Kant's ethics and philosophy of right augur the opposite of obedience to arbitrary, totalitarian rule.

Freedom and rationality are unquestionably the central themes of Kant's philosophy. Although his non-revolutionary, practical, and personal response to authoritarianism was inadequate (his insistence on freedom of conscience and expression as the only lawful forms of resistance), it is only correct to draw from Kant a form of liberalism rather than mute obeisance to the authoritarian state. The authoritarian element in Kant has been unduly amplified by the effects of an inverted "Whig" approach to German history which concerns itself with explaining the disasters of the twentieth century, sometimes to the neglect of many subtleties and misunderstood possibilities of the past. It is, therefore, important to emphasize that at one moment in German history, a regeneration of liberal values, fortified by the revival of Kant, was assayed by a prominent group of philosophers.

The critique of Kant does not end with the customary indictment of his defective liberalism; it goes on to portray him as a dissolver of the natural law. Kant represents, according to one historian's view, "the crisis of natural law in its most categorical terms and [he] developed the crisis to its most explicit denouement." Kant's dualism "was a classic statement invalidating, among other things, the traditional function of natural law."[75] A similar argument is found in Leo Strauss's essay on Max Weber's struggle with historicism: Weber's "'Kantianism' . . . forced him to sever every connection between moral duty and the common good."[76] In natural law moral duty and the common good are not identical but complementary; a fundamental opposition between the two would deny the practicability of natural law. Thus, the "dissolution of the total conjunction between the *is* and *ought*,"[77] which is found in Kant and his intellectual heir, Max Weber, would seem to constitute a decisive rejection of natural law, for it removed the "crucial middle link, the general principles that functioned simultaneously as truths of nature and morality."[78] Prima facie, this interpretation seems in conflict with the thesis that the revival of Kant was a departure from historicism and a return to a universal outlook akin to the spirit—though admittedly not the traditional basis—of natural law philosophy. The apparent disagreement here is important because it relates to the question of Germany's much-analyzed philosophical divergence from the West. Shortly after World War I, Ernst Troeltsch observed that the expressions *natural law* and *humanity* were disappearing from the intellectual vocabulary in Germany. Although those terms had once been meaningful, they had been replaced by values deriving from the Weltanschauung of historicism. [79]

Did Kant—and subsequently the neo-Kantians—undermine the assumptions of natural law philosophy and thereby assist in the triumph of historicism and state-oriented legal positivism, or did they try to formulate a philosophy of right as universal in scope as natural law but built on different assumptions and intended to counteract historicism? The critics of the Kantian tradition say that it destroyed the major premise of natural law by separating the Ought from the Is, the realm of morality and freedom from the domain of necessitous nature.[80] There is no doubt that Kantianism does make such a dichotomy, but it is a formal rather than an essential separation. In the *Foundations of the Metaphysics of Morals* Kant insists on the essential unity of reason: "I require of a *Kritik* of pure practical reason, if it is to be complete, that the unity of the practical reason and of the speculative be subject to presentation under a common principle because in the final analysis there can be but one and the same reason, which must be differentiated only in application."[81] Kant reminds us that "however much the applications of morality may change with varying circumstances, a good man is one who acts on the supposition that there is an unconditional and objective moral standard holding for all men in virtue of their rationality as human beings."[82] In Kant's own formulation of it, the moral law is given by pure reason to man a priori as a rational being.[83] In this sense, there is no reason to exclude Kant from the general observation that "all natural right doctrines claim that the fundamentals of justice are, in principle, accessible to man as man."[84] True, Kant did not seek moral law in the nature of man because "natural" man as such is ruled by his appetites and changing interests. And Kant did not find the moral law in "historical" man whose experience may be useful for practical rules but can never provide unconditional principles. The grounds of obligation must be sought, as Kant said, "solely in the concepts of pure reason."[85]

Kant's transcendental analysis of pure practical reason was his way out of the difficulties posed by the mechanistic physics of Newtonian science—a physics which, in fact, demanded the recasting of natural law theory. For if nature were henceforth the locus of causal mechanics, then the teleological Ought, the sphere of purpose and moral choice, had to be placed outside the plexus of causal processes. Kant abandoned man's *empirical* nature as the link between morality and nature because he found it untenable, but he did not destroy it. This had already been done by seventeenth-century science with its implicit exclusion of freedom and purpose from the workings of the natural universe. His formal distinction between the moral order and the natural order was, in his estimation, a necessary one if the universal basis of obligation was to be secured. To Kant's late nineteenth-century disciples, his transcendental method seemed to offer escape from the consequences of another intellectual revolution, the one brought about by nineteenth-century historicism with its insistence on the time-bound and conditional character of all values. Kant's transcendental solution was not entirely satisfactory, especially for those who found his formal, a priori analysis arid, bloodless, and remote from human experience. His pronouncements on the unknowableness of the thing-in-itself, and his restriction of cognitive knowledge to the forms and categories of the mind inspired some later critics to accuse him of subjectivism. His practical integration of nature and freedom in history and contemporary politics suffered in the opinion of one critic from imbalance—nature tended to dominate.[86] But Kant's intention was to restore man to a place of freedom and dignity by distinguishing his intelligible from his natural self, and by making history the scene of a ceaseless but meaningful struggle between the two. Later generations could look to Kant for lines of deliverance from the reduction of ethics to relative historical values.

The contention here is that Kant tried to preserve the spirit of natural law theory in new epistemological form, while discarding the eudaemonism of secular natural law.[87] That is, he denied that happiness or material welfare can provide universal criteria for natural right, although he was not an advocate of righteous misery as some have said. It was precisely this repudiation of eudaemonistic premises that later appealed to anti-historicists and non-Marxian socialists because it opened the way for an alternative to the relativity of values and the deterministic implications of both physical science and Marxian socialism. Kant altered the epistemological bases of natural law theory but salvaged its universality, and he did so in order to reconcile freedom and purpose with the Newtonian cosmology. The terms of the freedom-causality problem would be profoundly altered by the new physics of relativity, quanta, and indeterminacy, but this did not affect Kant or the early neo-Kantians. Kant spoke to the problem of the free personality versus the impervious clockwork universe. Kant's answer was imperfect but meaningful for a segment of the Wilhelmine intelligentsia. In an era of moral confusion and ethnocentrism, Kant's keynotes were, at least to an academic minority, moral clarity, intellectual humility, and the inviolable integrity of the individual.

By his formal dualism and his refusal to integrate nature and spirit, Kant had refrained from subordinating consciousness to reality and history to nature, so the individual would not be deprived of either his liberty or his obligations. Kantian dualism is an antidote to determinism, to any theory that sacrifices the individual to the ineluctable, impersonal forces of nature or history. Hence, Kantian dualism, in spite of its defects, is a doctrine of freedom and the antithesis of Hegel's philosophy of immanence. And if Hegel is inculpable of having fostered totalitarian thought as his defenders maintain, Kant should be recognized for having encouraged the opposite tendency, for his transcendental dualism is wholly incompatible with Nazism's monistic integration of blood and spirit in the racial myth. The return to Kant's practical philosophy was therefore a repudiation of positivist ethics grounded on experience and social utility. In Kant's words, "It is clear that all moral concepts have their seat and origin entirely a priori in reason . . . . It is obvious that they can be abstracted from no empirical, and hence merely contingent conditions."[88] Kant admitted that practical rules can be derived from experience but never moral laws, for maxims based on experience are contingent and therefore subject to change.

The Marburgers, particularly Rudolf Stammler, went back to Kant to find a pure concept of law above the shifting sands of experience. Here again they confronted the challenge of relativism: Contingent versus immutable standards of right. Thus neo-Kantianism was a reaction against Hegelianism and materialism, both of which were seen to have the same deleterious consequences—determinism and ethical relativism.[89] Kant's concrete political prescriptions were a more serious difficulty to social democrats in search of a mentor than the philosophical problems in his theory of freedom and moral autonomy. Kant was certainly no modern socialist or even social welfare liberal. If the Marburg neo-Kantians had followed him literally, they never would have broken with the traditional, middle-class antipathy toward universal manhood suffrage and state paternalism. Kant himself, as the most revered philosopher of liberal political values, was perhaps partly and indirectly responsible for the aversion of many liberals to democracy and social welfare. Like most liberals of his own time, he favored limiting the franchise to the economically independent citizenry, and his abhorrence of social welfare was violent: "The state where the subject is treated like a helpless child is the greatest despotism thinkable, and . . . the man who is dependent is no longer a man."[90] Kant's individual is, therefore, the educated man of the German classical period. The same humanistic ideal is found in Schiller, Goethe, Wilhelm von Humboldt, and other notables of the time; from them it passed into the mainstream of German liberal thought.[91]

Kant's political philosophy, it should be remembered, was radical in its historical context, which was the stratified and absolutist society of preindustrial Prussia. His abhorrence of state paternalism reflected a genuinely liberal aversion to the enlightened despotisms of his own century, especially Josephinism in Austria. And Kant never wavered in his support of the principles of the French Revolution. His advocacy of the property franchise seems predictably bourgeois in retrospect, but it could be deemed shrewdly realistic at a time when personal dependency was pervasive in a still feudal society. Less than a century later Bismarck instituted universal manhood suffrage for the Reich because he believed the peasants and workers would vote for their masters. The instinctive trust Bismarck counted on did not in the long run materialize on the scale he had anticipated. But a century earlier he would not have been disappointed. Kant recognized that those who have been placed in servile positions through birth or circumstances are scarcely capable of exercising independent political judgment even in a liberal state if vestiges of feudal or other forms of dependency exist.

But the Marburg neo-Kantians were not fundamentalists. In developing their theory of social democracy from Kant's principles of individual integrity and moral autonomy, they played down the aristocratic and cultural character of his individualism. Decisively breaking with Kant and the liberal tradition in this respect, they denied that education and property were the conditions of participation in civic life.

"Back to Kant" was considered a point of departure rather than an oath of allegiance to old-fashioned ideals.

The revival of Kant, however, was not a unitary phenomenon. It took varied and sometimes conflicting forms. In 1908, somewhat after neo-Kantianism had reached its zenith, Ludwig Stein wrote:

> The neo-idealism of our day manifested itself in many hues. From the phenomenalism of the Machian type, the pure logic and epistemological criticism of Hermann Cohen . . . from the ethical idealism of Theodor Lipp, the normative philosophy of Windel-band . . . [to the] orthodox Kantianism of Jakob Schmidt, the neo-idealistic prism displayed all the colors of the rainbow.[92]

A modern interpreter finds seven different species of neo-Kantianism but discerns among all of them four common Kantian assumptions: (1) They use the transcendental method as opposed to the psychological or empirical, that is, they seek the prior conditions of knowing and willing. (2) They are *conceptualists,* by which is meant that they deny intellectual intuition as a source of genuine knowledge and believe in the capacity of reason "for constructing a whole from its parts," the capacity for synthesis. Knowledge of contents or essences is ruled out. (3) Their epistemologies are *idealist.* "Knowledge is not the grasp but the construction of the object." (4) To understand Kant is to go beyond him. For instance, they all reject the unknowable ground of experience, the notorious thing-in-itself.[93] In regard to the neo-Kantians discussed in this essay, a fifth should be added: the primacy of practical reason. The willing subject supplies the conceptual forms of knowledge and the norms and values of morality and culture; these latter are beyond the realm of theoretical or pure reason but are nonetheless true, not ontologically but axiologically. Such values pertain to the realm of what-ought-to-be rather than what-is, as the neo-Kantians retain the theoretical dualism of their master's system.

To cover the full and variegated spectrum of neo-Kantianism is not the purpose here. The present concern is with early instigators of the movement, with the two most important "schools" in relation to historical and social thought (Marburg and Southwestern or Baden), and with the most significant and influential Wilhelmine heirs of neo-Kantianism, men such as Troeltsch, Weber, Meinecke, and Cassirer. Much was at stake in the neo-Kantian critique of Hegel and the German positivists. The outcome had a bearing on the future of Germany and the West. Whether moral reason and clear ethical standards would take primacy in German thought over power and the unreliable impulsions of will was a question of immense significance. There was much to draw upon in Germany's spiritual heritage for a healthy and constructive answer. We know the tragic outcome, but the irrational excesses of German politics in the twentieth century were not preordained, and totalitarianism was not then a foregone conclusion. Geoffrey Barraclough has recently said that even in the reign of William II, often treated as though its only importance was as an antechamber to the Third Reich, something altogether different might have happened. Neo-Kantianism must be considered with this in mind. I am not thereby implying that a massive conversion of the educated classes to Kant's humanism would have solved all of Germany's problems nor suggesting that ideas unilaterally determine the course of events. But German idealism expressed a particular form of historical consciousness. In its neo-Kantian manifestation idealism put forward a moral and teleological conception of history and community. In the words of one recent student of the subject: "In modern idealism, the notion of history as an immanent teleology came to the fore with important consequences for the role of the political community as a special participant in the stream of time." As for the effect of idealist historical consciousness on the course of events, he further observes: "When we remove the issue to the level of philosophical speculation, we cannot be so sure that a sense of destiny does not sometimes govern function, producing at the same time political change and expansion of consciousness."[94] We cannot say that a greater expansion of the German historical consciousness in the direction of neo-Kantian principles would have made a difference or had a salutary result, but we do know that such an expansion was attempted at a crucial time in the modern history of the German people. Moreover, it offends both common sense and logic to suppose that a society sufficiently imbued with the personalist spirit of Kantian ethics would not have been able to detect and defeat the threat of a racist dictatorship, however untoward the economic situation.

The revival of Kant did not begin overnight, nor was Kant entirely forgotten during the reign of Hegel and speculative metaphysics. It would be stretching the point to say that nineteenth-century philosophy in Germany was a series of footnotes on Kant, but there is no gainsaying that all subsequent German philosophers, in addressing themselves to the central questions of truth and value, were compelled to accept, reject, or modify Kantian principles. Several philosophers of the Restoration era considered themselves even closer to Kant than to Hegel. Johann Friedrich Herbart, who taught at Königsberg from 1790 to 1833, said in his *Allgemeine Metaphysik* of 1828, "The author is a Kantian."[95] Friedrich Beneke called for renewed appreciation of critical idealism in his *Kant und die philosophische Aufgabe unserer Zeit,* in 1832. Opponents of Hegelian pantheism like Carl Fortlage and I.M. Fichte sometimes appealed to Kant's religious and moral philosophy. In his opening address before the first Congress of German Philosophers at Gotha in 1847, Fichte gave Kantian thought a prominent place in his *Grundsätze für der Philosophie der Zukunft.*[96] In the same year appeared Christian Weisse's *In welchem Sinn die deutschen Philosophie jetzt wieder an Kant zu orientieren hat.*[97] Rudolf Haym's famous attack on Hegel ten years later concluded by advising German philosophers to return to the paths of Kant.[98]

Thus Kant's influence was always present and increasing long before the middle of the century. As the Hegelians fell to quarreling among themselves, younger philosophers, disillusioned with speculative idealism and unscientific *Naturphilosophie,* began to search for an alternative. In the 1850s, some found the answer in Kant's critical idealism, among whom many were former Hegelians or had been trained by Hegel's disciples. One of them, the philosopher-physician R.H. Lotze, who was among the most influential of the post-Hegelian generation, actually began the neo-Kantian movement.

2

Back to Criticism:
Rudolf Hermann Lotze

The Reconciliation of Philosophy and Science

Rudolf Hermann Lotze was not in any precise sense a neo-Kantian. His metaphysics owed much to the monadology of Leibniz, which put him a great distance from the antimetaphysical Kant. When he first gained recognition in the 1850s,"Back to Kant" was not yet the slogan of a movement. However his writings later became, in the words of one author, "a philosophical Septuagint" of the neo-Kantian movement.[1] Lotze joined the struggle against both Hegelianism and materialism. His weapon in the debate was an epistemological skepticism of Kantian provenance, and he expressly adopted some of Kant's arguments. His eclectic philosophy has been aptly summed up as Leibnizian pluralism modified by Kant's theory of freedom.[2] His critique of Hegel helped to sustain the new interest in Kant and made him the most important forerunner of the neo-Kantian movement.

Lotze is nearly forgotten today but his influence during his lifetime was very great. An English contemporary judged that, by almost universal consent, Lotze was the most popular teacher in Germany; he was well known in Great Britain and Holland, and in the last quarter of the century the French philosophers were also beginning to take notice of his work.[3] In 1912, an American scholar wrote: "It may be safely said that there are now few thinking men over forty-five in Germany who are not indebted to Lotze for mental poise, intellectual tastes or elements of a general culture which enable them to look beyond their own individual department of activity."[4] J.T. Merz, Lotze's pupil, in his massive *History of European Thought in the Nineteenth Century*, speculated that Lotze's attempt to create a unified Weltanschauung was "prophetic of the philosophical movement forty years after his time, as represented in the writings and school of Dilthey."[5] George Santayana, who finished his Harvard thesis on Lotze under Josiah Royce in 1889, admired his undogmatic attitude in contrast to the egotistic spirit he later identified as the main theme in modern German philosophy. Liberal Protestant philosophers of the 1880s and 1890s, most prominently Albrecht Ritschl, embraced his defense of theism, as did American Congregationalist theologians at Yale, Oberlin, and Grinnell. At Oxford, T.H. Green and his fellow idealists sponsored the translation of Lotze's logic and metaphysics, and R.B. Haldane went to Göttingen to study with Lotze himself.[6] By the 1870s, Lotze was the best-known German thinker outside of Germany. Royce was among his students; William James and Bernard Bosanquet were among his admirers. Perhaps the main reason for his popularity was his reputation as the man "who could see through the difficulties of adjusting the old biblical authority to the new authority of science"; this was exceedingly attractive to a generation of men experiencing difficulties in their Protestant faith.[7] At the core of this religious problem was the problem of knowledge, which was Lotze's primary concern. As with Kant, the center of Lotze's thought was epistemology. "Both Kant and Lotze begin their speculation by a reflection on the possibility of philosophizing."[8]

Lotze's early life and philosophical development fell between the classical era of Goethe and Hegel and the rebirth of idealism in his own lifetime. Goethe died in 1832 when Lotze was fifteen and just coming into intellectual awareness. He was born May 21, 1817, at Bautzen, once the home of Fichte and Schelling, and the county seat of Oberlausitz in Saxony. His forebears had come to Bautzen from Dippoldiswald, a few miles south of Dresden. They were mainly minor civil servants and professional people. Lotze's grandfather was a tax assessor; his father, a military surgeon in the Saxon army. Early in 1809, not long after being released from a Russian military prison, his father married Christiane Caroline Noack, the daughter of a Dresden schoolmaster. Lotze's background was, therefore, in the bureaucratic and professional bourgeoisie, the social base of German idealism and liberal politics, and he rarely deviated from the social and political attitudes of that class.[9] Although his scholarly attainments were beyond the ordinary, Lotze's education was typical of his class. He attended the gymnasium at Zittau, a city near the Bohemian border where his family had moved in 1819. The humanistic curriculum struck a responsive chord. He was enraptured by German classical literature, and soon tried his hand at belles lettres, writing a precocious novel entitled *Die Deutschen,* devoted to the Romantic thesis that inner religious life is the most profound source of poetic and artistic creativity.[10] At no great loss to German literature, the novel was never published, but it was an accurate indicant of things to come.

Frederick Copleston said rightly that Lotze came to philosophy through art rather than from his later medical training. The hero of Lotze's novel is Lothar, an idealized mirror of the author, who, as an ascetic young aristocrat, is faced with the problem of choosing a career. He decides to ignore all practical concerns and to live the life of the mind. Unlike his idealistic contemporaries, Lothar has no desire to join political crusades and fight for the rights of the common people (*Pöbel*). He is apolitical and thoroughly scornful of the political marketplace. Accused by his friends of aristocratic egoism, Lothar replies that there is nothing more insufferable to him than the masses with their clamor for natural rights; the people must attain greater dignity before they will be capable of using their rights properly. Lothar is an advocate of *Bildungsaristokratie,* an elite of the educated and refined. He is suspicious of popular government and places inner freedom above positive political rights. Lothar, in the hands of his author, becomes a fictional spokesman for German idealism.[11] As Lotze matured, his social views became somewhat more generous, to the extent that one writer could refer to his thought as "idealism fitted to democracy and industrial civilization."[12] *Die Deutschen,* in spite of its callowness, conveyed a metaphysical theory Lotze never abandoned. In it he tried to express his conviction that everything animate and inanimate in this world is endowed with spirit. The unity of all things, the final metaphysical and moral ground, Lotze believed, is in God whose spirit permeates all things, even though we may be unable to perceive His presence. Here, in the youthful effusions of *Die Deutschen* were the main ideas of *Mikrokosmus,* Lotze's three-volume opus which began to appear in 1856. He wanted the *Mikrokosmus* to become the philosophy of man as Alexander von Humboldt's *Cosmos* had attempted earlier to be a science of nature. One of Lotze's principal aims in this ambitious work was to rescue the concept of a personal God from the pantheism of the absolute idealists.

Lotze's brief excursion into fiction also set forth the philosophical problem that became the focus of his life's work: How can a transcendent God, a spiritualized universe, and a mechanistic theory of nature be reconciled in a consistent, defensible system? Lotze searched for unity, but his scientific, critical turn of mind pushed him into dualities.[13] His effort to harmonize metaphysical unity and moral idealism with the mechanical processes of nature guided him back to the critical and practical philosophy of Kant—or pushed him forward to Kant, since he began with the metaphysics of Leibniz and Spinoza.[14] Lotze agreed with his Leipzig professor Gustav Fechner that all things possess spiritual properties and that God is the ultimate consciousness of the universe. But he did not follow Fechner into his theory of parallelism between psychical and physical events, which was his solution to the mind-body problem and the problem of knowledge. The ethical idealism of Fichte, which in many ways was just as important to neo-Kantianism as Kant's, was also significant for Lotze and formed part of his theism. Fichte's notion of an ultimate moral principle expressing itself in finite objects, and thus creating a teleological unity, made a great impact on Lotze in determining his philosophy of values. And his philosophy of values was his principal bequest to the Baden neo-Kantians.

Lotze began his studies in medicine and philosophy at Leipzig in 1834 with Christian Weisse, a Hegelian, as his philosophical mentor. He was first Weisse's pupil, then friend and disciple, and eventually his philosophical opponent.[15] As I have noted above, Lotze, like many neo-Kantians, was first associated with Hegelianism. He learned from Weisse both the merits and shortcomings of Hegel's philosophy. But Weisse was no Hegelian purist. He was a theist who argued that free acts not only of the Divine Will but also of individuals contribute as much to the unfolding of history as the march of Idea. Weisse's theories of theism and freedom, however, left a permanent mark on Lotze. Both men based their philosophy of freedom on the familiar Kantian argument that without free choice, moral action is unthinkable. Weisse also leaned toward Kant in his theory of knowledge. In an academic address of 1847, three years after Lotze had come to Göttingen, Weisse recommended that greater attention be paid to Kant's critical method.[16] Later Lotze believed that his teacher had not gone far enough in this direction. Yet the now-forgotten Weisse should be counted among the earliest of those to beckon German thought back to Kantian criticism. His case illustrates how intellectual movements often begin among minor figures in the ranks of preceding traditions as tensions arise in their encounter with new ideas and situations. In the specific instance of neo-Kantianism, Weisse is an example of the gradual and usually overlooked drift back to critical philosophy by some Hegelians even before the middle of the century.

Lotze took his degrees in medicine and philosophy in 1838, and spent the following year practicing in Zittau. Returning to Leipzig to prepare for his habilitation, he was accepted by the philosophy faculty in 1840, the year he began work on his first major treatise, the *Metaphysik*. During his six years at Leipzig, Lotze was part of a distinguished circle of academicians and artists, including Fechner, Salamon Hirzel (Lotze's publisher), Weisse, the Schumanns, and Mendelssohn. Lotze's friend Härtel was director of the Drapers' Concert Hall where Mendelssohn was Kapellmeister.[17] The Leipzig circle, which had counterparts in university towns all over Germany, exemplifies the German intellectual aristocracy in microcosm.

In 1844, Lotze left Leipzig for Göttingen to accept the chair of philosophy left vacant in 1841 by the death of Johann Friedrich Herbart. It was fitting that Lotze should follow Herbart at Göttingen, for he owed much to his predecessor. His pluralistic view of the universe and his belief that the task of philosophy is to find unity behind the manifold of experience were indebted to Herbart's anti-Hegelian postulate that the world is composed fundamentally of many real things. The Herbartian influence also helps to explain Lotze's interest in Lucretius and Leibniz.[18] Göttingen was Lotze's home for the next thirty-seven years, until 1880 when he went to Berlin under the sponsorship of Eduard Zeller. He was soon involved in the rejuvenated intellectual life of the Hanoverian university. He joined the Friday Club, a group of young Turks who met on Friday evenings for dinner and conversation—usually about the shortcomings of Göttingen. The *Verein* had its own publication, *Göttinger Studien*, created to invigorate the intellectual climate at the university.[19] The vitality of Göttingen's intellectual life had declined since the affair in 1837 of the seven liberal professors who had protested the suspension of Hanover's constitution.[20] The memory of the "Göttingen Seven" was still fresh, and the *Verein* worked to keep it alive. Lotze's membership in this group was his closest brush with any kind of academic radicalism.

Although Lotze was no hermit, he did not allow association with the *Verein* progressives to pull him into the vortex of university politics. He was contemplative and often melancholy, and an increasingly serious heart condition held his non-scholarly activities to a minimum. In 1848, he wanted to join a Free Corps which upheld the regime, but his health would not permit it.[21] The sight of crumbling political authority was distressing to Lotze; his reaction to the revolutionary upheaval was dour and pessimistic. In March he wrote to a friend that he wondered "whether next semester there would be a University of Göttingen other than in name."[22] He complained to Hirzel about the spottiness of the news reaching Hanover and expressed the hope that "reasonable people in Saxony would come forward and bring the revolutionary movement to a sane outcome."[23] In the midst of revolution, though, Lotze seemed more occupied with revising his *Pathologie* for a second edition than with politics.[24] When he was invited to serve on a governmental reorganization committee, he declined. After the first year of revolution had passed and some of the dust had settled, he summed up the feeling of disillusion at Göttingen: "Whenever possible the subject of politics is avoided."[25]

Lotze showed just as little enthusiasm for Prussian leadership and was much relieved when Austria regained her mastery of German affairs. The tumults of 1848 having left him exhausted and discouraged, he moved from Nicolai Strasse in Göttingen to a home in the country to restore his health.[26] He was thirty years old in 1848, still fairly young by any yardstick, and might have been expected to share the hopes of pre-March, at least vicariously. But he was far too absorbed in his work and too skeptical about the ideals of the revolution; like his fictional hero Lothar, he was essentially a nonpolitical man.

Lotze's first important involvement in an intellectual controversy was the convention of natural scientists at Göttingen in September 1854. He was drawn into the famous *Materialismusstreit*, the materialism controversy, which proved to be the last fling of simple materialism as a respectable academic philosophy.[27] This debate was also called the "struggle for the soul," because one of the main points at issue was the independence of consciousness or spirit from bodily functions. The 1854 convention revealed a deep rift in the scientific community between the materialists, led by Ludwig Büchner and H.C. Czolbe, and prominent scientists like Helmholtz, who rejected the crude monism later purveyed by Büchner's *Kraft und Stoff*. The materialism debate was the immediate background leading to the publication of Helmholtz's classic treatise on optics, *Über das Sehen des Menschen*, which called for a revival of Kant's critical epistemology.[28]

Lotze, somewhat to the surprise of those who considered him a mechanist because of his works on physiology, joined the anti-materialists. His early writings had seemed to represent an unequivocally mechanistic position; hence, in spite of his warnings that they revealed only half of his philosophy, the materialists considered him an ally. The *Mikrokosmus*

soon made clear that he was not. When it became evident where Lotze
stood in the "mind-body" controversy, he quickly became a favorite of
the anti-scientific preachers and theologians. G.S. Hall relates this story,
suggesting Lotze's influence in America:

> The Boston Monday Lectureship, which in the later seventies
> crowded Tremont Temple for twenty Monday noons per annum
> for five years to hear the Reverend Joseph Cook, some of whose
> annual volumes reached a sixteenth edition, first made Lotze, who
> was the lecturer's oft-mentioned hero, popular in this country. He
> was described as "on his knees before a personal God" [a man
> who] "rent materialism thus and thus," as Mr. Cook tore his manu-
> script before a transported audience.[29]

Without expressly adopting Kant's theory of knowledge, Lotze spoke
more and more with the accent of philosophical criticism, especially in
Mikrokosmus. The Göttingen convention was, as I have maintained, a
spur to the early neo-Kantian movement. It was also perhaps the nadir
of nineteenth-century German philosophy and, by bringing the problem of knowledge into the limelight, the beginning of an intellectual
renaissance that culminated in the last two decades of the century.

In the meantime, Lotze's political attitude was changing only slightly.
In December 1863, during Bismarck's battle with the Prussian Diet,
Lotze complained to Hirzel that because of the present discord, "we
shall lose for some time all pleasure ... in every undertaking."[30] He
was worried about the adverse effect Prussian politics might have on
the university. And soon the events of Bismarck's *Realpolitik* began to
impinge on his life at Göttingen. After the incorporation of Hanover
and its great university into Prussia, Lotze was appointed to the Board
of Examiners for academic candidates. In this capacity he was able to
observe firsthand what he called "the pathetic fruits of Prussian gymnasium instruction." He remarked bitterly to Hirzel "how provincially this
department of a great state has been organized."[31]

Lotze was unable to escape his new administrative responsibilities. In
December 1869, he was reappointed to the Board, but continued to
take a dim view of Prussia's educational bureaucracy: "God must take
special care of the administration of examinations in the North German Confederation."[32] However, a reconciliation with the Prussian
state began during the Franco-Prussian war. In August 1870, he in-
formed his friend Strumpf that one of his sons had already been sent
to the front and another was on the way.[33] Eight years after the war, he
recalled in an address at a faculty dinner that his resentment of Prussia

had begun to diminish when his son Konrad won the Iron Cross. He concluded his speech, though, with an encomium for the deposed Hanoverian dynasty: The House of Hanover had always treated the university as a great treasure.[34] Lotze accepted the new Reich, but not without some qualms—and with no little nostalgia for the good old days. That Lotze could make his private peace with Prussia was partly the result of Göttingen's renascence under the new regime.[35] His doubts of 1866 were not confirmed while his growing cordiality toward Prussia was helped along by an honor he received in 1876. He described it to Hirzel: "Yesterday I was made, for no reason, a privy councillor, but I think of myself as no more important—perhaps this is just a sign of age."[36]

After nearly forty years at Göttingen, Lotze accepted an offer from the University of Berlin.[37] At first he was reluctant, but it was a signal honor, and Zeller, who visited Lotze in April 1880, was a persuasive emissary. The following year Lotze moved to Berlin. In June 1881, he returned to Göttingen to set his affairs in order and visit friends, and while there, contracted a serious lung inflammation. He died on July 1, 1881. When William James heard the news of Lotze's death, he wrote to George H. Howison: "As you are in Berlin I suppose you are lamenting Lotze's loss. He seems to me the most exquisite of contemporary minds."[38]

Lotze did not leave behind a Lotzean School. His influence was great but diffuse—and it was certainly international, appealing particularly to those young Anglo-Americans struggling with the apparently incompatible demands of scientific knowledge and religious experience. He was also without question the main transitional figure in German thought. He, probably more than anyone else, helped to bring about the change from an age of speculative systems to a new period of epistemological criticism and was a leader in the search for independent humanistic values in a culture captivated by scientific method. He belonged to both periods, which Saint-Simon would have distinguished as "organic" and "critical." He was perhaps the central thinker in a neglected phase of German intellectual history which is sometimes dismissed as several decades of *Epigonentum* between Hegel's radical critics and the Nietzsche-Dilthey era. Although hostile to the Hegelian *espirit de système*, Lotze was, as it turned out, a systembuilder too. In a sense, he was one of the last German metaphysical architects, not of Hegelian stature but worthy of notice, especially as a forerunner of neo-Kantianism. The lineaments of German intellectual history in the second half of the century become obscure without reference to his work.

Lotze on the Limits of Conceptual Thought

The *Metaphysik* of 1841 marked Lotze's break with Hegelianism, set him apart from his teacher Weisse, and established his Kantian orientation. "Lotze turned back decisively to epistemological criticism on the foundations of Kant."[39] The *Metaphysik* also pointed to his increasing emphasis on Kant's practical philosophy and on the primacy of practical over theoretical reason. His concluding comment in his treatise is that "the beginning of metaphysics is not in itself but in ethics," a tenet that recurs in the philosophy of Windelband and Rickert.[40] Lotze anticipated Windelband and Rickert in another respect, too. He conceded that the unity of phenomena may be grasped in scientific concepts, but the true essence of being is the individual, the particular.[41] In simple form, this anticipated Windelband's distinction between the generalizing procedure of science and the individualizing method of history. To anyone familiar with the German background it will seem obvious that Lotze did not originate this distinction, which perfectly expresses the tradition of Ranke, romanticism, and historicism. Not only was his position on the particularity of experience consistent with this tradition but his teleological theism was also close to Ranke's belief that behind the succession of individual events, the historian intuitively perceives the hand of God. But the unfolding of history is not the exfoliation of an abstract Idea—this was Ranke's objection to Hegel—rather, it is the manifestation of the Divine Personality in concrete moments of a real historical process. Thus the neo-Kantian philosophers who expressed the late nineteenth-century version of what Georg G. Iggers has called the German conception of history could readily borrow ideas from Lotze for their hermeneutical theory of historical method. And here *hermeneutical* means that the historian is looking for the deeper meaning of events and their immanent values rather than trying to discover general laws or a purely causal sequence of happenings.

The quarrel with Hegel came from Lotze's skeptical view of conceptual thought which he passed on to the later neo-Kantians. Hegel's error was that he had "identified thought with reality, and converted the rich, living world of concrete facts into a fixed system of abstract categories."[42] Depreciation of individual life in favor of Idea gives us stone instead of bread. Lotze and the Baden neo-Kantians believed that conceptual reason cannot be exhaustive; it cannot do justice to individuality or to the richness of experience. A good example of his epistemological skepticism is found in the eighth book of *Mikrokosmus*, where he wrote: "What everything is in itself, what its true nature is by

which it exists . . . this may remain forever inaccessible to thought."[43]
But then he made an important distinction: "[Idealism] believes that in
knowing the import of what thus happens it possesses all essential
truth; that it is only for the realization of this truth that things exist."
This is the central doctrine of Lotze's philosophy. He believed that the
immediate, phenomenal world exists not for itself but for some purpose—for something that ought to be. He used this doctrine against
the panlogism of the Hegelians who, in his opinion, had said that all
meaning and purpose are eventually realized in thought—and he also
used it against those materialists who denied that reality possesses any
transcendent significance.

The dominant theme in Lotze's theory of knowledge is the antithesis
between thought and things. He never wearied of arguing that
"thought, in the last resort, is tentative, and is debarred by the frailty of
human knowledge from the possibility of arriving at absolute certainty."[44] For him, thought was only a part, and a comparatively
insignificant and dependent part, of man's mental equipment.[45] Lotze's
whittling down of conceptual thought brings to mind Kant's famous
comment in the *Critique of Pure Reason* that he wanted to demolish
thought to make room for faith. Lotze's final concern was belief. The
spiritual link between purpose and necessity, between values and mechanical laws, is a personal God. Much like Kant, he set definite limits
to cognitive knowledge, and assigned ultimate metaphysical questions
to the category of necessary assumptions, regulative ideas, and faith.

In the *Metaphysik* Lotze presented a strong case for immediate perception as opposed to the reduction of experience in concepts. We are,
he said, immediately aware that the content of consciousness is too rich
to be exhausted in thought.[46] Some other faculty besides reason is
required to perceive the fullness of conscious experience. Lotze knew,
though, that this denigration of conceptual reason was two-edged—
epistemological skepticism exposes the errors of the absolute idealists,
but it can also destroy indispensable beliefs: "For both the strength and
weakness of our position, and our hopes with regard to the future,
depend equally upon that chained spirit of criticism which . . . more
easily accomplishes the inevitable demolition of error than the recon-
struction of truth, and, in the zeal of its analytical incursions, runs the
risk of injuring unperceived the most necessary foundations of ordered
human existence."[47] Indeed, Lotze chastised Kant for his excessively
critical procedure and consequent failure to work out a comprehensive
philosophy of experience: "The constant whetting of the knife is tedi-
ous, if it is not proposed to cut anything with it."[48] But his solution to

metaphysical problems was closer to the Königberg philosopher's than he realized. Similar to Kant, he based his moral, religious, and onto-logical arguments on the preeminence of practical reason: "Hence it is only in practical conviction that we can hold fast to the thought that all beings and all events have their ultimate ground in that which is re-garded as the highest end of the universe."[49]

Lotze believed that thought is secondary and formal, while feeling, willing, and believing bring us closer to reality and reveal a meaningful world which cannot be reached by cognitive reason. His skepticism and insistence on the limits of conceptual thought reappear with an even keener edge in the philosophy of Windelband and Rickert. Thus, Lotze had an important but usually underestimated influence on the logic of the humanities in the last quarter of the century.

Lotze's Theory of Value

Many neo-Kantian philosophers were vitally interested in the problem of value. Their search for universality was a reaction to the cultural and epistemological relativism which had become characteristic of social and historical theory. Lotze's philosophy of value underlay his ethics; he was a eudaemonist, deriving his value theory from feeling rather than from Kant's unconditioned moral law. Even the pursuit of truth, he held, emerges originally from the feeling that truth is good.[50] Thus, the origin of values is psychological, and values arise from feelings, originally from the nature of sexual experience. The truth-seeker is actually a value-seeker. But, in keeping with his skepticism, Lotze said that there is a broad chasm between the world of forms (accessible to reason) and the world of values. No matter how "energetically our receptive mind may work its way backwards in thought to spell out from the actual forms of nature their ethical significance, we cannot proceed from that to prove from the consciousness of highest value the necessity of their taking shape in these and no other forms of nature."[51] The forms of nature are related to values, however, because they (that is, the mechanical pro-cesses of nature) are necessary conditions for the realization of the high-est good. "The world of things finds its most adequate description or logical expression in an all-prevading mechanical order, but it finds its interpretation through the world of values."[52] However, Lotze admitted the undemonstrability of this teleological concept. The machinery of the natural world has been created for a higher purpose, but this idea re-mains, in so many words, a postulate of practical reason. He willingly conceded that his theory was essentially no different from Christian teleology: "Religious belief in understanding the world as a divine creation has always cherished and expressed the same conviction in another way . . . [that] the most essential part of . . . [nature] consists in what God meant or willed that it should be."[53] Up to this point, the orthodox Christian Hegelians could have agreed with Lotze, but not in his dissent from the Hegelian doctrine that all values are eventually realized in thought through the progression of Reason. Here his moral individualism came through clearly:

> There is no real subject, no substance, no place in which anything worthy or sacred can be realized except the individual ego, the personal soul; beyond the inner life of the subjective spirit with its consciousness of ideas, . . . its effort to realize them, there is no superior region of a so-called objective spirit, the forms and articulation of which are in their mere existence more worthy than the subjective soul.[54]

Lotze agreed with Hegel that history contains the emerging ideas of humanity and freedom, but he criticized Hegel for exaggerating the universal form of Idea at the expense of its individual expressions. The consequence of Hegel's panlogism, he maintained, was the denial of free will and the subordination of individuals to partial and passive roles in history: "That which ought to be is determined only by universal ideas which, as ideas, form no part of the real world, and always have to wait until human wills give them some special definite form under which they become part of the world of reality."[55] "The fulfillment of an historic doom," Lotze concluded, "will be found only by him who counts every accomplished matter of fact among the necessary phases of development of an idea that rules the world."[56] He would have nothing of Hegel's idealist monism. He believed that history is the realm of freedom where individuals strive within a social framework for a higher moral and cultural existence, toward the creation of values with universal meaning.[57] He would not allow universal notions, in Dilthey's phrase, to "spread their gray veil over the historical world."

Yet Lotze's moral individualism brought him into the difficulties of relativism. If values are derived from individual feelings of worth, what guarantees their universal validity? The Baden philosophers were later beset with the same dilemma in their effort to place the individuality of historical events in the matrix of universally valid judgments. What benchmarks can be used to measure human events without robbing them of their concreteness and individuality? Lotze tried to find his way out of extreme individualism by asserting that pleasure and pain are not purely individual, but like our judgments of truth and false-hood, they have a universal side and "are a means of discovering an objective order of worth or value in things."[58] Here we find a clear anticipation of Windelband's later postulate that there is a universal normative consciousness. Values are historically neither contingent nor transitory: "The worth of human actions is not temporarily determined by arbitrary institutions of local prevalence or changing taste . . . but it depends on universal moral Ideas of an absolute good, just and beauti-ful, and only exists in proportion as these Ideas are reflected in the various and changing forms of action."[59]

This passage makes it painfully evident that Lotze did not succeed in solving the problem of values; he took refuge in teleological idealism and in a Platonic theory of moral ideas. He did not claim to have cut the knot; he recognized the problematic character of his views. He wanted a value theory derived from individual moral experience but sanctioned by a universal and transcendent moral ideal. The base of his value theory is the individual's subjective awareness of worth; its apex is the perfect will of a personal God. Thus, there may be some justice in the ironic observation by one of his critics that he began by doubting everything and ended by believing anything.[60] Yet Lotze confessed that the imposing assumptions of his value theory were undemonstrable. He came close to the position of modern pragmatism that certain un-provable postulates are necessary "fictions" of judgment, that for prac-tical reasons we must act "as if" certain ideas are universally true. The neo-Kantian Hans Vaihinger, founder of *Kant-Studien*, expanded this idea in his philosophy of "as if."[61] Lotze's practical resolution of truth and morality also foreshadowed William James on whom he was an important influence.[62]

While contending that values in human experience have no meaning apart from feelings of pleasure and pain, Lotze perservered in the con-viction that values are ultimately transcendent and immutable.[63] In try-ing to extricate himself from these apparent contradictions, he outlined the normative value theory later worked out by Windelband. Even though values derive from feelings of pleasure and pain, is it not possi-ble, Lotze asked, to contemplate the data of the senses apart from our individual reaction to them? Can we not perceive the objective value of an experience independently of the way in which it affects us?[64] He contended that we are capable of ascribing values to things without having our judgment warped by affective responses, and that among peoples on comparable cultural levels, the faculty of value judgment speaks with approximately the same voice.[65] There is something like a value consensus which is a reflection of absolute values.[66] With these arguments, unsatisfactory as they seem today, Lotze was trying to elude relativism without resorting to Hegel's doctrine that historical values are imperfect embodiments of the evolving Idea. In the process, he created the main outline of Heinrich Rickert's theory that historians can ascribe values to events without interjecting subjectivity or cultural bias.

Lotze's Ethics and Theory of Freedom

Lotze's ethics came from the same eudaemonistic roots as his value theory. Happiness, he said, is the natural and unblameworthy standard of human conduct.[67] Ethical rules are meaningless without reference to pleasure and pain. But these eudaemonistic standards must correspond to "universally-binding commands or moral ideals."[68] Once again, he was attempting to have the best of two worlds, the empirical and the ideal. He could not accept Kant's alleged ethical rigorism but he brought it in by the back door in modified form. Individual rules of conduct, Lotze asserted, could be drawn neither from Kant's categorical imperative nor from Hegel's principle that individual activity is measured by its role in the fulfillment of the highest world purpose. Hegel, he said, was guilty of "perilous dependence on metaphysical wisdom," because it would be necessary to have a clear idea of this highest world purpose in order to deduce rules of conduct from it.[69] This rejection of Kantian and Hegelian ethics was based on the failure of both to provide rules for actual moral decisions. The Highest Good, Lotze explained, is the binding power over all our activities, but even the Highest Good is meaningless without sensible beings to derive pleasure from participation in it.[70] Kant would have called his ethics heteronomous because it was based on motives other than unsullied obedience to moral law.

Lotze was Kantian, however, in his insistence on the primacy of conscience and autonomy of persons. In his lectures on practical philosophy, he expressed his own version of the moral law: "Conscience says this: It is unpraiseworthy to treat any object so casually as to impair it without justification; whatever is, and thereby has an intrinsic nature, is to be respected and not baselessly altered."[71] Lotze enlarged the reverence of conscience to include both people and nature, but he never confused the two. His ethics was built on a theory of freedom only partially in accordance with Kant's. Lotze said that if good and bad acts are not mere delusions, freedom is a necessary supposition. But he did not embrace Kant's doctrine of intelligible freedom: "It is useless to speak with Kant of an intelligible freedom through which the soul has freedom in its character as thing-in-itself in opposition to the actual course of events in time. Such a freedom does not interest us. That which we seek must reside in the possibility of initiating a new act within this temporal life."[72] Ethical freedom is, therefore, the freedom to choose among different values without being forced by nature or circumstances.[73]

The purpose of ethical action, said Lotze, paraphrasing Schleiermacher, is to produce moral values and to imbue natural relationships with moral qualities.[74] He summed up his moral philosophy in this manner: "Thus the universal moral ideals transmute themselves in real life into a series of specific rights and duties, which set the boundaries within which the corresponding actions must remain in order to be recognized by all others without misunderstanding, and . . . at the same time to serve the general welfare."[75] Lotze's moral philosophy was concrete and socially oriented. He rejected Kant's much maligned rigorism and theory of intelligible freedom. Like the Marburg neo-Kantians later, he refused to consider freedom, duty, and right apart from their actual social context: "For the benefit of the commonweal, the unconditional moral right becomes a conditioned juristic right."[76] He believed that this circumscription of natural rights was not historical but original, for social existence would be inconceivable without such an a priori limitation.

Lotze on Society and State

Although Lotze shrank from personal involvement in politics, he had a great deal to say on matters of political and social theory. In private life he was somewhat like the middle-class "men of honor," described by Gustav Freytag, "who tried with a touching conscientiousness to hold ignoble things at a distance . . . the noblest [of whom] ran the danger of becoming victims rather than heroes in political and social struggles."[77] Yet Lotze devoted much space to practical political questions in *Mikrokosmus* and went into the subject even more fully in his lectures on practical philosophy. The essence of his politics is found in a dictum he borrowed from Kant: "If law ceases, all worth of human life on earth ceases too."[78] The paramount obligation of the state is to uphold the rule of law, and the purpose of law is to protect the integrity of individuals: "Whenever law and society shall treat individuals as though they were things, there our civilization is marred by a remnant of barbarism."[79] Within society, Lotze said, there is constant tension between individual wills and the objective order, between the material wants of individuals and the mechanism of ordered political life which cannot satisfy all those wants.[80] The task of social authority (the state) is to regulate these conflicts firmly and fairly. Lotze's political thought is trenchantly practical. He held that political philosophy should be concerned only with the world as it is, not with utopian ideas of what it should become.[81] Genuine moral action is requisite to the good society; the mere disposition to do good is not enough. You must "do something in the world" by putting your principles into practice rather than sitting around waiting for a favorable opportunity.[82] Here Lotze was obliquely criticizing Kant's greatly misunderstood saying that the only absolutely good thing in the world is a good will.

Moral acts, like rights, have no meaning for Lotze outside their social setting. The hallmark of moral activity in society is striving for the well-being of others.[83] But because few are capable of following this selfless rule, it is necessary for the state to become a "timeless conscience" above the struggle of individual and group interests. Yet he did not elevate the state to metahistorical dignity. And he strongly condemned the Hegelian idea that the state has been "concatenated into a series of stages in the development of the World Soul."[84] He believed in minimal government—although his idea of the proper minimums far exceeded the limits of laissez-faire liberalism.[85] Society is the place for the healthy interplay of interests, regulated by the standards of morality and equity which are embodied (but not permanently enshrined) in the positive law of the state. Beyond these general tenets, it is not easy to sort out Lotze's political ideas and arrange them in a coherent system. His political views were hybrid; they ranged from modified laissez-faire to conservative corporatism. Although he described his politics as moderate socialism, this expression says very little about his syncretic political philosophy.

The only consistent element in Lotze's politics is his contempt for dogmatism. He believed that limited monarchy was the most suitable form of government in Germany, but democracy might be more feasible elsewhere. He deplored the alienation and dehumanization of the worker in modern industrial society, but believed that working-class associations were divisive and ineffective.[86] He thought that the organic theory of society was indefensible, yet he said that corporative forms of organization—an idea usually identified with organic conservatism— might restore the laborer to his former dignity and security. He was against the perpetuation of unearned wealth through inheritance, but defended the principle of private property. Lotze shunned the cant of orthodox liberalism. Free competition, property, and profits are not, he said, sacrosanct. They contribute to a healthy social environment, but property and wealth are a stewardship rather than inherent attributes of political liberty. If a business becomes wastefully inefficient or if wealth is misused, then the state is obligated to intervene.

The state has two main functions: (1) Its authority represents the claims of social conscience—for only a supra-class institution can apply the rules of conscience equitably. And (2) the state develops within itself the coherent historical life of society, past, present, and future.[87] The state is not given the role of ubiquitous magistrate; its job is rather to "protect all free and lawful personal activity, affording merely the possibility of general human culture."[88] The government of ancient Rome, according to Lotze, had the right blend of freedom and authority. The Romans combined "in satisfactory practice, respect for transmitted rights, provision for new wants, and the conditions required for the growth and continuance of the whole."[89]

If the authority of the state is to operate as a timeless conscience *au-dessus de la melée,* it is best embodied in a living, personal sovereignty, such as hereditary monarchy. The function of the hereditary monarch is to "bring to bear the historical idea in opposition to the alternation of passions and the clash of opinions."[90] Lotze's theory of the state thus emphasized the practical need for a continuing, transcendent authority so that moral and cultural life may develop in an optimally free political environment.[91] Limited monarchy is a real institution answering to the needs of society, but it is also, or so Lotze believed, above the struggle of parties and the battle for power. Limited monarchy, as the capstone of the state, represents the enduring interests of society. Hence, monarchy is a viable source of stability—it saves society from itself, because only the monarchy is free to identify itself with the general welfare.[92] Like many German liberals of his era, Lotze had scant respect for party politics and the idea of parliamentary sovereignty. If the constitution calls for an element of democracy, then the franchise, in Lotze's estimation, should be limited to those of superior *Bildung,* and to the citizens whose talents warrant them the vote because of service to the state or because they have created a material stake in society.[93] The masses, because they are usually inert, need inspiration and leadership; they are best served by the energies and discoveries of individual minds, the meritocracy of German *Bildung,* that is, by the educated, professional, and propertied classes. In this respect, Lotze remained well within the political traditions of German idealism at mid-century.

In his view of the nation-state, Lotze conformed to the canons of orthodox German liberalism as well. He did not subscribe to the cosmopolitanism of Goethe, the idol of his youth. He responded to it with: "Every individual nation is called forth to historical attainments only through zealous cultivation of its own peculiar qualities and through the impulse of self-preservation from which the love of these qualities springs. Without a doubt, the history of mankind would be dull fare indeed and would not arouse the lively interest it does but for that constantly invigorating competition [among nations]."[94] No nation can become truly great without so-called national hatred of others. The theory that rivalry among nations is a necessary cultural stimulant was one of the more dangerous assumptions of the nineteenth century. But among his own contemporaries, both within and without Germany, Lotze had no monopoly on this dubious notion that national rivalry sparks the dynamics of progress.

Lotze, admittedly, added nothing new to the politics of German idealism. He was perhaps more keenly aware than earlier idealists of the social dislocations arising from modern industry, and he acknowledged the need for political interference in the marketplace in the interest of social justice. Measured by twentieth-century standards, however, Lotze was conservative. There was no room in his philosophy even for such a thing as Fichte's *geschlossene Handelsstaat*, which guaranteed to all both property and the right to work. And his notion of who should participate in political power conformed to the bourgeois dimensions of nineteenth-century liberalism. His importance does not rest on his political philosophy. His contributions to neo-Kantianism were constructive skepticism, a distrust of purely conceptual thought, a deep interest in the problem of values and an admirable effort to bring philosophical idealism into harmony with nineteenth-century science.[95] The importance of Lotze for James and many others was, in the words of one recent authority, "that he formulated the problems for them and managed in his eclectic or dialectical way to state the alternatives that seemed to be viable: idealism, realism, and pragmatism."[96] This certainly suggests the truth of John Passmore's comment that Lotze was "the most pillaged source," and supports Paul Kuntz's opinion that from 1880 to 1920 there was a Lotzean period in the history of thought.[97]

It cannot be said that Lotze succeeded in resolving the baffling issues that confronted him, but in the attempt he gave fresh impetus to undogmatic thought and to the revival of critical philosophy. He tried to remedy what Merz described years ago as the most serious defect in the Hegelian system, "the absence of a specifically ethical teaching, of an adequate treatment of the moral problem which had been such a marked characteristic" in Kant.[98]

3

Hegelians Manqués:
Kuno Fischer and Eduard Zeller

Kuno Fischer and Eduard Zeller, together with their older contemporary J.E. Erdmann, did much to free nineteenth-century German historiography from the cramped quarters of politics and diplomacy. They made the history of philosophy an integral and worthy branch of historical studies, and in the process they liberated philosophy from the old tradition of studying philosophical systems in a historical vacuum. In keeping with their Hegelian training, Fischer and Zeller brought philosophy into history and, in effect, historicized philosophy. The significance of their contribution to the future of intellectual history would be difficult to exaggerate. Wilhelm Dilthey's work in the historical emergence of Weltanschauungen; Weber's inquiries into the relation between spiritual values and economic practices as well as his theories on the rational ideal and the rise of bureaucratic forms; and Meinecke's classic study of the transition from cosmopolitanism to the national idea are all indebted to the "history of philosophy" school inaugurated at the University of Tübingen in the second quarter of the century. Both Fischer and Zeller became Hegelians manqués, that is, they defected to a certain extent from Hegel by remanding their contemporaries back to the critical method of Kant. But they stayed close to Hegel in their conviction

58

that philosophy is the crimson thread of history because it reveals the progressive stages of human consciousness.

Fischer's two-volume study of Kant, appearing in 1860-61 as part of his opus *Geschichte der neueren Philosophie*, and Zeller's academic lecture "On the Significance and Task of the Theory of Knowledge" in 1862 were landmarks in the genesis of neo-Kantianism.[1] Fischer's admirable exposition of Kant's epistemology and Zeller's appeal for a revival of *Kritizismus* shook the academic pillars, while Fischer's interpretation of Kant put a sharper edge on the growing epistemological debate.[2] Although both men remained essentially Hegelian as to the history of thought, they actually were the first formally to become neo-Kantians by explicitly endorsing the return to criticism.

The Harassed Hegelian

Kuno Fischer's family was associated with the Protestant church and the army; his father was a minister and his mother was the daughter of a Prussian cavalry officer.[3] He was born in the pastorage at Gross-Sandewalde in Silesia on July 23, 1824, and educated at the gymnasium in Posen. He then went to Leipzig, where he matriculated in the summer of 1844, the year Lotze left Leipzig for Göttingen. The line of descent from Fischer and Lotze, through Windelband to Heinrich Rickert provides an interesting study in the transmission and gradual modification of ideas from one generation to the next. This particular descent moved from belief in the immanent and irresistible progression of the Hegelian Idea in history to a reassertion of the individual consciousness and will in the form of Kantian and Fichtean voluntarism, a rebellion of individual personality against the seeming fatalism of Hegel. It would not require a Marxist to see this development as a protest of the bourgeois liberal spirit in Germany against historical passivity. And it was probably not an accident that this rebellion coincided with the liberal awakening and the so-called New Era in Prussian politics beginning in 1858.

At Leipzig Fischer attended the lectures of Lotze's Hegelian teacher Christian Weisse. He later transferred to Halle where he studied under two other followers of Hegel, Johann Eduard Erdmann and Julius Schaller; in 1847 he finished his doctoral thesis, "De Platonico Parmenide." At Halle he had much in common with the other neo-Kantians. Zeller was also a student of Platonic thought. Hermann Cohen and Paul Natorp of Marburg were to write treatises on Plato. The Marburg philosophers looked upon Plato as the first genuine philosopher of science. Both before and after he took his doctorate, Fischer contributed to Oswald Marbach's *Literatur und Kunstblatt* and two other publications, *Die Epigonen* and *Die Akademie*. These early writings are of more than casual interest because they anticipate some of the ideas central to his later philosophy. In one of the early Marbach articles Fischer defended Hegel's doctrine on the reasonableness of emerging reality. He never questioned the Hegelian proposition that immanent reason forms the linkage in the history of thought. In these journalistic forays he began to conceive what he considered to be the chief task of his work: To discern "the philosophy of history in the history of philosophy."[4]

Fischer's essays assumed political overtones when he began to attack Hegelians of the extreme left, particularly Max Stirner, the left-Hegelian ego anarchist. Fischer, however, was a very flexible Hegelian. From the beginning he urged the reshaping of Hegel's doctrines, and when revolution came in 1848, he proved that he did not consider Prussian institutions exceptionally advanced. Although he did not join the liberal rebels actively, he made it clear that he favored "a thorough rejuvenation of public life."[5] The rising historian was extremely wary of being distracted from his scholarly work. Like Lotze, he rarely descended into the political marketplace, but he was not as detached as Lotze. His essays on the young Hegelians led to friendship with Arnold Ruge, editor of the *Hallische Jahrbücher* and leader of the group.[6] Fischer's political reputation was later compromised in the eyes of the reactionary government because of his personal contact with left-Hegelian circles.[7]

After taking his degree in 1848, Fischer was in such financial straits that he could not afford immediately to become a *Privatdozent* living solely on students' fees. He took a tutoring position in Pforzheim in the home of a factory owner. In 1849, he moved to Karlsruhe where his already broad range of interests was expanded by his discovery of dramatic literature; he later wrote studies of Lessing, Schiller, and Goethe.[8] But his stay in Karlsruhe did not have a happy conclusion. In 1850, he was told to leave the city by an official who was suspicious of his earlier associations with the young Hegelians.[9] This was not his last painful experience with the nervous post-1848 regimes.

In September 1850, Fischer was finally able to begin his academic career. He was appointed to a position at Heidelberg, later a vital center of neo-Kantianism, and soon he had to obtain a larger lecture hall to accomodate his burgeoning audience. One reason for his success was a new technique he pioneered, which he called the *freien Vortrag*—a less formal style of lecturing which broke away from explication of a set text and allowed digression without altogether abandoning the text as format. He quickly acquired a reputation as a spellbinding lecturer which he held for the remainder of his life. Today an oil painting of Fischer charming a crowded classroom hangs in a special section of the Palatine Museum in Heidelberg dedicated to the university's distinguished professors. A bust of Heinrich Rickert stands nearby. Fischer's success behind the lectern, however, brought him dubious rewards. His popularity apparently aroused the jealousy of some of his colleagues, who later refused to support him when he came into conflict with the church and the Ministry of Education.[10] In 1852, Fischer's prospects brightened. The first volume of his *Geschichte* was published in June, and in September he married Marie Desirée Le Mire, who, like his mother, was the daughter of a soldier, in this case a French officer on liaison duty in Heidelberg.

But there was another political contretemps ahead. Daniel Schenkel, professor of theology and director of the Heidelberg Seminary for Ministers, was offended by some of Fischer's lectures and sent word to the High Consistory in Karlsruhe that the young docent's interpretation of Spinoza had a pernicious influence on the students. He accused Fischer of being sympathetic to Spinoza's pantheism, which to the orthodox was rank heresy.[11]

This time many of the faculty came to Fischer's support and he was backed by the University senate, but a reactionary minister of education had come to power in June 1853. There was small chance for a fair hearing. Fischer's permission to hold lectures was revoked; with a stroke of the bureaucratic pen, his promising career was interrupted. He accepted this decision with a certain amount of resignation but still became a symbol of trammeled *Lehrfreiheit*—the precious academic freedom held dear by German professors, although it had been frequently violated even before the Third Reich. Fischer fought his battle with his adversary, Professor Schenkel, in print.[12] There was a flurry of polemics, and his predicament as a symbol of violated principle became even greater. Soon he won the interest and political support of important figures in Berlin.

The two and one-half years Fischer was forced to spend in academic limbo were not wasted. He continued work on the *Geschichte* and also wrote his *Grundriss der Logik und Metaphysik oder Wissenschaftslehre* in which he reformulated Hegel's principle of identity in light of Kant's critical epistemology.[13] In his historical work he anticipated his student Dilthey's *Verstehen* theory on use of psychological empathy for grasping the meaning of past events. He called his method *nachzuerleben*—to reexperience. Yet Fischer was not willing to accept the implications of historicism. He believed that intellectual problems are typical and recurring. Philosophical ideas are expressed in a timebound frame of reference, but at the core they express the perennial questions of conscient humanity.[14] These were the lean years of Fischer's life, but gradually his fortunes improved. He befriended two important pre-March liberals, Gervinus and Haüsser, and in 1854, David Friedrich Strauss, who could well understand the rigors of academic ostracism. At the same time influential people in Berlin were applying pressure to get Fischer a new appointment. Alexander von Humboldt and the historian August Böckh were working behind the scenes to persuade Frederick William IV to end Fischer's academic exile. Humboldt wrote a personal note to the king which finally resulted, in September 1856, in Frederick William issuing a cabinet order which authorized Fischer's appointment to a Prussian university. Yet the fight was not over. Another reactionary minister, Karl von Raumer, delayed forwarding the order, and Fischer had to wait for his appointment until late autumn.[15]

In November 1856, Fischer received a letter from Moritz Seebeck, curator at the University of Jena, inviting him to become an honorary professor in ordinary (*ordentliche Honorarprofessor*). Humboldt rejoiced that "once again little Jena has saved the honor of Germany."[16] Fischer spent the next sixteen years at Jena, where he established his reputation as a powerful spokesman for the idealist heritage in an age of naturalism and pessimism. Fischer was swimming upstream, for this was the decade when Arthur Schopenhauer was enjoying belated popularity and the poems of pessimistic resignation by the Italian Giacomo Leopardi were in vogue.[17] But certain similarities between Fischer's and Schopenhauer's thought no doubt made him seem more in tune with the temper of the time.

Fischer was involved in a network of relationships among the early neo-Kantians that helped to spread the renewed enthusiasm for critical philosophy. He had met Strauss, who was Zeller's teacher at Tübingen; then Zeller became his friend and correspondent. Fischer left Jena for Heidelberg in 1872 to fill the chair Zeller had resigned to accept an offer from Berlin while, at Berlin, Zeller took the initiative in luring Lotze from Göttingen, finally succeeding in 1881. When Lotze died shortly thereafter, Fischer was invited to Berlin to take his place but declined. He befriended and corresponded with another early neo-Kantian, Otto Liebmann. Thus, an informal association of intellectuals with Hegelian backgrounds and Kantian inclinations became established. They were bound by personal friendship and common philosophical interests, and were active in the same academic milieu. Neo-Kantianism had a strong interpersonal and institutional basis which facilitated its rise to prominence.

His call to Jena ended Fischer's difficulties with the authorities. Ill-treatment at the hands of the education ministry had not visibly sharpened his interest in politics or turned him into a critic of the monarchy. He picked up his career where it had been interrupted almost three years earlier and quickly proved that he had not lost his touch as a fascinating lecturer. Early in 1857 he began a series of lectures on Kant entitled the *clavis Kantiana*.[18] His presentation of Kant in the classroom revealed the line of interpretation he would follow in his *Geschichte der neueren Philosophie*. In the following decade Fischer's career finally blossomed. His heralded two-volume study of Kant, comprising the fourth and fifth volumes of the *Geschichte*, was welcomed as an oasis in a desert of undistinguished philosophy. The grand duke of Weimar was so impressed with Fischer that he sent his son, and heir to Jena, and in 1865-66 Fischer accompanied the young prince on a tour through Italy and Sicily.[19]

After rejecting several offers from Heidelberg and Vienna, Fischer relented and returned to the Baden university in 1872, to finish his work "and to die," as he put it. While he was at Heidelberg, the *Geschichte* was completed, and he found time to write essays on literature and drama. Honors came his way in predictable conformity with the official manner of rewarding (and co-opting?) distinguished academics. He received the honorific title *Geheimrat,* a customary civic accolade for outstanding professors. Of more significance was his admission to the Berlin Academy of Sciences as a corresponding member, and to the Accademia dei Lincei in Rome.[20] The death of Fischer's second wife in 1903 actually brought his career to an end, although he lived four more years, for soon thereafter he terminated his lectures and formally retired in 1906. He died on July 5, 1907. Wilhelm Windelband had been given his chair in 1903.

Fischer on Kant

By all accounts Kuno Fischer's volumes on Kant in the *Geschichte* were of paramount importance in the genesis of neo-Kantianism.[21] In the opinion of his student Windelband, "Fischer's study of Kant since its publication has had an immeasurably wide influence, and . . . the literature on Kant has swollen unbelievably. Fischer himself, therefore, occupies a pre-eminent place in the revival of Kant. . . . "[22] Fischer's ideas on history and his interpretation of Kant are of particular significance in early neo-Kantianism. He believed, like any conventional Hegelian, that the history of philosophy reflected the growing self-awareness of human reason, but he held with Kant that thought could never become absolute.[23] He was too steeped in Kantian criticism to ignore the limits of thought. Like Lotze, he was skeptical and, therefore, unwilling to dissolve reality in reason. And, as Windelband expressed it, "he was among those Hegelians who believed that Hegel was not the end of philosophy."

Fischer met the problem of historicism obliquely. He stressed both the continuity and contingency of philosophical thought. The history of philosophy is an unbroken process of emergent reason. Even through the great turning points of philosophical history and the great revolutions in thought, spiritual continuity remains intact.[24] But philosophy is also time-bound. It assumes a life-form peculiar to the era of its formation. The historian of philosophy has the task of sympathetically penetrating this life-form to get to the essence, and to find the perennial human question hidden beneath the historical shell.[25] He must follow the dialectical relation that always exists between thought and its historical context. Modern philosophy was first in conflict with its historical conditions; this conflict was sharpened to complete opposition, followed by reconciliation.[26] Fischer saw this dialectical process at work in the opposition of will and intellect, and found a historical example of it in the evolution from Kant to Fichte to Schopenhauer.[27] Here he gave a hint of his own voluntarism, a tendency which became clear in his exegesis of Kant.

Fischer asserted that historians of philosophy have erred in assuming that the sciences of philosophy and history are incompatible. In their view, philosophy looks for truth, history looks for the succession of events in time. The truth is one, the events of history are many; therefore, never the twain shall meet. Fischer rejected this splitting of spiritual reality. The separation of history from philosophy frustrates the historian of philosophy, and the barren result is "history without philosophy and philosophy without history."[28] He therefore raised the characteristically Kantian question, "How is the history of philosophy as a science possible?" For Fischer, the answer lay in his Hegelian theory of history. Philosophical knowledge is a process, the gradual development of reason in consciousness. Hence, every idea has a history, and external historical conditions play an important part in the formation of every idea. All the sciences, he insisted, are creations of history. Yet, with his usual note of caution, he added that our ideas are never complete, the work of intelligence is never over, and the objects of thought themselves are not immutable. The objects of philosophy do not evolve according to mechanical laws; they have a living, spiritual nature; thus they have to be seen in the progressive development of the mind.[29] The history of philosophy is the growing self-knowledge of the human spirit.

Fischer had a faith in the liberating and consoling powers of philosophical contemplation akin to Schopenhauer's. The historian of philosophy, he exalted, is freed from transitory concerns. While he contemplates the course of reason, he is momentarily detached from his historical situation; it loses its power over him. As the philosopher turns from life, inwardly he is liberated, cut loose from mundane moorings.[30] For Fischer, this elevated state was beginning of true philosophizing and spiritual freedom. The idea of ascending to knowledge through resignation doubtless came from Schopenhauer, and it is tempting to infer that Fischer first began to appreciate the haven of private contemplation during his vexations with the educational bureaucracy. The private sphere as a refuge from unpleasant and intractable political realities was not an uncommon notion after 1849, and, as many historians have suggested, it may have served as a rationalization of declining political vigor among the middle classes. Yet this mood passed. Fischer was also a philosopher of freedom. It would be just as sensible to see him as a symptom of reviving, bourgeois confidence in the late 1850s and early 1860s.

Fischer's Idea of Freedom

The type of freedom usually adopted by German idealists has been condemned as elegant in theory and defective in practice. At least as far back as the eighteenth century, German intellectuals "turned from politics to the cultivation of their private lives and to the exploration of the world of the spirit."[31] Hermann Lotze, in a modest way, broke with this "ethical suspension of the practical"; so did the Marburg and socialist Kantians. Kuno Fischer's position was somewhat ambiguous. But in 1875 he gave a public lecture in which he explored the question of human freedom.[32] His conclusion was that "in the Kantian doctrine of intelligible and natural character ... which Schopenhauer called the greatest achievement of human profundity and took as the point of departure for his own doctrines, the question of freedom was for the first time recognized in its true meaning."[33] Fischer did not want to commit the fallacy of the stone "which was thrown but believed itself to be flying."[34] Nevertheless, he wanted to avoid the deterministic conclusions of the materialists. He discussed the problem of freedom with wit and irony. He pointed to the paradox that Christians from the time of St. Augustine have argued the theological impossibility and moral necessity of freedom, while the materialists have been equally contradictory. They insist on the physical impossibility of freedom because they are determinists and mechanists—but they assert the practical necessity of freedom because they are reformers.[35]

Fischer tried to disarm the determinist argument by first accepting most of it, and then resorting to Kant's theory of intelligible freedom. "Our actions," he said,"are all grounded in natural character."[36] A fool will act foolishly, and a wise man wisely. Now, if this natural character itself is determined, then there is no freedom, but if character is a free act of will, then we are free.[37] Implying that character *is* a free act of will, he proceeded to the idea of a consciousness that recognizes our acts as *both* determined and free. This moral consciousness, as he called it, is the basis of ethics; it makes us responsible for our actions. For him, the awareness of both freedom and necessity is no ordinary conscience. It does not say "you have done wrongfully, do better the next time." On the contrary, it admonishes,"you have done wrongfully because that is the way you are, but you should be otherwise."[38] In other words, conscience does not judge the single act but the total moral character of the actor. By recognizing the wrongful act as a result of defective character, the conscience is an even more severe judge; it affirms moral responsibility. At that point Fischer concluded, moral consciousness tells us our actions are determined because they are necessary expressions of character, but free because we are responsible for them.[39] Going along with Kant, he held that freedom was part of the intelligible rather than the natural order. His doctrine of freedom also retained Kant's dualism; he did not, it should be stressed, merge consciousness and reality, freedom and nature in the Hegelian principle of identity. Although Fischer did not work out a systematic moral philosophy, he helped turn the ethics of German idealism away from Hegel and toward Kant. But he virtually ignored the practical social implications of Kant's ethics. He adhered to Kant's doctrine of intelligible freedom as Schopenhauer had left it—with the emphasis on determinism in nature and the idea of freedom up in the noumenal clouds.

Schopenhauer's philosophy, it should be noted, was an important part of the neo-Kantian ferment in the 1850s. Schopenhauer had made barely a ripple until the middle of the century, then suddenly his philosophy became an intellectual fad. After the disillusionments of 1848–49, there was a trend toward hard-nosed realism and at least a temporary canalizing of bourgeois energy into nonpolitical pursuits, until the short-lived revival of liberal hopes started by the accession of William I. Von Rochau coined the term *Realpolitik* in the early 1850s. Rapid economic progress contributed to the realistic and apolitical temper of the decade. Railways shot out across the country, the Tax Union was founded, the first credit banks established, and Germany entered the machine age. Even the student songs and ballads, at one time exaltations of high hopes and youthful idealism, became mocking and cynical.[40] Material prosperity and political impotence imbued the middle class with some of those philistine qualities which Nietzsche would later single out for his wholehearted contempt.

Schopenhauer is important in the history of neo-Kantianism because of the prominence he gave Kant in his own philosophy. He claimed to be Kant's true successor, and asserted that nothing had happened in German philosophy between Kant and himself. "I cannot see," he wrote, "that anything has been done in philosophy between him and me; I therefore take my point of departure directly from him."[41] He also claimed that to understand his own ideas one must first comprehend Kant.[42] Schopenhauer should also be ranked as the most intemperate enemy of Hegel and Fichte (whom he once simply dismissed as a windbag). His heavy-handed anti-Hegelianism jibed nicely with the current revolt against Hegelianism, but it was his extreme voluntarism that influenced Fischer's interpretation of Kant, which reflected Schopenhauer's apotheosis of will. Although Fischer criticized the way Schopenhauer construed Kant's forms of knowledge as functions of the brain,[43] he himself interpreted the thing-in-itself as will.[44] According to Fischer, the thing-in-itself was what saved Kant's philosophy from being a solipsistic dream, and preserved the idea of freedom. The thing-in-itself resides in a supersensuous, intelligible world as opposed to the contingent, sensible world of nature. So far this is true to Kant, but Fischer added that the intelligible realm of freedom resides in pure will. Thus, as in Schopenhauer, the supreme world principle is will. This is not a "heavenly world of spirits," said Fischer, "but where the laws of freedom are valid and fulfilled." This is the "World as Will."[45] But he did not reach Schopenhauer's dire conclusion that will is a relentless cosmic force.

Fischer believed that he was following Kant to the letter: "In other words, the actual or true world principle according to Kant is not cognitive reason, but the will."[46] Fischer was here only partially correct. The principal doctrine in Kant's philosophy is the primacy of practical over theoretical reason, of moral over cognitive activities. As Leonard Krieger explains,

> The will [for Kant], the active faculty of desire in man standing between his reason and his natural inclinations, is the principle of his integration, his individuality. . . . The moral law here obliges the individual to obey the absolutely unconditioned precepts which his practical reason presents to his will, and this obedience constitutes freedom because the universal and unconditioned precepts of action embodied in the moral law and produced by pure reason liberate man from the compulsions of the sensible world and positively make the will of man self-legislating.[47]

This expresses clearly the role of will in Kant's philosophy, and indicates that Fischer's expansion of will into the intelligible world principle is not entirely of Kantian provenance. In Kant, it is *reason* that gives moral laws to will. Kant believed that a good man is "one who acts on the supposition that there is an unconditional and objective moral standard holding for all men in virtue of their rationality as human beings."[48] Reason, therefore, discerns an intelligible *moral* order and prescribes to will. The will neither constitutes this supreme principle nor informs reason. Will is instrumental but not constitutive.

Although Fischer's fidelity to Kantian fundamentals is open to question, he was one of the instigators of the coming renaissance in German thought. As he observed in a later edition of the *Geschichte*, German philosophy was bogged down in a "morass of eclecticism" about the time he began to teach.[49] In his lifetime, the idealist tradition was given new life; it was imbued once again with the critical spirit of Kantianism and momentarily purged of the confusions prevalent around mid-century. Fischer deserves some of the credit for this and for the renewed vitality of German intellectual life later in the century. As for the naive materialism of the 1850s, he was a major participant in its defeat. But it could also be charged that his brand of neo-idealism was a retreat from unpleasant realities and from the earlier effort by the young Hegelians to come to grips with new social and political problems.[50]

Zeller and the Psychological Interpretation of Kant

None of the early neo-Kantians was more deeply involved in the young Hegelian milieu than Eduard Zeller, Germany's foremost historian of Greek philosophy in the nineteenth century. A student of the Hegelian biblical critic F.C. Baur at Tübingen, editor of the official Tübingen journal, the *Theologische Jahrbücher*, and friend of Hegel's most radical young disciples, Zeller was constantly embroiled in religious controversies. His philosophy of history was, like Fischer's, of Hegelian pedigree, and he was also among the first to recommend a return to Kantian criticism.

Zeller was born on January 22, 1814, at Kleinbottwar bei Marbach in Swabia. His family's background was typical of the bourgeois intelligentsia; his father served forty-two years as a minor treasury official in Württemberg.[51] When Zeller was eight years old, he was sent to the Latin school to prepare for the difficult seminary entrance examinations; by parental decision he was headed for the ministry. In 1827, he enrolled for one term in the gymnasium at Stuttgart before entering the seminary. While he was a young seminarian at Maulbronn, he took a summer course under Strauss, who was there briefly as a professorial regent. Later at Tübingen, they became close friends, although Strauss's religious ideas strained their professional relationship. Zeller would eventually be one of Strauss's biographers and literary executors.[52]

In the fall of 1831, Zeller entered the evangelical theological seminary at Tübingen, soon to become the home of F.C. Baur's controversial work on biblical literature. The most famous Tübingen *Stiftler* had been Hegel himself, whose classmates in the early 1790s were Hölderlin and Schelling.[53] The philosophical persuasion at Tübingen was Hegelian, but the ambience of critical biblical scholarship was no doubt conducive to a critical attitude in other areas such as epistemology. D.F. Strauss was on the faculty (until his dismissal over the scandalizing *Leben Jesu*) and was one of the principal bearers of Hegel's philosophy from Berlin. Another member of the Tübingen faculty was the democratic poet, Ludwig Uhland. When Uhland was forced to resign over a political dispute with the Württemberg government, Zeller was chairman of a delegation of students who presented him with a gift to express their esteem.[54] Later Zeller suffered Fischer's misfortune of guilt by association with such allegedly revolutionary figures as Uhland.

Zeller's first studies at Tübingen were in philosophy, but he shifted to theology under F.C. Baur, whose interpretations were not yet as unorthodox as they became later in his books on early Christianity and the New Testament. He finished his theological studies in 1835, but remained at Tübingen for another year to attend lectures on Greek and Platonic philosophy. After a short apprenticeship in the ministry as a vicar in Nellingen, he visited Hegel's widow in Berlin, bringing with him a letter of reference from the luminaries of South German Hegelianism, Eduard Gans and Strauss.[55] Early in 1839, Zeller returned to Tübingen, first as tutor in the *Stift*, and then *Privatdozent*. He soon became a critic for the Berlin and Halle *Jahrbücher*, the latter a journal of young Hegelianism. Then in 1842, the Tübingen school created its own polemical organ, the *Theologische Jahrbücher*, edited by Zeller.[56]

Compared to the radical Hegelians, Zeller was a moderate. He objected to Strauss's use of science as a solvent of religion, but he was equally critical of all lopsided approaches to religion, such as Schleiermacher's emphasis on feeling, Feuerbach's on will, and Kant's on morality. He preferred to judge religion in the totality of spiritual life rather than in isolation.[57] As he expressed it in the preface to his *History of Greek Philosophy*, his aim was to get from the "outer appearance of the spirit to its secret workshop."[58] Increasingly his ties with Baur and Strauss brought him grief from the religious conservatives. In 1843, he was attacked by Fischer's journalistic opponents on the *Evangelische Kirchenzeitung*, the voice of narrow Christian orthodoxy. In 1844, the Pietist spokesman Christoph Hoffmann, incensed at the teachings of F.T. Vischer, another close associate of Zeller, wrote twenty-one thundering theses against the "heterodox" Hegelians. Hoffman, not one to suffer the enemy calmly, declared that whoever publicly attacks or impugns Christian doctrine should be promptly thrown out of the community and "to the dogs."[59]

The political tide was still running with Hoffmann and the conservatives. In 1845, Vischer was suspended from his teaching position for two years, blocking Zeller's path to promotion for nearly four years; he therefore accepted an offer from Bern in 1847. When Strauss had been called to Zurich eight years earlier, such an outcry arose that the liberal government was forced to resign. Zeller's acceptance of the Bern offer almost caused the same reaction, but the ministry stood behind its decision and weathered the storm of Pietist protest.[60] But hostility toward him did not subside immediately; his friends were so concerned for his safety that they assigned a night watchman to his home. Their solicitude was not unwarranted; on several occasions angry townspeople threw rocks through his windows.[61] Zeller did not stay in Switzerland long. The reactionary situation in his homeland had forced his exile. But when liberal ministeries came into power in 1848, the political climate improved temporarily, and Zeller was eager to return. The March ministry in Electoral Hesse called him to the chair of theology at Marburg, but the elector was in no hurry to confirm the appointment.

Zeller was not officially accepted until the revolution had spent its momentum and the liberals were again out of power, forcing him to settle for less than full academic freedom. He was given a chair in philosophy and forbidden to give lectures in theology.[62]

For the thirteen years Zeller stayed in Marburg he was part of a dazzling intellectual circle, including the eminent historians Heinrich von Sybel, Johannes Gildemeister, and Georg Waitz. Their rallying point was the weekly Tuesday Club (Dienstag-Club), another miniature of Germany's academic middle class. A number of important academic and civic responsibilities at Marburg frequently took Zeller away from his research. He collaborated with Sybel on the *Historische Zeitschrift*, which the latter founded in 1859, and on local civic projects. In 1855, they created an association for the abolition of mendicancy and a Society for the Poor.[63] Zeller's civic work was indicative of a growing social awareness at the University of Marburg which came to fruition later in neo-Kantian socialism.

In 1857, Zeller became embroiled in an issue which presaged the position he and other German liberals would take during Bismarck's *Kulturkampf* in the 1870s. He wrote an article in Bran's *Merkur* attacking the proposed Concordat between Württemberg and the papacy. The treaty was eventually rejected by the Württemberg Chamber of Deputies, and Zeller was given some of the credit for defeating it.[64] Sixteen years later, Zeller was still sticking to the anticlerical beliefs he had held during the *Kulturkampf*. He denounced the alleged pretensions of the Roman hierarchy, and assailed the Catholic Church as a threat to free thought in Germany.[65] Ostensibly, German liberalism was the party of toleration, but the *Kulturkampf* proved that the liberal ambit was limited to certain confessions as well as to classes. Zeller's diatribes did not help to widen the circle. It should be remembered, however, that anticlericalism and suspicion of the ultramontanes had been traits of European liberalism since the beginning of its struggle with the old regimes.

In 1862, Zeller moved to Heidelberg and joined the company of Helmholtz, Robert Bunsen, Ludwig Häusser, and later, Treitschke.[66] His inaugural lecture at Heidelberg was the occasion of his famous appeal for a return to Kant as well as his first major departure from the master, Hegel, though in 1847 he had argued for free will and individual autonomy against Hegel's panlogism in a *Theologische Jahrbücher* article.[67] But this was a minor heresy compared to his invocation of Kant in 1862. When he was offered a chair at Berlin in 1872, he found the invitation difficult to resist. Helmholtz persistently encouraged him to accept and many of his old friends from Marburg and Heidelberg were already there. He accepted and could then bask in the glory of the imperial capital. At Berlin Zeller reached the top of the academic Olympus. Soon he, Helmholtz, and Theodor Mommsen became the unofficial triumvirate of the Berlin *Akademie der Wissenschaften*. On the centenary of Frederick the Great's death in 1886, Zeller produced a monograph entitled *Friedrich der Grosse als Philosoph*,[68] in which he wisely decided to rank Frederick the historical figure above Frederick the philosopher. He attempted to illustrate how Kant's moral philosophy and Frederick's sense of service to the state grew from the same soil of the German Enlightenment. This thesis had its merits, but Zeller failed to delineate the cynical side of Frederick's character.

In 1894, with the highest academic honors bestowed upon him, Zeller retired to Stuttgart. Recipient of the order *Pour le Mérite*, rector emeritus of the University of Berlin, and still active on a number of scholarly journals, he enjoyed a busy retirement in Nesenbach, a suburb of the Swabian capital.[69] In 1899, he fired a broadside at the philosophies of Schopenhauer and Nietzsche, which, in his opinion, were not philosophies at all but inchoate bursts of emotion. He wanted to see a revival of logical, scientifically grounded metaphysics in place of disordered intellectual spontaneity.[70] He also used the greater leisure of retirement to edit the correspondence of his old friend, D.F. Strauss.

By the end of the century, Zeller was the unchallenged "Nestor of German Philosophy."[71] His work in ancient philosophy had been improved upon by more refined philological methods, but he was still accorded great respect. Several generations of scholars were indebted to his systematic historical study of Greek thought. When he died on March 19, 1908, it was the end of the pre-March Tübingen school, and an epoch of German intellectual history was over.

Zeller and Erkenntnistheorie

Zeller intended to accomplish for the history of religious thought what Fischer was doing for the history of philosophy. He wanted to understand Christianity historically, in the context of its early milieu. His early studies in the Old Testament and Greek philosophy had convinced him that early Christianity owed more to those traditions than had hitherto been acknowledged. At the same time he was becoming more and more uneasy with his Hegelian presuppositions. This discontent brought him back to Kant's theory of knowledge. He was, of course, familiar with Fischer's exposition of Kant, and his close friend Helmholtz had already recommended Kant's epistemology to the German scientific community in his essay of 1855, *Ueber das Sehen des Menschen*. Zeller, in his inaugural lecture on October 22, 1862, "Ueber Bedeutung und Aufgabe der Erkenntnistheorie," set forth his own program for renewing critical epistemology. According to Zeller, the main flaw of Hegelianism was its equating of logic with the ontological part of metaphysics.[72] Confusing the process of thought with the overall processes of reality was, he believed, a serious error. Therefore, he took up the principal neo-Kantian criticism of Hegel (already propounded by Lotze): The erroneous identification of thought with reality. This identification is the crux of Hegel's monism, and any departure from it is a movement toward the duality of mind and reality.

Zeller advocated the Kantian position that logic must consider the universal forms of thought before examining its determinate content. Logic should serve as a scientific methodology, propaedeutic to the study of material reality.[73] He saw Kant as the enemy of rationalistic dogmatism such as represented by Leibniz's disciple Wolff and the Hegelians:

> Kant's immortal service is that he led philosophy away from this dogmatism, and directed the question toward the origin and truth of our ideas, not merely inaugurating the inquiry but answering it more soundly and comprehensively than any of his predecessors, who had one-sidedly deduced our representations either from experience or from our minds. Kant recognized that they arise from both these sources; and he asserted this not in the eclectic sense; on the contrary his belief was that there is not a single representation in which both elements are not present.[74]

The basis of Kant's appeal to Zeller's generation is clear in this passage. Kant had brought the theory of knowledge into harmony with the great scientific formulations of the seventeenth century. He demonstrated, to the satisfaction of many, that universal scientific laws were intellectually possible, and indeed necessary, according to the equally universal a priori forms of thought. But in his first critique, Kant made the strongest empirical statement imaginable when he said that no idea arises in our minds without the company of sensuous experience.[75] Thus Kant reshaped the idealist tradition without demolishing it, and at the same time became the epistemologist of empirical science. The mind was active, not reduced to a mere sponge or *tabula rasa*, registering impressions and making arbitrary connections. By the same token, the empirical data of the senses were not reduced to solipsistic fictions. Kant's great synthesis did not prove impregnable, but it corresponded to the intellectual needs of the mid-nineteenth century. Kant's epistemological synthesis of mind and experience, which kept each sphere separate but indispensably coordinate, was appropriate for an age of empiricism when the idealist tradition, only temporarily in retreat in Germany, was struggling to the fore again. The revival of Kant promised to protect both the autonomy of spirit from Hegel's ineluctable monism and the integrity of consciousness from the onslaughts of materialism. Neo-Kantianism was not, as at least one commentator had suggested by the title of his book, an idealistic reaction against science.[76] Indeed, it was precisely the opposite—a revolt of scientists against discredited idealism and naive positivism. Kant was brought back to arbitrate a potentially fruitless struggle between idealism and science.

Zeller looked upon Kantian criticism as a constructive method rather than an inflexible creed. Kant could be improved upon, and his errors must be corrected in the spirit of his own critical method.[77] Like so many of Kant's followers, Zeller was disturbed by thing-in-itself. He believed that Kant's treatment of this intelligible realm, which is also somehow the unknowable ground of experience, was ambiguous and unsatisfactory. Otto Liebmann asserted that the entire post-Kantian movement had foundered on the hidden reefs of thing-in-itself. Zeller's solution to this problem took him in the direction of psychologism, one of the two main lines of divergence among neo-Kantians. His explanation, similar to F.A. Lange's, turned Kant's a priori forms into the physiology of the brain: "Now the manner in which we receive the impression of things, the quality and strength of the sensation . . . is conditioned by the constitution of our sensory equipment and the laws of our sensory faculties.[78]

To Zeller, Kant erred in saying that we cannot know the real nature of things, the hidden reality behind phenomenal experience. Fichte had twisted Kant's mistaken doctrine of the unknowable thing-in-itself into complete subjectivism. Zeller believed that he was correcting both Kant and Fichte by restoring the empirical side of Kant's philosophy and thereby giving back to idealism its lost equilibrium. In a postscript to a later edition of his 1862 lecture, Zeller suggested that "space, time and causality reside in the physical nature of man."[79] In trying to bend Kant toward modern physiology, he lost the meaning of Kant's transcendental criticism. Zeller's 1862 exegesis of Kantian epistemology suggests that his vision had been affected by the intervening epoch of empirical science. In his eagerness to demonstrate the aptness of critical philosophy for his own day, he forced a false analogy between Kant's a priori forms of the mind and contemporary findings in brain physiology.

Modified Kantian Moralist and Intellectual Liberal

Zeller's interpretation of Kant's moral philosophy was also affected by the "empirical prejudice" of the nineteenth century. He saw Kant's ethics, just as he saw the Kantian theory of knowledge, through the lens of modern naturalism; therefore, he tried to soften Kant's ethics with eudaemonism, just as Lotze had done. Although he never bothered to develop a systematic moral philosophy, he presented two lectures before the Berlin Academy on the subject of ethics.[80] Kant's predecessors, Zeller explained, had derived their ethics from material grounds—the a posteriori motives of pleasure and pain.[81] But empirical moral principles do not possess universality. Kant expunged these material motives from ethics, and made the form of our will as such the measure of moral worth. Kant's formalism, his purging of all empirical elements, was, Zeller thought, unacceptable. He reiterated Lotze's criticism that Kant's a priori moral principle was useful only in a cloud-cuckoo land; it could not provide practical rules of conduct. Practical rules must be based on cause and effect, on probable consequences. Although it seems clear in Kant that the purpose of the moral will is to inject good into the real world, Zeller construed his ethics so that there was no provision for practical results. But by introducing practical motives and thereby impairing the autonomy of Kant's moral principle, he found himself faced with the problem of ethical relativism. Moral laws derived from experience, and ultimately based on pleasure and pain, either individual or social, do not have a universally binding character. Yet Zeller was not willing to accept the relativistic consequences of his eudaemonism. His solution was to combine apriorism with empiricism, basing his ethics on the universal rational nature of man. Psychology can discover what the universal characteristics of man are, and under what conditions they have developed.[82] Zeller suggested, not entirely clearly, that man has an a priori moral nature which comes into play only in real situations, in light of consequences or purposes. There is no such thing as a pure ethic. Eudaemonism is thus the only alternative, but only in the broad sense in which the Greeks understood it: Serving the fulfillment of human life.[83]

Zeller stated the eudaemonistic principle unequivocally: Pleasure is good, pain is bad. But these feelings are not necessarily capricious or egocentric. As rational beings we learn from experience to compare ourselves with others, to be circumspect.[84] The good of the individual rational being more often than not corresponds to the good of the whole. Here Zeller was not far from the "invisible hand" and the greatest happiness principle of utilitarianism, but he would not relinquish a vestige of a priori rationalism: "The universal validity and binding power of [moral laws] rest on the fact that these [human] activities and relationships are established from the moral standpoint as the activities and life-conditions of free, rational beings."[85] From the characteristics and laws of human nature revealed to us by psychology, we are able to deduce prescriptions for willing and doing.[86] Hence, ethics must have its foundations in psychology. Zeller believed that Shaftesbury and his successors were correct in deriving morality from the original, universal inclinations of man.[87] One might add that the critics who claim Kant undermined the natural law by separating the natural and moral orders would have to see in Zeller a restoration of their unity. It was undoubtedly his familiarity with Greek ethics that brought him back to a pre-Kantian natural morality.

The inherent dignity of man, and the idea of humanity, Zeller added, should be the highest criteria for ethics and law. Without abandoning these traditional tenets of humanistic idealism, he tried to graft the shoots of modern empiricism and psychology onto Kantian ethics. When he was through, the eudaemonistic foliage was so thick that the Kantian trunk was barely visible. His moral philosophy was the common-sense eclecticism of a mid-century idealist under the influence of Greek ethics and the empirical temper of his own age. His ethical theory is significant in the history of neo-Kantianism because it reveals both an increasing realism and a tendency to transmogrify Kant's philosophy into a psychology of the mind.

Zeller's reaction to Bismarck's German policy was, as revealed in an essay he wrote on the question of Alsace-Lorraine, less grudging than Lotze's. He acknowledged the ascendancy of Prussia as a natural and constructive solution to the German problem. He came to Berlin not long after Bismarck's victory over France and the annexation of the provinces. Caught up in the perennial liberal dilemma of power and moral responsibility, he would not sacrifice the principles of natural law and humanity to the demands of *Realpolitik*, but at the same time he believed that without a strong national framework, German culture would perish. He realized that the newly won German power brought sobering obligations, but to disgorge the conquered provinces was not one of them.[88] He tried to reconcile national power with ethics and right. Here he encountered the most crucial problem facing intellectual liberalism in the *Gründerzeit*. Confident that the ideas of humanity and nationality were compatible,[89] he believed that the German people had been for too long preoccupied with cosmopolitan ideas of humanity to give proper attention to the nation-state, but then they discovered that science and culture are best served by national institutions. Yet once nationhood is attained, the *völkisch* impulse can get out of hand. These words of Zeller's now seem prescient: "As political greatness is pursued, and a political nation emerges, the object of a nation's original pride may be forgotten—its *Bildung*, its idealism, its cosmopolitan humanity."[90] National interest conflicts with humanity only when the education and development of a nation have become one-sided, when the nation sets goals which cannot be reconciled with the welfare of other peoples.[91] Questions of power divide nations. Ideal interests, such as morality, art, science, and education, bring them together. A common respect for European culture is, therefore, the best protection against European fratricide. Zeller did not live long enough to see this proposition severely tested by events.

Although Zeller was very proud of the new German nation, he criticized immoderate countrymen who looked upon national power and greatness as valued ends in themselves.[92] Duty to nation and obligation to humanity must not be separated, for the greatest fulfillment and most worth deserving fruit of national life are humanity. Zeller, in his lecture, "Politics in Its Relationship to Law," said that the moral foundations of a society are destroyed by a policy that flaunts the concept of right; this principle holds true no matter whether injustice is done to the people themselves or to other nations.[93] Zeller was seemingly a staunch defender of a nation under the rule of law. Yet he wrote an essay shortly after the fall of Sedan in September 1870, justifying the seizure of the French provinces which seemed to contradict his previously moderate principles.[94] Although he professed to be examining the question of national self-determination *sub specie aeternitatis*, his article was an exercise in special pleading. He defended the annexation as essential to Germany's security and as a buffer against further French depredations. At least he was being more candid and realistic than the nationalists who defended annexation in terms of historical legality and the ethnicity of the provinces.

The French, Zeller charged, were hypocrites. They had seized Algeria, Cochin China, and other colonies without consulting the inhabitants or holding a plebiscite to see if they wanted to become part of France.

And in Italy, where Cavour had actually permitted plebiscites, the charade of self-determination was merely a disguise for Piedmontese conquests.[95] The foreign press threw the principle of self-determination in Germany's face, but to Zeller it was an empty gesture. He justified the annexation of Alsace-Lorraine on neither ethnic nor historical grounds but instead on the perfidy of France. "France has broken the old treaties."[96] When treaties are broken, the people no longer have the right to free self-determination; it becomes a matter for sovereign nations to decide. Only governments can enforce international obligations. Because the question of sovereign authority is involved in Alsace-Lorraine, it is an issue for the nation-states to resolve.[97] Zeller was implicitly making power the final arbiter and submitting the liberal ideal of self-determination to the verdict of battle. His essay is full of angry fulminations against the predatory French and the ultramontane clergy who "undoubtedly participated in the attack on Prussia, as has been proved by the connection between this attack and the plans whose fruit was the Vatican Council."[98] For once Zeller had lost his classical sense of proportion. Regardless of France's part in causing the war (and the reckless diplomacy of Napoleon III was certainly among the causes), Zeller's francophobia and suspicions of an ultramontane conspiracy were unfortunate symptoms of liberal bias. He had reached the limits of his liberalism; it did not include France or the Catholic clergy.

Although Zeller did not go as far as the ideologues of 1914 in asserting German genius and uniqueness against the hostile West, many of the liberal intellectuals did espouse a feverish cultural chauvinism in 1914, and among them was the neo-Kantian Paul Natorp, who developed a German metaphysics based on the special qualities of the German "soul."[99] But in allowing himself to be blinded by distrust of France and hatred of the Catholic clergy, Zeller was giving power to the negatives of German liberalism—xenophobia and anticlericalism— and he was narrowing the idealist political perspective just when it needed to be opened up. By his break with Hegelian metaphysics and his exposition of Kant's critical method Zeller made an important contribution to neo-Kantianism. He and Kuno Fischer were the most important among second generation Hegelians to speak out in favor of critical philosophy, a fact that was not ignored.

Liebmann and Kant's Epigones

Otto Liebmann, a much younger contemporary of Fischer and Zeller, gave neo-Kantianism its slogan in his first book, *Kant und die*

Epigonen, published in 1865, three years after Zeller's Heidelberg lecture. It was soon recognized as an important monograph in the growing volume of literature on Kant[100] and as a sign of the incipient Kant revival. Liebmann was born on February 25, 1840, by which time Zeller was a young tutor at Tübingen and Lotze had begun teaching at Leipzig. Liebmann's birthplace was Löwenberg in Silesia, where his father was a court tax assessor. In 1848, the family moved to Frankfurt where Liebmann's father was a member of the revolutionary parliament which met in the Paulskirche. In 1849, the father was called to Berlin to be a councillor in the municipal court, and Otto attended the Friedrich-Wilhelms gymnasium, whose director was the brother of Leopold von Ranke.[101] Later Liebmann prepared for the university at the famous Schulpforta school and in Halle. Beginning his university career in 1859, he studied at Jena, Leipzig, and Halle, concentrating on mathematics and natural sciences. One of the strongest impressions of Liebmann's youth, according to his son, was hearing Treitschke speak from the balcony of the Leipzig city hall on the occasion of the German Turnfest. But it was Kuno Fischer at Jena who aroused his interest in philosophy and converted him to Kant.[102]

In 1864 Liebmann settled in Tübingen as a private tutor, a position allowing him enough leisure to prepare *Kant und die Epigonen*. While at Tübingen, Liebmann became acquainted with the left-Hegelian, Friedrich Theodor Vischer, who had been harassed by officialdom when Zeller was there.[103] In 1870, Liebmann volunteered for military service and participated in the seige of Paris. His patriotism was even keener than Zeller's, and from this first-hand experience came his patriotic war memoir, *Vier Monate vor Paris*. In war, his admiration of Treitschke found concrete expression.[104] The friendship with Vischer continued after they went separate ways, Liebmann going to Strassburg in 1875, and Vischer to Stuttgart. Liebmann taught at Strassburg until 1882 when he went to Jena, remaining there until his death on January 14, 1912. His closest associate in later years was the founder of Baden neo-Kantianism, Wilhelm Windelband.

The German academic world in the second half of the century seemed intimate, small, and interconnected. Friends parted to accept new positions, and then arranged (or not infrequently obstructed appointments of their enemies) invitations for colleagues left behind. There were both professional and personal links among the leading neo-Kantians. One man's work was encouraged, complemented expanded—or criticized—by another. However, the academic and social homogeneity of the neo-Kantians did not prevent widely divergent interpretations of Kant. Indeed, the movement was marked as much by feuding as by friendship.

Liebmann was something of an angry young man. His *Die Epigonen* was a colorful, contentious diatribe. Every chapter ends with the expostulation: *Also muss auf Kant zurückgegangen werden*! He arraigned his older contemporaries for obscurantism and interminable haggling over the philosophies of men whose work dwarfed their own: "Thus, the Babylonian Tower of German philosophy in our century does not distinguish itself from its biblical counterpart in that its architects believe that they have succeeded in extending it into Heaven; it differs from the Bible version in that a confusion of ideas has emerged from the confusion of tongues."[105]

Liebmann saw Kant as the parent of four nineteenth-century philosophical trends: (1) the idealistic, through Fichte, Hegel, and Schelling; (2) the realistic, through Herbart; (3) the empirical, through Fries; (4) the transcendental, through Schopenhauer.[106] But these four sister philosophies were built on a "rococo embellishment" of Kant rather than representing the core of his thought, and they all incorporated his errors. To Liebmann, the briar patch of metaphysics after Kant grew from Kant's contradictory handling of the thing-in-itself. First it was a problematic substratum at the base of appearance, but then Kant asserted its existence with certainty.[107] None of Kant's successors, Liebmann argued, had seen that the thing-in-itself was "a drop of alien blood" in Kant's critical philosophy. Liebmann, a typical neo-Kantian skeptic, said, "All knowledge begins and ends in a question."[108] The idea of an unknowable thing-in-itself is simply evidence of the human thirst to know the ultimate ground of things—something that can be felt, imagined, or dreamed, but never known by theoretical reason.[109] Along with Lotze, Liebmann stressed the limitations of conceptual thought, but this did not lead him to irrationalism. He said that a "knowing feeling" in philosophy is as absurd as a "hearing eye" or a "seeing ear."[110] Feeling is not a source of knowledge.

Liebmann examined the main post-Kantians one by one and found them guilty of perpetuating Kant's alleged hypostatizing of the thing-in-itself. Fichte turned Kant's idea of spontaneous self-consciousness into absolute subjectivism. Schelling followed the course of intuition, unassisted by careful criticism and made his "rudderless trip . . . to the shadowy coasts of mysticism."[111] To avoid Schelling's errors, Hegel found the dialectical method but then, reducing all he touched to abstract intellect, dissolved everything in pure thought. They all exceeded the limits of reason that Kant had already set. Liebmann devoted an entire chapter to the faults of Hegelianism, and praised Fischer's critique of Hegel in the latter's *Logik und Metaphysik*.[112] Hegel's system, he wrote, ends, as the French put it, with a "Chateau en Espagne." The World Spirit is the thing-in-itself in metahistorical robes, only with Kant's dualism dissolved by the principle of identity.[113] Herbart, on the other hand, had tried to find the empirical basis of appearances. The idealists had sought an independent subject, the Absolute I, but Herbart wanted to find an independent object—a real existing thing independent of the subject.[114] He also erred in explanation of the thing-in-itself, only in converse manner. But the most brutal treatment Liebmann saved for Schopenhauer, whose assault on post-Kantian idealism he thought was scandalous. He could not understand how Schopenhauer had become the philosophical hero of the day.[115] Schopenhauer's worst gaffe was his reduction of space, time, and causality to functions of the brain. He had transmuted Kant's autonomy of pure thought into the autocracy of will.[116] Here was the source of fallacious psychologism, a result of his apotheosis of will. The thing-in-itself was the culprit behind these misunderstandings which led Kant's epigones into serious error.[117]

In spite of Liebmann's brisk dismissal of the speculative idealists, he turned more toward metaphysics in his later writings, and the mysterious thing-in-itself reappeared in semantic disguise. He resembled the other neo-Kantians in his attempt to negotiate a middle course between the extremes of absolute idealism and naturalism while incorporating features of both. He said that there is an unknown magnitude beyond our senses from which appearances arise. It is the relation between an unknown Y and another equally unknown X. The latter appears to us as our body, from which every sensible impression emerges to consciousness. This relation between X and Y he called the transcendental factor of intuition. This formulation, as some of his critics observed, seems not far removed from the troublesome Kantian thing-in-itself which he saw as the nemesis of post-Kantian idealism.[118]

Liebmann's affinity with Marburg neo-Kantianism was revealed in his *Zur Analyse der Wirklichkeit* (1876), in which he explains the task of philosophy as the transcendental analysis of facts in consciousness.[119] And as he moved toward what he called "critical metaphysics," Liebmann came closer to his friend Windelband and Baden neo-Kantianism. He held that ultimate truth is not of the physical world but consciousness itself, which produces both all we can know theoretically and also the values of morality and culture. He came to define philosophy broadly as the examination of man's total cultural consciousness. The purpose of critical methaphysics is to study human views and hypotheses about the nature of things. Between this metaphysical realm and the theoretical truths of science there is an area left open to values and judgments which are determined by our will as shaped by culture. This sounds very much like the normative consciousness of Baden neo-Kantianism.

In 1912 Liebmann was eulogized by Windelband as the "truest of the Kantians."[120] There is much truth to this, even in the unresolved difficulties in his critical metaphysics. He brought the diverse symptoms of early neo-Kantianism into clear focus with his *Kant und die Epigonen*, and his subsequent efforts continued to encourage the rise of critical philosophy to its preeminence at the turn of the century. In his writings the two main tendencies of later neo-Kantianism—the phenomenology of consciousness or the philosophy of values—are found. Windelband, for his work in the latter, was probably as much indebted to Liebmann as to Lotze. And in Liebmann we see a decisive refutation of the psychological interpretation of Kant's apriorism. Psychologism was characteristic of the early neo-Kantians, most conspicuously Zeller and Friedrich Lange. Hence Liebmann's interpretation of Kant was a prelude to the rejection of psychologism by the Baden and Marburg philosophers.

4

Friedrich Albert Lange:
Kantian Democrat

The Kantian Intellectual in Politics

Friedrich Albert Lange, as the only genuine political activist in the early phases of neo-Kantianism, occupies a special niche in its history. His efforts to make epistemology a matter of secondary interest, to place the "social question" at the focal point of his work, and to imbue the working class with a sense of independence and political awareness went far beyond the limits of liberal orthodoxy.[1] He was the first to deny that Kantianism was the special philosophy of the educated, propertied, and professional middle class and to put Kant's ethics in the service of social democracy. Although Lange believed that Marx was the true voice of the German working class, he could not accept the dialectical apparatus of Marxism, and he was as opposed to proletarian collectivism as he was to the Prussian statism of Lassalle. He was an individualist, but not of the laissez-faire Manchester sort. He believed that individual effort could be effective only through social cooperation, and he did much to encourage the cooperative movement in Germany. Theodor Heuss called him one of the most notable "marginal" figures in German political and intellectual life.[2] But Lange's role in the German radical movement of the 1860s was far from marginal as was his influence in the later 1890s when his ideas were revived by a revisionist leader of Bernstein's prominence.

Today, Lange is remembered more widely for his *Geschichte des Mater-*
ialismus, which in its time was considered the outstanding critique of the
subject.[3] In spite of his opposition to materialism, he was singularly
practical and science minded. With a reverence for facts bordering on
naive positivism, he was intrigued by statistics and empirical data. Yet
like Helmholtz, he believed that science had definite limits which were
to be found through epistemological criticism in the Kantian spirit.
Lange accepted the "physiology of the mind" interpretation of Kant, a
reflection of his own scientific bent and of the generally empirical cast
of early neo-Kantian theory. He believed that brain physiology was
"developed or corrected" Kantianism. His most important contribution
to neo-Kantianism was in his use of Kant to go beyond the boundaries
of liberal social philosophy. With Lange, intellectual liberalism (if indeed it is justifiable in this case to call him a liberal) finally dirtied its
hands in the grime of industrial society by descending from the accus-
tomed heights of cultural elitism and entering the tumult of everyday
politics. Free of the arid pedantry and myopic specialism toward which
much of neo-Kantianism was tending, Lange was a lucid, engaging
writer and an effective public speaker. If neo-Kantianism eventually
failed as a progressive doctrine because it did not attract enough mass
support, Lange does not bear the blame.

Lange was born at Wald bei Sollingen on September 28, 1828. His
father, Johann Peter Lange, was a minister and later professor of theology at Bonn,[4] and his grandfather was a drayman who wore the blue
overalls (*blauekittel*) of the peasant.[5] Perhaps Lange's concern for the
rural classes, generally neglected in nineteenth-century social theory,
came from his peasant ancestry. The Langes lived in Duisburg and
Langenberg until 1841, when Pastor Lange was called to Zurich by the
conservative church officials to teach at the university. He was appointed to that position because of the uproar over the withdrawal of
D.F. Strauss; Lange was, of course, a safer prospect.[6]

Young Lange became an expert gymnast, but does not seem to have
been affected by the athletic nationalism associated with the gymnastic
clubs from the time of Father Jahn. These clubs were among the many
popular associations which proliferated in the 1860s and fostered the
liberal cause.[7] Enthusiasm for gymnastics was quite in keeping with
Lange's ebullience and zest for action. Whatever early philosophical
influences he encountered as he grew up are difficult to determine precisely. He heard lectures on Hegel's phenomenology, although he later
exhibited even fewer vestigial traits of Hegelianism than the other early
neo-Kantians. He also studied Herbart's mathematical psychology,

which appealed to him at first, but was then cast aside. Herbart, however, may have reinforced Lange's empirical or realist tendency, but the significance of Herbartian realism for Lange is difficult to assess.[8]

In April 1848, Lange left Zurich for the University of Bonn. On his boat trip to the Rhine city he had a long conversation with a young working-class radical who apparently filled his mind with the new social ideas of the revolutionary era.[9] He did not, however, become a democrat until later. Studies in Latin and philosophy, and his fiancée in Langenberg seemed more important to him at that time than politics. Yet he was impressed by the national parliament, and remarked to a friend that it was the first time men of all groups had come together to represent Germany. His exposure to revolutionary ideas also brought a sharp turn toward agnosticism, much to the consternation of his father. Lange soon believed that the absolute difference between Christianity and other religions, devoutly stressed by the orthodox, was more apparent than real. He concluded that religious dogmas are superflous, but science and art are indispensable to civilized life. His rejection of dogmatic Christianity, his appeal to the comparative method of reducing all religions to their anthropological rudiments, and his acknowledgment of science as the secular creed of post-religious man were typical reactions of the educated to free thought at that time.[10]

During the revolution Lange was not active in politics, for he was deterred by admonitions from his parents who insisted that he stay away from the student rebels. The events of 1848-49 did, however, inspire a cosmopolitan spirit and a freedom from national partisanship which he retained the rest of his life. Angered by the chauvinistic narrowness he saw in some of his friends, he wrote to his friend Kambli in Zurich that he hoped for an "open road from Berlin to Paris . . . .[11] Within your own borders build an altar to cosmopolitanism." For Lange saw no conflict between cosmopolitanism and genuine national feeling. It was said that he and the poet Arndt were the last of the intellectuals in Bonn to take off the cap of imperial black, red, and gold after the revolution had run its course. At Bonn, Lange joined the *Novemberverein*, a student society devoted innocently to culture and intellectual conversation, as he reassured his parents. The members were mainly theology students, seemingly untainted by Tübingen radicalism, keeping Lange still in respectable company. Yet at the same time, he was beginning to feel that it was wrong to isolate *Bildung* from everyday problems, and noted, "I have a burning need for the practical and immediate life."[12] He despaired of ever becoming a great scholar. He looked upon his studies as a means to an end and dreamed of setting up a small private school along English lines. That he had no academic pretensions was undoubtedly one of the keys to his later success with ordinary people, in contrast to many of the German intellectuals who were not known for their modesty.

Faithfully obeying parental advice against getting involved in "red radicalism," Lange thanked one of his Zurich correspondents for not mentioning the subject of politics; but the social question soon became an inescapable concern. He was skeptical about the new French Republic because the Bourbon-Bonaparte apparatus was still in evidence. The full life of men can never develop in a machine state. Only the greater freedom and independence of individuals, he believed, would lead to a true social republic.[13] Thus, the deep-grained individualism of Lange's political outlook took the form of hostility to impersonal bureaucratic *étatisme*. For Germany, he wanted neither "Manteuffel nor Red Revolution." He playfully called his own political theory "organized anarchy," based on free associations and cooperatives, an idea he eventually put into practice.

Near the end of his university days Lange had a disturbing emotional encounter with the mother of one of his fellow students. Evidently his friend had written home that Lange was cultivated and brilliant, but also charming and personable. His prospective hostess, who was looking forward to having him as a house guest over the spring holidays, had recently been snubbed by a bookish acquaintance in Frankfurt. When Lange visited her in Altenkirchen, her new prejudice against academicians was still strong, and she not only took him for a cultural snob but also told him so in a tempestuous scene. He was hurt and outraged, and in a lengthy letter to his hostess, denied any such pretensions.[14] His natural reticence, which he later overcame, had probably created a false impression, for he was determined not to be a supercilious pedant. Indeed, the taciturn scholar eventually became an unaffected and trusted tribune of the working class.

In 1851, Lange took his degree *eximia cum laude* and then served his year of military service in Cologne. He continued his teaching by offering a course on Caesar's *bellum Gallicum* to the officers and enlisted men.[15] During his tour of duty he also conceived a plan for making available to the masses popular penny pamphlets on science and literature, a dream that materialized in 1864 when he became his own publisher. After separation from active duty, Lange took a teaching position in the gymnasium at Cologne where he taught Latin, Greek, and German. A minor disagreement with his fiancée's guardian, who would not give his ward permission to marry him on the meager salary of a probationary teacher, was disturbing. Because his father counseled patience, he waited, only to find out later that Rhenish law did not require a guardian's consent. This was Lange's first encounter with the ambiguities of bureaucracy, the kind of statism he had already condemned in theory. But the matter was settled and he married Fredericke Colsman of Langenberg in September 1853.[16] Still a gymnastics enthusiast, he wrote a short monograph entitled "Ueber die Verbindung des Turnens und der militarischer Ausbildung." (In contrast to Charles Kingsley, his contemporary in England, Lange exemplified a kind of "Muscular Free Thought," as opposed to Kingsley's famous Muscular Christianity.) Lange evangelized for the clean, wholesome life of an open mind and a limber body, a theme later found in the German youth movement. His activity as a social reformer began with his involvment in the movement to democratize secondary education by broadening the standard classical curriculum of the gymnasium. He believed that the dispute between humanistic and practical education would eventually be resolved at the expense of the classical program unless it was modified.[17] Lange's desire to widen the social base of *Bildung* put him in the forefront of the liberal thinkers on education.

From 1852 to 1858 Lange taught at the University of Bonn. There he tried to create interest in educational theory, but his lectures on pedagogy were poorly attended. He did much better with his course in psychology. In the fall of 1855, he met Friedrich Ueberweg, author of *Grundriss der Geschichte der Philosophie des neunzehnten Jahrhunderts*. When Ueberweg later went to Königsberg, he became Lange's epistolary sounding board on philosophical matters.[18] Both men were influenced by the physiological theories of Johannes Müller on sensory perception, but they came to opposite conclusions.

For the summer semester of 1857 Lange planned a lecture series on the history of materialism. This was the beginning of his opus, *Die Geschichte des Materialismus*, which came to fruition nine years later. From 1858 to 1862, he was a full instructor in the gymnasium at Duisburg, where he had been a student. He was so deeply engrossed in teaching that his literary production was limited to a series of short articles for an encyclopedia of education being edited in Stuttgart.[19] During this period his interest in Kant increased as some of his letters show. "I think that Hegel's system," Lange wrote, "is a regression to scholasticism." Speculative philosophy is passé. "Herbart," he continued, "with whom I originally agreed, was for me only a bridge to Kant, to whom many genuine scholars are now returning."[20] But Kant went only halfway. It would still be necessary to destroy metaphysics completely. "I believe that every metaphysics is a form of delusion, with only aesthetic or subjective justification. My logic is probability statistics, my ethics is moral statistics, and my psychology rests entirely on physiology." It was characteristic of early neo-Kantianism to be very suspicious of metaphysics, but Lange went much farther and sometimes fell into the clichés of popular empiricism.[21] His uncritical empiricism was somewhat mellowed by an appreciation of music and art.

Kant impressed Lange greatly in his proof that the ideas of God, Freedom and Immortality were theoretically undemonstrable, and in his emphasis on practical reason.[22] It was Kant's limitation of metaphysics that made him so compatible with the empirical predilections of Lange and many of his contemporaries. Far from being exclusively a revival of idealism, the original resurrection of Kant was inspired by suspicion of metaphysical monism, both Hegelian and materialist. Lange's idea for a sequel to the Kantian critiques was one on psychology, a book he planned but never wrote. His ambition to write such a critique places Lange among the early converts to neo-Kantianism who, under the spell of empirical science and recent discoveries in brain physiology, equated Kant's transcendental method with psychological analysis of the mind.

Lange remained, however, just as skeptical of political formulas as of philosophical dogmatism. In the autumn of 1858, when Prince William became regent for the mentally disabled Frederick William IV, he dismissed the reactionary ministry of Otto von Manteuffel and appointed a new cabinet composed of conservatives and moderate liberals.[23] Lange was not greatly impressed by the dawn of the New Era: "This coquetry with liberalism," he said, "we have lived through before."[24] Even if reforms come, the masses are not ready for political responsibility.[25] Within a comparatively short time Lange had changed his mind about democracy. But like most German liberals, he was never able to extend his toleration to the Catholic Church. The Catholic influence on education was especially harmful. "Catholicism stupefies, stupidity impoverishes, poverty destroys." He showed only slightly less rancor in his anticlericalism than Zeller, for dislike of Rome was one thing liberals, radicals, and socialists had in common.

In spite of his political skepticism, Lange was gradually pulled into the vortex of New Era liberalism. He joined the *Nationalverein* in 1860 and became involved in other civic activities.[26] He revealed to one of his friends that he hoped to gain from these new commitments the experience and reputation necessary to win election to the Prussian parliament. But he would not achieve his goal of elected office until he moved to Switzerland and was elected to the Swiss Constitutional Commission and the canton assembly of Zurich.[27]

Early in 1864 Lange became embroiled in a fight with the school authorities, a not uncommon predicament of many early neo-Kantians. In January, the provincial school board at Coblenz warned the teachers of the Rhineland to refrain from political activities. Lange felt that his academic freedom was being attacked by the reactionaries. He wrote a strongly worded letter of protest and shortly thereafter became unemployed for his pains. On March 22, 1862, he gave a public speech on the occasion of the king's birthday, on "The Position of the School in Public Life." Lange asked rhetorically, "Are not teachers citizens too" and is not part of their responsibility to exemplify the qualities of good citizenship? He recalled the example of Thomas Arnold, headmaster of Rugby, who had also been criticized for his outspokenness, but Arnold's great success proved that teachers could express their opinions on politics and religion without compromising their role as teachers. Lange also wrote an editorial for the *Rhein-und-Ruhr Zeitung* in the same vein, which earned the paper a sharp reprimand from the censors. In June, Lange received a blunt admonition from the Interior Ministry accusing him of making false insinuations against the state. On July 4, 1862, he went to Coblenz and submitted his resignation, but from the time he received the 1862 official circular constraining gymnasium teachers from free speech, Lange became a determined enemy of the state monopoly on education. Two years later he explained to a friend, "I can conceive of no political freedom which does not include full freedom to teach as well."[28]

After leaving the Cologne gymnasium, Lange turned to journalism. In late 1862, he became coeditor of the *Rhein-und-Ruhr Zeitung,* at about the same time Bismarck became minister president of Prussia. The New Era was over, and the former protégé of the *Kreuzzeitung* party of ultraconservatism had come to power. In the columns of his paper, Lange fought the new regime as far as censorship and the laws of libel would allow. He denounced what he called the "invasion of the French imperialistic system," and accused the Protestant churches of allowing themselves to be used as spiritual swords against the oppressed rather than the oppressors. In June 1864, Lange fulfilled his dream of starting an inexpensive popular press. He opened his own small publishing house and brought out penny pamphlets aimed at the interests of the lower classes. He also founded a workers' weekly, the

Rheinisch-Westfälsche Arbeiter-Zeitung, a shoestring operation which soon folded.

Throughout the era of the constitutional conflict (1862-66), Lange was a crusading editor. He waged a three-cornered battle against the government, the "potentates" of wealth and power, and the Progressive party, which he indicted for its tepid defense of the constitution and neglect of the social question.[29] At the same time he joined the nascent social democratic movement, just then in the midst of a civil war between the Lassalleans and the followers of Liebknecht and Bebel.[30] Lange found that his editorial struggles left him tired and discouraged and, in 1866, he began to hunt for an academic appointment. F.T. Vischer had recently left Zurich for Tübingen and Lange hoped to succeed him, but he had to wait five years before receiving his invitation to Zurich. His *Die Geschichte des Materialismus,* first published in 1866, had been well received, but Lange's optimism that it would open the doors to an important university chair was premature.

Because of Bismarck's victory in the constitutional struggle and his own interminable bouts with the censors, Lange decided that the German atmosphere was no longer congenial. He moved to Winterthur near Zurich, where his family had lived for many years. Printer's ink was still in his blood, and his friend Bleuler was able to provide the capital; together they founded a new paper, the Winterthur *Landbote,* with Bleuler handling the management and Lange doing not only the writing but much of the manual printing operation as well. *Landbote* flourished, shortly becoming the leading democratic journal in the canton of Zurich.[31]

Lange left Germany at the end of one political crisis and arrived in Switzerland at the beginning of another.[32] He jumped into the fray with renewed energy. Respite in academic life seemed farther off than ever. Four years later, his appetite for action finally satisfied, Lange joined the Polytechnical School of Zurich, ready at last for the scholarly life.

In 1872, Lange returned to Germany, first to a medical clinic· in Tübingen for palliative surgery, and then to a new, and his last, academic post at Marburg. His Marburg lectures were immediately popular. One listener was the young *Privatdozent,* Hermann Cohen, soon to be the leader of Marburg neo-Kantianism. Lange's principal literary production at Marburg was the completion of a revised edition of *Die Geschechte des Materialismus.* Deteriorating health would not permit much more. He died on November 21, 1875, but not before having planted the seeds of social Kantianism at Marburg.

From Liberalism to Social Democracy

From 1862 to 1870, Lange was active in politics, first in Germany and then in Switzerland after Bismarck's triumph over the liberals. This was also the period of his greatest literary productivity. His book on materialism and his polemical work, *Die Arbeiterfrage*, were published in the middle sixties; in the highly charged political atmosphere of the sixties Lange's career reached its highest point. While many German liberals were becoming reconciled to the reality of Prussian power, Lange held to his cosmopolitan credo and, in his social philosophy, moved farther to the left. The grandson of a peasant mule skinner, he never had felt constrained by the conventions of intellectual liberalism[33] nor had he been effectively intimidated by the anxious bourgeois proprieties of his parents. In fact, Lange had become a radical democrat. In the political turmoil of the 1860s, largely through his efforts to promote political cooperation between the German labor movement and petty bourgeois democracy, he became a militant social democrat.

Lange's clash with the educational bureaucracy in 1862 intensified his already strong individualism; thereafter, he began to sound increasingly like an English Benthamite.[34] The authority of the state should be limited to general police powers and should have no authority whatsoever over education. The schools, he argued, should be controlled locally, by free, self-governing communities.[35] The constitutive principle of society should be a federation of semiautonomous associations for education, religion, industry, and trade. However, Lange was not suggesting a medieval or prefascist corporatism. His model was the English cooperative association, and in 1862 he started a consumer cooperative in Duisburg based on the English example.[36] He looked forward to the development of the consumer cooperatives into productive societies somewhat on the lines of Louis Blanc's national workshop scheme. In spite of his aversion to bureaucratic control, he hoped for financial assistance from the state; thus, in the *Staatshilfe* versus *Selbsthilfe* controversy, Lange was an eclectic and not always a consistent thinker. Yet in at least one respect Lange's comprehension of social realities was far broader than Lassalle's, or for that matter, Marx's. He recognized and wanted to remedy the general neglect of rural labor by socialism, and he perceived the danger of the industrial labor movement producing a blue collar aristocracy of its own at the expense of the unorganized country proletariat. His solution was state provision of credit for agrarian cooperatives.[37] His most radical proposal was to call for redistribution of the great estates to peasant landholders.

Because he believed cooperatives were the keys to a democratized economy, Lange followed the efforts of Hermann Schulze-Delitzsch in the field with keen interest, but he believed that the Schulzean movement favored the elite of labor at the expense of the *Lumpenproletariat* and agrarian labor.[38] His aims were close enough to those of the embryonic socialist movement so that he decided to take a direct hand in the *Arbeitervereiene* conferences of the early 1860s. Subsequently he earned the respect not only of August Bebel but also of Marx and Engels, who never perceived him as anything more than a sympathetic bourgeois fellow-traveler but recognized that his introduction of the urgent social question to democratic circles was very important.[39] In October 1864, Lange was a delegate to the convention of the German *Arbeitervereine* in Leipzig and was elected to the steering committee along with Bebel, Hirsch, and Sonnemann. This happened during the period of cordial if shortlived relations between the socialists and democrats. When he found he was caught in the middle of a quarrel between the advocates of laissez-faire individualism and state socialism, he tried to mediate. Although his conciliatory overtures did not succeed, he won further stature in the eyes of both sides.[40] Lange, however, was torn between the two alternatives. He agreed with the Lassalleans in their concern for industrial labor but he was chary of their statism. He supported the Schulzean concept of self-help through cooperatives but could not abide its apparent indifference toward unskilled and rural workers. The orthodox Marxism of Wilhelm Liebknecht was equally unacceptable because it seemed doctrinaire and deterministic. Although Lange was unaware of it at the time, there was no intellectual home for him in the German socialist movement.

Lange, before his final separation from the labor movement in 1866, used his considerable oratorical skills as a peripatetic speaker throughout the Ruhr valley, in Mülheim, Essen, and Elberfeld, exhorting factory workers to use their economic initiative in the cooperatives. He singled out for particular abuse the German habit of "accepting everything from the top."[41] He wanted the German working class to assert its strength through its own economic and political institutions. An independent and militant spirit would be sufficient. Violent revolution was contrary to his temperament and to his faith in democratic evolution.

The most important product of Lange's crusade was *Die Arbeiterfrage*, published by his company in 1865. The original edition was unabashed social propaganda, and Lange admitted that the first version had been written in three weeks; but he later spent more time on a revised, expanded, and much more thoughtful edition.[42] *Die Arbeiterfrage* was a mélange of nineteenth-century ideas. The first chapter is an excursus on Malthus and Darwin. Darwin's struggle for existence in nature, Lange argued, has been transmuted into a struggle for subsistence in industrial society. The conflict has become doubly grim because man no longer owns the means of his own livelihood; the resources of nature and the tools of production are no longer in his possession. His only weapon is his labor which he now must offer on the open market as a commodity, thus exposing himself to Ricardo's tyrannical iron law of wages. He can thus never rise permanently above the level of bare subsistence.[43] In a later edition, Lange cited Marx's passages on entrepenurial exploitation with approval and borrowed Marx's theory of surplus value. Although he found Marx's thinking congenial on many counts, he could not accept either his dialectical apparatus or his revolutionary solution. He believed that society as an industrialized version of Darwinian nature could be redeemed through democratic evolution and the cooperative efforts of an independent proletariat. Conflict is not inherent in human relations; it is the pernicious consequence of maldistributed political and economic power.

Certainly one of the most pervasive assumptions in nineteenth-century thought was that conflict is not only endemic to the human condition but is also the source of social energy and the fuel of progress. Struggle was not only the primordial force behind the evolution of the species but also the whetstone of economic efficiency and the forge of great nations in war. Taken from its theoretical context, the thesis became a justification for ruthless amorality in the pursuit of individual and national power. This notion of incessant conflict, so crucial in classical liberalism, voluntarism, Hegelianism, Marxism, Darwinism, and nineteenth-century nationalism, was, in Lange's opinion, diminishing in its validity. Since the 1840s, rational and moral considerations had begun to mitigate the struggle.[44] Either in fear of revolution or out of genuine sympathy, the capitalist class was gradually curbing the excesses of industrialism. Urban life itself, by bringing people of different classes into closer contact with one another, was producing an empathy that cut across class lines. The social conscience of Western Europe had been awakened. And the worker himself, through trade unions and cooperatives, was becoming more self-reliant. The union movement, as Lange accurately observed, had not made the proletariat more revolutionary but more conservative. The trade unions were an escape valve for class hostility, a source of working-class solidarity, and a constructive means of improving the worker's lot.[45]

Lange's solution to the social question was to change the laws of the state to permit full freedom of association so that the workers could "enter the arena of production."[46] Cooperatives and credit unions, politically independent but subsidized by the state, would generate a socially equitable workers' capitalism. Private property on a modest scale need not be abolished but social property, in the form of industrial cooperatives, would eventually become predominant. Lange's formula for social progress would indeed "enrage the Marxists and please the pragmatists."[47] In the parlance of French socialism, he was a possibilist. First, the workers must acquire political influence to obtain freedom of association, that is, universal, direct, and secret manhood suffrage. Then, they must organize into consumer and producer cooperatives, both industrial and agrarian. Because large concentrations of private property are obstacles to cooperatism, they must be broken up by abolition of the right of inheritance: Hereditary property and private property are not inseparable rights.[48]

Lange could not accept the traditional middle class justification of property as derived from Locke. Locke's defense of private property does not "satisfy the demand made by Kant . . . that the freedom of one should not diminish the freedom of others."[49] Private property is indefensible if it intrudes on or inhibits the freedom of others. Here Lange became the first of the neo-Kantians to measure freedom and social justice by the yardstick of Kant's ethics. He was essentially a moral idealist and a humanist in spite of his emphasis on practical reform. He believed that the ultimate purpose of his cooperative society should be to encourage the unfolding of man's spiritual, intellectual, and artistic capacities.[50] But cultural *Bildung* is a social ideal, not a prerequisite for political activity.[51]

Lange's philosophy is based on individual liberty; it must never be sacrificed to considerations of power, political expediency, or even patriotism. In 1865, he wrote in the *Landbote*: "Germany must be free and unified; however, a unity in which freedom is oppressed and despotic military government is introduced is not progress but the greatest of conceivable dangers."[52] Although Lange's biographer claims that he was later reconciled to Bismarck's policies, it is not evident in his writings.[53] However, toward the end of his life Lange did show signs of world weariness and mental exhaustion. Although he wrote an antiwar pamphlet in 1870, calling for an end to Franco-German hostilities in the name of reason and humanity, he confided to Ueberweg that it was written as a favor to friends; he himself "lacked faith in the undertaking."[54] The embattled journalist of the 1860s was not losing faith in his principles, but he was beginning to doubt the efficacy of the printed word.

Although Lange clearly made the transition from liberalism to social democracy it was not done without holding on to some residual liberal beliefs, most notably individualism and hostility to revolution.[55] His political philosophy pointed in the direction liberalism might take in order to free itself from economic bias and to attract the mass support necessary for it to combat the authoritarian state. He broke with the sectarian aspects of bourgeois liberalism, rejecting both its Manchesterism and its stubborn adherence to private ownership as a sacred cow. He was equally contemptuous of liberal welfarism, which he believed was inspired more by a desire to mollify the masses and steal the thunder of socialism than by a willingness to concede real social power to the workers. Among the formal social philosophies of the era, Lange's most closely resembled that of Lujo Brentano, a "Socialist of the Chair," but more accurately a "social liberal."[56] Brentano was an advocate of free associations for workers and employers alike.[57] Lange's ideas also bore an affinity to those of the later John Stuart Mill, his main exemplar among English social theorists.

Lange's social philosophy cannot be identified with any particular school because he was remarkably free of the *esprit de système* characteristic of German academic thought. His ideas were not constricted by class or by the customary liberal predilection for *Bildung*, the supercilious concept of an academic culture inaccessible to the new industrial masses. Lange, not only in his social philosophy but also in his civic activities on behalf of the cooperatives, constitutional reform, and democratic suffrage, achieved an integration of theory and practice, and of intellectual freedom and political responsibility rare in the history of German liberalism. The Marburg neo-Kantians who inherited his social liberalism carried on the intellectual tradition but were not as militant in its practical application.

Lange's Critique of Materialism

Materialism, the philosophical persuasion of many democratic intellectuals in 1848, became the object of mounting criticism in the 1850s, especially by those who found it an inadequate basis for science or politics. Lange's formative years coincided with the period of the materialism controversy and the ultimate rejection of materialism by Helmholtz and other scientific intellectuals. A decade before Lange wrote *Die Geschichte*, Büchner, Moleschott, and others had denied the independence of consciousness from matter, of mind from the physical processes of the body. The famous "struggle for the soul" found its first important public airing at the Göttingen convention of natural scientists in 1854, but was virtually a dead issue in academic circles by 1860 because prominent philosophers and scientists such as Liebig, Helmholtz, and Lotze had repudiated the rather primitive materialism of Büchner and his associates. In the 1860s Büchner was a key figure in the ill-fated effort to organize a democratic People's party outside of Prussia, a movement aimed at an effective coalition of petty bourgeois democrats and Bebel socialists.[58] Lange, to whom political reform was more important than philosophical disputation, collaborated with Büchner in his promising but short-lived experiment in uniting social classes and resisting Prussian authoritarianism.

The materialism debate, despite its frequent philosophical inanities, performed an important service in calling attention to the limitations of science and in exposing the banality of popular scientism. Immanuel Kant, who had demolished dogmatic metaphysics of a different kind, was invoked in the antimaterialist cause. He had argued that our scientific knowledge is limited by the modes of perception which determine the form of sensuous experience. Our minds work in conjunction with sensuous experience, but the modes of perception are a priori. Hence, Kant's concept of pure reason was singularly appropriate for the antimaterialists because it preserved the autonomy of consciousness, while neither making ungrounded metaphysical claims for its powers nor denying the indispensability of experience. Kant's theory of knowledge had great relevance for intellectuals who sought to comprehend the possibility of scientific knowledge without yielding to the simplicities of metaphysical materialism.

Lange, following the lead of Helmholtz whom he had heard lecture at Bonn in 1857, accused the materialists of failing to explain the facts of consciousness. Modern psychology and physiology, he believed, had shown that the world investigated by physical scientists is a world that depends on our perceptions; it does not have an independent existence—nor is the observer a mere reflector of it.[59] Lange's objection to materialism was epistemological rather than spiritual or religious. This was recognized by his outstanding disciple, the Marburg neo-Kantian Hermann Cohen, who called Lange the "apostle of the Kantian Weltanschauung."[60] In his introduction to a later edition of *Die Geschichte des Materialismus* Cohen wrote that Lange had met the two great challenges of the age: To base science on its own appropriate principles and to regenerate the masses through the ethical ideal of socialism.

Lange's own description of his intentions was that he had wanted to demolish the cardinal points of the materialist argument. It was no accident, he said, that the last chapter of his book pointed to a practical solution to the difficulties raised by materialism for this "is in the nature and import of my entire critique."[61]

The cornerstone of Lange's critique is Kant. Kant's philosophy, as Lange understood it, was essentially an attempt to destroy materialism without falling into skepticism in the process.[62] But Kant's method, in Lange's estimation, was of more enduring value than his system. As a systematic philosopher Kant sometimes erred. Thus, for Lange and the neo-Kantians, the *neo* prefix was not a terminological conceit. Far from desiring to enshrine Kant's doctrines on the altar of infallibility, they wanted to resuscitate philosophical criticism in the spirit rather than according to the letter of the master. Lange was among those early neo-Kantians who deviated appreciably from Kant in giving his epistemology a hard turn toward what was called psychologism. Lange, Helmholtz, and Zeller were decisively influenced by recent findings in the physiology of the sense organs. In fact, as noted, Lange called this new physiology "developed or corrected Kantianism."[63] This suggests the close relationship between the early Kant revival and the spirit of empirical science, and supports the thesis that neo-Kantianism was a revolt against *scientism*, not against science itself.

Lange's ideas provide a useful summary of the recurrent attitudes found in the early years of the movement: Respect for modern scientific procedures while insisting on their limits; rejection both of *Naturphilosophie* and metaphysical materialism; suspicion of Hegel's panlogism; and emphasis on the practical side of Kant's philosophy. But *Die Geschichte des Materialismus* is much more than an examination of issues in the materialism debate; it is a history of materialistic philosophies in their changing historical context. Lange made an analysis of materialism from antiquity to the present, and then explored the forces that had encouraged a materialistic world view in his time. He dated the end of post-Kantian idealism and the beginning of modern materialism in Germany with the July Revolution in France.[64] Sharply aware of the intimate connection between politics and Hegelian idealism, Lange explained that "philosophy lost its magic the moment it was placed in the service of absolutism." Heine's migration to Paris, Lange believed, was symbolic of the intellectual situation after 1830. And Hegel's identification of the reasonable with the real "heightened the mistrust of philosophy." France, the country of realism and bourgeois rule, was the harbinger of the future. The spirit of enterprise, trade, and industry coincided with the scientific climate of the era and hastened the temporary demise of idealism. Material interests became supreme.

Lange did not attribute modern materialism to the nature of politics and economic interests alone. Hegel and some of his left-wing disciples were also responsible. Hegel had confused reality with its manner of appearing to us; then Ludwig Feuerbach transformed Hegel's identity principle into quasi-materialism with his equation, "truth, reality, and sense are identical."[65] He was also known for his notorious quip that misleadingly identified him with the materialists, "man is what he eats," which in German is a pun, *Mann ist, was er isst*. Feuerbach and the materialists equated sensibility with reality—an understandable but erroneous inversion of Hegel's monism.[66] His anthropocentric modification of Hegel was easily converted into an attack on existing religious and secular authority. Arnold Ruge's *Hallische Jahrbücher* then forged the philosophical and scientific arguments of radical Hegelianism into a weapon of political opposition in the 1840s.[67] The failure of the aspirations of 1848 not only discredited the identification of political institutions with progressive ideals but created an even greater zeal for regenerating society through material and industrial progress. "Coal and iron were the redemptive words of the era."[68] Six years after the revolution, the Göttingen convention of physical scientists met which, in Lange's phrase, assumed the passionate tones of a great religious dispute.

But materialism was ephemeral, at least among the academicians, because the roots of idealism were too deep in German soil to be permanently annihilated. Speaking of the speculative and abstract bent of the German character, Lange remarked, "Germany is the only country in the world where the pharmacist cannot even fill a prescription without thinking about the connection of his activity with the fundament of the universe."[69] Materialism as a Weltanschauung proved untenable in the land of spiritual depth and *Innerlichkeit*. Lange had little respect for his contemporaries among the materialists. He dismissed his political ally Büchner as a dilettante and shallow popularizer. Czolbe and Vogt were at least reputable scientists, but they were poor philosophers. By ignoring the phenomenal nature of experience—which Kant had already proved—they hypostatized perceptions. Energy, matter, and atoms are merely useful constructs which illustrate relations and processes as scientists perceive them. But these scientific hypotheses do not give us a literal description of reality. The real nature of things is forever inaccessible to thought. Lange blamed Hegel's identification of subject and object for the confusion of our perceptions with things-in-themselves. "The theory of identity is the apple which tempted philosophy to fall into logical sin."[70] Thus, Lange's critique is double-barreled, aiming at both Hegel and the materialists who ignored Kant's proof that the thing-in-itself cannot be known.[71] By neglecting Kant's critical method, his successors went in the direction of either metaphysical absolutism or anthropocentric humanism, the latter represented by Feuerbach.[72] Lange built his analysis of materialism on Kant's distinction between phenomenal experience and the unknowable ground of reality. The Kantian thing-in-itself Lange saw as merely a limiting concept, that is, as an insuperable barrier between our phenomenal world and an unknown realm inaccessible to thought. He criticized Kant for failing to recognize that this noumenal realm, although beyond the reach of reason, is the source of the sublime and holy, the noncognitive sphere of music, art, poetry, and religious feeling. Yet he found in Kant's dualism an effective refutation of materialism which is inherently, and in Lange's opinion fallaciously, monistic.

Ethics and Freedom

Lange disliked Hegel's lofty preoccupation with the world spirit and his consequent neglect of freedom and self-determination,[73] yet he did not share Kant's confidence in the possibility of a scientific foundation for ethics.[74] He consigned the metaphysics of morality to poetry, which to him meant "the Ideal in which the world of Being and the world of Becoming are brought into unity and harmony."[75] Lange did not entirely disallow metaphysics; rather, he called it a "constructive art of forming concepts," an activity in which the mind is perfectly free to indulge so long as the theoretical limits of knowledge are not forgotten.[76] This supraintellectual activity finds its highest expression in art—and who could refute a note of Beethoven's or accuse Raphael of error in his Madonna?[77] Lange agreed with Kant that faith, moral action, and art require ideas that are beyond the province of theoretical reason. These ideas can be denied no more than they can be proved. He could not go along with the exegetes who thought that Kant had cleared everything away to prove the ideas of God, Freedom, and Immortality.[78] These interpreters, Lange said, did not understand the purpose of Kant's first critique, and apparently Lange was not too clear on those parts of the second and third critiques in which the limits of theoretical reason are surpassed by moral and aesthetic judgment. Lange perceived Kant as a demolisher of dogmatic metaphysics, of Humean skepticism, and as a fideist in morality and religious belief. It was Kant the epistemologist of empirical science whom Lange admired. Neo-Kantianism as represented by Lange was not yet a means of liberating the moral sciences from the natural.

Kant's moral theory, Lange concluded, is full of difficulties, and his deduction of it is unsatisfactory, but its gist is correct, "otherwise the beginning of ethical experience would not be thinkable."[79] Lange's moral philosophy is a mixture of eudaemonism and teleological idealism with a voluntaristic twist typical of early neo-Kantian ethical philosophy."Whatever moral progress there is, rests on the gradual extending of our view of the world beyond the crude perturbations of impulse and violent impressions of pleasure and pain. Moral ideals progress only so far as man is able to shape his own world."[80] Although Lange's formulation is deficient in logical rigor, his moral philosophy has the merit of being designed to inspire practical action. Therefore, the very least that can be credited to Lange is that he tried to meet the most frequently asserted criticism of German ethical idealism since Luther: Its alleged separation of freedom from practical responsibility and from the actual consequences of moral choice.

Lange believed that the idea of freedom is just as irrefutable as the principle of causality and that there is no conflict between the two. The consciousness of freedom unites with a sense of responsibility and is then capable of influencing our actions just as much as impulse, desire, or external circumstances. His theory of freedom is thoroughly pragmatic, without pretense of logical proof. For him, the antimaterialists who used Kant's intelligible freedom to support empirical self-determination were in error.[81] He did not tinker with Kant's dualism—nor was he greatly disturbed by the paradox it poses. He accepted moral ideals as real elements in the causal process, but the precise way in which ethical freedom affects the phenomenal world can never be known.The commonsense flavor and philosophical imprecision of Lange's ethics are exemplified in his advocacy of "moral sympathy," an idea he found in Adam Smith which he believed the classical economists had wrongly neglected. He attached great significance to the emotions of sympathy and sociability in human relations, paying little heed to the abstruse discussion of ethical freedom that figures so prominently in the history of German idealism.

Lange's *Die Geschichte des Materialismus* was a literary success. By 1921, it had gone through ten editions. But more important than this was his impact on the revisionist intellectuals of the Social Democratic party. In addition to imparting his social Kantianism to the Marburg philosophers, Lange made a strong impression on nonacademic intellectuals such as Eduard Bernstein and Franz Mehring. In fact, there was a Lange revival at the end of the century, instigated mainly by Bernstein to whom Lange was the first modern proponent of Kantian socialism, and the one who had cleared the way for democratic, evolutionary socialism by replacing dialectics with ethical idealism.[82] Young Max Weber and his cousin Otto Baumgarten also read Lange's opus. After several weeks of struggling through Lotze (presumably the ponderous *Microcosmus*), Weber found Lange a stimulating change of pace.[83] Indeed, Lange's refutation of both materialistic and Hegelian metaphysics with Kantian arguments was a signal event in the history of neo-Kantianism.

Yet Lange's place in German intellectual history goes beyond his writings. His public life was far more important than his writing, for he contrasted vividly with the conventional intellectual liberals of his day. His active political life was an exemplary demonstration of progressive democratic ideals in practice. "In his political thinking," writes Karl Jaspers, "Kant develops the idea of a realization of reason. . . . Man is destined by his reason to live in society with men, and in it to cultivate, civilize and moralize himself by means of art and the sciences. . . . His rational task is actively, in battle against obstacles, to make himself worthy of mankind."[84] F.A. Lange succeeded more fully than most in living up to these Kantian precepts. In his person, intellectual liberalism encompassed both academic philosophy and democratic politics. The dangerous gap between thought and social reality was momentarily closed.

5

Neo-Kantian Socialism

The Marburg School: Hermann Cohen and His Disciples

The emergence of the Marburg School under Hermann Cohen marked a new phase in the history of the neo-Kantian movement. The Marburg philosophers abandoned the psychologism of Lange and rejected the untenable analogy between brain physiology and Kant's forms of perception. Thus, they were more careful students of Kant and less enamored of midcentury positivism than their predecessors. But the Marburg group retained Lange's democratic socialism and continued his attempt to interest the working classes in neo-Kantian politics. It broke with Lange only by restoring Kantian epistemology to the level of transcendental criticism; it made a purely logical inquiry into the prior conditions of thought.

The Marburgers have been accused of narrow epistemological specialism, and the school has been described as a purely academic phenomenon with little social or political significance.[1] But it is wholly inaccurate to describe them as arid logicians who were indifferent to social problems; several recent studies have shown clearly their strong interest in reform.[2] Although much of the Marburg literature is abstruse epistemology, especially that part of it devoted to the logic of mathematics and science, a large portion deals mainly with ethical, political, and social questions of an eminently practical nature.

Hermann Cohen and Paul Natorp in their work give at least as much attention to social philosophy as to logic. In Rudolf Stammler's legal philosophy, the social interest is unquestionably paramount although Stammler was sometimes rebuked for empty formalism. The formal philosophies of these three were conceived to sustain their principal concern: social justice in a democratic state. Their younger followers, men such as Franz Staudinger, Karl Vorländer, Kurt Eisner, August Stadler, and Leonard Nelson, were just as interested in bringing the neo-Kantian message into politics. One can readily agree with Mosse's view that they represented the search for a third force in German life, "an attempt to solve the problems of the modern age by creating a force that could eliminate the unpalatably capitalist and materialist present."[3] But his opinion that the neo-Kantians rejected practical compromise and gradual reform in favor of an ethical absolute represented by the categorical imperative of Kant is not so readily acceptable.[4] In proper Kantian fashion, they saw history and politics as a process of education guided by reason and by the moral idea of free men exercising their rights and responsibilities in a constitutional state.[5] Undeniably their approach had an element of elitism in the implication that neo-Kantian philosophers best understand the moral outlines of the future; still, they did not propose a conflict free utopia in some mythical German New Harmony. Their specific proposals pointed to the social welfare capitalism realized in West Germany today. If their approach was impractical, it was because of their failure realistically to assess the social, institutional, and cultural obstacles in their path— obstacles which could not be removed completely even by the improvised and aborted revolutions of 1918-19. It took the Hitler period and the catastrophe of 1945 to reduce these obstacles sufficiently to permit the rise of the broad social liberalism characteristic of the Federal Republic today. In other words, the realization of neo-Kantian goals would require the physical destruction of the Old Regime. As bourgeois humanists opposed to revolution, a violent solution to the social problem was abhorrent to them; moreover, the majority were loyal to the state and believed, however erroneously, in its reformability. It was not that they were lacking in practical ideas, but that their radicalism was deficient and their reformist optimism politically naive. This fault is certainly not the same as a flight from reality into the mystical domain of the Absolute, which has been alleged.[6] Although the Weimar heirs of neo-Kantians, in their increasing frustration and estrangement from existing politics, tended to evade cooperation with the existing socialist movement, that was a deviation from the spirit of Cohen and prewar neo-Kantianism.[7]

Yet it must be admitted that the Marburg philosophers reveal not only the strengths but also the weaknesses and ambiguities of neo-Kantianism. Their academic writings, like most of Kant's formal philosophy, are difficult and stratospherically abstract. Esotericism invites only a small audience; therefore, they denied themselves a wide middle-class readership. Cohen, and to a much greater extent Natorp, tended to turn the logical operations of the mind into ontological absolutes and even to make the mind productive of its own reality; thus, they drifted into a metaphysical idealism contrary to Kantian criticism and closer to the neo-Hegelianism of the late nineteenth century. But the neo-Kantian ethics of the Marburg school was used to propose a new democratic, evolutionary socialism as an alternative to both the revolutionary dialectics of Marx and the bourgeois liberalism of the educated classes. This effort, measured by its practical results, was a failure. Although Marburg socialism did succeed in arousing interest among revisionist intellectuals of the Social Democratic party, it appeared too late, its influence beyond academic environs was too weak, and the commitment of the middle classes to the Hohenzollern military monarchy was too strong for it to have any influence. The apogee of Marburg neo-Kantianism unfortunately coincided with Wilhelmine *Weltpolitik*, the Pan-German movement, the rise of giant industry, the spread of fashionable irrationalism, and the erratic diplomacy of Bismarck's successors. The social liberalism, humanism, and moral rationalism of Marburg philosophy were overwhelmed by the political rhetoric and clanking machinery of empire. Eventually, the Marburg group itself was shattered by the frequently conflicting loyalties of humanism and patriotism. Paul Natorp became a latter-day prophet of the German soul; during the war he preached about the incompatibility of German *Kultur* and Western civilization. His Kantian ideals had no foolproof protection against nationalism. Although Cohen and Stammler were militant patriots, they still sought for some kind of reasonable middle ground, while Ernst Cassirer, a younger disciple, remained closer to the Marburg cosmopolitan tradition. Cohen's distinguished students—Natorp, Stammler, and Cassirer—lived into the Weimar era; Stammler and Cassirer witnessed the collapse of Weimar democracy and the rise of Hitler. The war, and then Cohen's death in 1918, brought the Marburg movement to an end, though its overall influence lingered on until it was eclipsed by the philosophies of two former Marburg students, Husserl's phenomenology and Heidegger's philosophy of *Existenz*. Marburg neo-Kantianism actually began to lose its momentum and unity in the time between Cohen's retirement in 1912 and the outbreak of the war. After the war, its importance remained as a diffuse moral and political influence. Natorp and Vorländer were active in educational reform and politics; Leonard Nelson, who was perhaps closer to Kant's student Fries than to Kant, was vigorously involved in the same areas. The Kantian categorical imperative continued to function as a social ideal for such humanists as Heinrich Mann and the intellectuals of the *Weltbühne*.[8] Few members of the left-wing, non-Communist intelligentsia were left untouched by the ethical personalism of neo-Kantian social philosophy. But one can hardly speak of a Marburg school after Cohen's death in 1918 and the assassination of Kurt Eisner, his most militant pupil, early the following year.

Cohen, Lange's Heir Designate

Hermann Cohen, another second generation neo-Kantian, was born on July 4, 1842, in Koswig, Anhalt, where his father, Gerson Cohen, taught at the synagogue school. His Jewish background and rabbinical training had a decisive effect on his outlook. At that time German Jews were working both for civic emancipation and for the reform of their own faith. Jews had been given full juridical equality by an ordinance of July 3, 1869, but still it was usual for them, if they were to attain important official and academic positions, to submit to Christian baptism.[9] Cohen declined this "passport to modern culture," as Heine once bitterly described it. He believed that disloyalty to the ancestral creed would be unGerman.

Cohen's cosmopolitan and liberal beliefs at the University of Marburg were naturally reinforced by his plight as a Jew in the historic Protestant land of Hesse. He spoke out for the freedom of his own people and for relief from the civic disabilities that barred them from full participation in German life, but he had no love for Zionism and its dream of a Jewish national state, a question over which he later argued with Martin Buber. Cohen believed that the Jewish prophetic tradition, Kant's ethical idealism, and the values of German culture were complementary and compatible. As an enemy of confessional intolerance, he fought for the liberalization of his own religion, emphasizing that Judaism in its essence was a rational, nondogmatic religion of morality. Later, he devoted more time to his studies of Jewish philosophy, gradually losing his taste for social and political controversy. But a resurgence of anti-Semitism in the 1870s moved him to defend liberal Judaism as congenial to German culture. His main opponent was no other than Heinrich von Treitschke, the nationalist historian and editor of the *Preussische Jahrbücher*. Cohen first disarmed his antagonist by agreeing with his appeal for a homogeneous German culture; he then invoked Kantian ethics as the unifying element between German idealism and enlightened Judaism. Treitschke was greatly impressed and confessed that he found Cohen's reply the most thoughtful one to come from an opponent. The incident has particular importance because Cohen, for the first time, was responding to a social issue specifically from a Kantian position.

The Treitschke encounter was not Cohen's last public battle against the forces of anti-Semitism. In 1888, he engaged Paul de Lagarde in an argument over the questions of whether there should be Jewish schoolteachers and their trustworthiness in Gentile society. A schoolteacher had charged that Jews were free to behave treacherously toward their colleagues because they were not bound by their own religious laws in their relations with Gentiles; they were, therefore, free to commit all kinds of moral abominations. Lagarde had testified on behalf of the German teacher who had impugned the fidelity of Jews in his profession. Cohen attacked Lagarde's testimony in the so-called Talmud trial of 1888, and received a much more friendly response from the Jewish press than he had during his exchange with Treitschke in the preceding decade.[10] This second experience further strengthened his commitment to the identity of Judaism and Germanism, and had a decisive impact on his reaction to World War I.

Cohen attended the gymnasium in Dessau and in 1859 entered the Jewish Theological Seminary at Breslau, where he joined the moderate Reform Judaism of Zacharias Frankel.[11] Frankel, who headed the historical or Breslau school of Judaism, was between the conservatives and liberal reformers in his beliefs; he encouraged critical research of religious sources but supported tradition when it was upheld by conscientious scholarship. He believed that reform was both justifiable and necessary, provided that it was not merely inspired by the clamor of the laity but was also sustained by reason and impartial research. When he was a young rabbi in Dresden, Frankel crusaded for abolition of the special oath required of Jews before the civil courts which was eventually abolished throughout Germany. Cohen was imbued with his teacher's devotion to Jewish emancipation and later followed him into Talmudic scholarship, but his interest in secular philosophy won out over the rabbinate. In 1861, he enrolled at the University of Breslau, and three years later at Berlin to study philosophy under Kuno Fischer's former antagonist, Adolf Trendelenburg. The Aristotelianism of Trendelenburg may have augmented Cohen's antipathy toward speculative philosophy; it is certain that Trendelenburg's debate with

Fischer on the subjectivity of space and time was responsible for Cohen's conversion to Kantianism.[12] Cohen, however, was first enthusiastic about the comparative philology of Hermann Steinthal and Moritz Lazarus; the latter had published his first scholarly articles in the newly founded *Zeitschrift für Völkerpsychologie und Sprachwissenschaft.*[13]

As Cohen began to master Kant, he shifted from Steinthal's linguistics to epistemology. In 1871 the modest but lucid treatise, *Kant's Theory of Experience,* announced his espousal of critical method and his rejection of the older neo-Kantian psychologism. At first, his book was either scorned or ignored, except by Lange, who was so impressed by it that he modified his own interpretation of Kant in the third edition of the *History of Materialism.* When Lange came to Marburg in 1872, he recommended that Cohen be offered the chair in philosophy. Within the year, his advice was followed; in 1873, Cohen made his habilitation, and when Lange died three years later, succeeded as full professor.[14]

Since the University of Marburg had been created as the first Protestant university in Germany by Landgrave Philip of Hesse in 1527, it had experienced alternately prominence and obscurity. It was the scene of the famous colloquies between German and Swiss Protestants in 1529 and the center of Protestant scholarship, but by the middle of the eighteenth century it had declined almost to oblivion. In 1761, the enrollment had dwindled to thirty-one. Marburg remained in the doldrums for another century, whereupon, in August 1866, it was incorporated into the Prussian system.[15] Twenty years earlier, the prince elector of Hesse had helped prepare the revival of Marburg by inviting Zeller to take the chair in philosophy. Because he had been Strauss's student, it was assumed by the uninformed that Zeller was an atheist and his appointment at first caused a great uproar. But it subsided, and Zeller remained at Marburg long enough to spread the new Kantian gospel and prepare the way for Lange and Cohen.

Before Cohen evolved his own systematic philosophy, he completed his commentaries on Kant's three critiques, publishing *Kants Begründung der Ethik* in 1877, and *Kants Begründung der Aesthetik* in 1889. Between 1877 and 1889, he turned his attention to the theory of mathematics and the philosophy of infinitesimal calculus. At the same time, he was exploring the thought of Plato, whom he considered a forerunner of criticism and the first philosopher of science.[16] In the decade preceding his retirement in 1912, he wrote his own trinity of critiques: *Logik der reinen Erkenntnis, Ethik des reinen Willens,* and *Aesthetik des reinen Gefühls.* Cohen's intellectual life began with religion, moved to linguistics, then epistemology, ethics, and science, and finally returned to religion. He was the most versatile and wide-ranging of the Marburg philosophers, remarkably vital as a teacher in opening new areas for critical study by his students. Disillusionment with German politics and personal suffering under the shadow of unofficial anti-Semitism in Germany was apparently the reason he returned to religious inquiry. Persistent in his conviction that both Judaism and German idealism were, basically, religions of moral reason, he grieved that so many Germans looked upon Jews as unassimilable.[17] Cohen predicted that all religions would one day be replaced by pure theism and a higher morality, doubtless a great overestimation of the rational element in religious experience.

When Cohen reached seventy, he resigned his Marburg professorship and joined the *Akademie des Judentums* in Berlin where he resumed his study of Jewish thought. He was not as fortunate as Lange in being able to designate his own successor. His choice was his brilliant pupil, Ernst Cassirer, but the chair was given to an experimental psychologist now forgotten.[18] Marburg neo-Kantianism was nearing the end of its eminence. Its most effective propagator, Hermann Cohen, died on April 4, 1918.

Cohen's Attack on Psychologism: The Primacy of Logic

Neo-Kantianism could be summed up as a campaign to prevent the subordination of consciousness to undifferentiated experience and to protect the integrity of the free individual from all forms of monism and determinism. Cohen raised consciousness to an even higher level than had Lange; he explored the limits of pure logic in the formation of concepts in science, ethics, and art. He started with the Kantian question, "What certainty does our thought possess?" but went far beyond Kant in his answer by elevating mind to an almost Hegelian pinnacle with his doctrine that thought not only determines the forms of sensuous experience but also produces its own reality. Being (*Sein*) is not independent. It first arises in thought.[19] Only thought can produce what we know as Being.

Truth, according to Cohen, is that which is always in agreement with reason—and the laws of reason are independent of experience. Thus, the ontological problem of Being is transformed into the problem of validity, metaphysics is replaced by logic, and the realm of Being is replaced by the realm of values.[20] Here Cohen goes beyond the limiting principle in Kant—the thing-in-itself. There is no objective world outside of cognition; therefore, cognition is no longer finite, as it is for

Kant. By hypostatizing thought itself, Cohen verges on a form of absolute idealism that neo-Kantian philosophy had originally attempted to refute.[21] Indeed, one of the traits of later neo-Kantianism was the circuitous return to metaphysics, a repetition of the course followed by German philosophy after Kant in the transition from critical to absolute idealism.

Cohen did remain truly Kantian in proposing that the a priori forms of knowing are the bases of scientific logic. He looked upon Kant as the epistemologist of Newtonian physics and conceived of his own work as an effort to adapt Kant's transcendental analysis to the new demands of nineteenth-century science. The philosophical error of his youth, Cohen confessed, had been to interpret the Kantian forms of thought as part of man's psychophysiological constitution—the heresy of psychologism as found in Lange. The "lawful elements" that make experience possible are not vessels, grooves, or empty molds of the mind; rather, they are the rules or processes used by the mind in organizing experience—they are the formal conditions of thought.[22] Here Cohen renounced the physiological interpretation of Kant's apriorism, and thereby liberated epistemology from the empiricism of Helmholtz, Zeller, and Lange. The result was something of a paradox: By dropping the empirical bias of earlier neo-Kantianism, Cohen made his epistemology a purely formal study of conceptualization; by insisting that this process of conceptualization actually produces its own reality, he veered toward a metaphysics of the mind which had provoked the original neo-Kantian attack on Hegel.

To Cohen, logic was the queen of the sciences, but he was not satisfied with pure formalism. Philosophy does not end in logic, but logic must clarify the conditions of all cultural activity, from morality to art. Logic is indispensable in the understanding of human culture as an integral whole. Logic discovers the laws of form and function— laws which are themselves the mainsprings of culture in its three main divisions: science, morality, and art. Therefore, Cohen's theory of knowledge is the core of his humanism because the conditions for producing general human culture are found in logic. In ethics, which is the logic of jurisprudence, is found the conditions for creating a just society within the state.[23] Cohen used logic as an organon of universal culture. His deepest concern was for the logic of social justice which is ethics, and in his theory of experience he devised a way to solve the ethical problem. Kant's transcendental method was the key, for it analyzes the possibility of rationality in experience. Transcendental criticism must be applied to ethics in order to find "the law of rationality of the will in the production of the object."[24] The universality of the moral law is in its validity for all rational beings, but the precise form of the moral law can be discovered only by the transcendental method.[25] Following Kant closely in this regard, Cohen used formal criticism to show that morality is autonomous conscience —the pure will to do good.

The Political Possibilities of Marburg Socialism

Cohen first sought the formal conditions of experience and then the universal rational conditions of right conduct. His students, Natorp and Stammler, followed the same method. Although they did not admit natural law as such, they were implicitly following Western natural law tradition by seeking the universal character of justice and right. In the pursuit of a universal ethic, the Marburg philosophers disavowed both Hegel and the historical school of Von Savigny. The neo-Kantian restitution of *Aufklärung* universalism in ethics and legal philosophy was not generally accepted in Wilhelmine Germany, but nonetheless it was an encouraging sign; it bore witness to the durability of the cosmopolitan tradition. The separation from accepted Western ideals was clearly discernible during the Second Reich, but neo-Kantianism, at least until 1914, favored convergence; it was a counterforce against the centrifugal influence of German cultural nationalism.

Marburg neo-Kantianism also clashed with another powerful ideology of that period—German Marxism. The Marburg philosophers found in Kant's ethical idealism what they believed was a moral mandate for socialism.[26] By giving primacy to ethics over economic dialectics, they surrendered the alleged scientific rigor of Marxism to make room for an ethics of freedom. In depriving socialism of its dialectical inevitabilities, they also denied the necessity of revolution, thereby making democratic socialism theoretically conceivable—and making socialism more respectable from a bourgeois point of view. The Marburgers apparently found a formula for socializing liberalism—or for liberalizing socialism. Even though the practical possibilities of this ethical socialism were never realized, they should be given credit for recognizing the moral dimensions of the problem, the need for tolerance, understanding, and a more generous attitude toward fellow Germans of different classes. The divisive forces were too strong, mutual suspicion too deep-seated, and the reformist attitude of the neo-Kantians themselves too sanguine to produce a successful democratic coalition based on ethical idealism alone. The neo-Kantians suffered a weakness which was both the glory and downfall of the entire idealist tradition: the conviction that rational consciousness is the most powerful agent in history, that the Is will march toward the Ought, and ultimately the rational will unite with the real. Although the neo-Kantians were not utopian and knew with Kant of what crooked wood men are made, they still harbored a gradualist optimism that took too little account of the real situation in Germany.

The growth of German social democracy after 1890 into a mass movement coincided with the rise of both Marburg ethical socialism and revisionism within the Social Democratic party which, by 1912, not only had the largest popular base but had become the largest delegation in the Reichstag. Its electoral strength still came mainly from the working class, but the huge glacier of bourgeois hostility was beginning to melt. Political cooperation between the Social Democrats and left-wing liberals seemed to promise the development of a genuine democratic opposition to the Junkers and industrialists. In 1912, the Progressives and Social Democrats formally coalesced at the polls, each party giving its second ballot support to the leading Progressive or Socialist candidate.[27] In the subsequent contest for the Reichstag presidency, August Bebel, the former bête noire of Bismarck, received the vote of the entire Progressive bloc and twenty National Liberals as well. Bebel was narrowly defeated, but Philip Scheidemann, his Social Democratic colleague, was elected to the vice-presidency.[28] It could be argued that this liberal-socialist alliance was created by special circumstances of the election year and did not represent a genuine synthesis of democratic forces, but the 1912 campaign did prove that middle-class resentment of regressive Junkerdom and absolutism was powerful enough to overcome the perennial fear of working class radicalism, at least temporarily. Had this political experiment been given an adequate period to germinate, it might have led to the genesis of a workable left-of-center opposition, but instead it became one of the first casualties of the war. This coalition was, of course, reborn with Weimar, but suffering such congenital damage as nearly to destroy its prospects for a healthy, independent political life. Yet in 1912, Friedrich Naumann's appeal for a progressive alliance extending from "Bassermann to Bebel" seemed to some people not a wild dream.

If the tactics of their party leaders are any indication, a modest accommodation was developing between the middle class and the laboring masses. Social integration of those groups considered inherently disloyal by Bismarck was dangerously overdue in Germany, and now the process was underway. Marburg socialism and its political corollary, revisionism, were symptomatic of this belated conjunction. Unfortunately, the process was still embryonic when war and social dislocation struck Germany in 1914. The setback was a disaster, for it is unlikely that the National Socialists could have come to power in a national community where social attitudes were sufficiently adjusted to the realities of modern industrial civilization. Hitler's successful exploitation of the Bolshevik fear and the virtual extinction of the nonsocialist left by 1930 testify to the failure of adequate social integration and to the serious deficiencies in bourgeois political philosophy. The historical significance of Marburg socialism is that it was prospectively a formula for the rapprochement of progressive democracy and parliamentary socialism. The historical tragedy is that it failed. Both German liberalism and socialism eventually fell victim to their largely self-imposed isolation from each other.

Cohen's Democratic Socialist Ethos

Cohen's contribution to democratic socialism created an ethics in which individual freedom is meaningful and purposeful only in a community of free individuals. His theory of freedom was derived from Kant's distinction between causal determinism in the world of appearance and autonomy in the intelligible world of moral freedom. But he tried to conquer the practical difficulties in Kant's dualism by converting the categorical imperative, the law of the self-legislating individual, into the social imperative, the law of the self-legislating society. The social imperative demands that one should "act as though the element of humanity in one's own person, as well as in the person of every other individual, is treated at all times as a purpose, never merely as a means."[29]

Cohen's thesis was that the intelligible sphere, where Kant placed the thing-in-itself and noumenal freedom, is beyond reason but can be comprehended by other forms of consciousness as a goal or task. The meaning of moral thing-in-itself lies in its function as a task for ethics; it poses the demand of the *homo noumenon* for the *homo phenomenon* to become a rational, self-legislating person. The *homo noumenon* expresses the "vocation of man" as man.[30] For Cohen, individual freedom becomes the entelechy of man's moral development in society and sustains a teleological optimism somewhat more sanguine than that contemplated by Kant.[31] Cohen also goes beyond Kant in his assertion that freedom is a transcendental idea which produces its own world of realities—ethical realities which possess Being but not phenomenal existence. Noumenal freedom possesses Being "insofar as it commands a purpose."[32] Freedom is a regulative idea necessary in the purposive development of humanity; its existence resides in what ought to be rather than in what phenomenally Is. Both the Marburg and Baden neo-Kantians agreed on the priority of the ethical Ought over the phenomenal Is. Following Kant, they raised practical over theoretical reason, but going beyond Kant, they gave ethical ideas a quasi-ontological status. Cohen's reason for expanding Kant's ethics was eminently practical. "One demands," he said, "more of freedom than a hypothesis for ethics. One demands that freedom be a real force for living men. It must mean . . . the capacity for developing [ethical] principles."[33] The possibility of moral action has nothing to do with interrupting causality or initiating a new series of phenomenal events. The old metaphysical argument about freedom versus determinism in nature was rendered irrelevant by Kant when he based ethics on the possibility of a moral law rather than on empirical freedom: "Thus there arose from the concept of universal moral legislation the idea of self-legislation or autonomy."[34] Cohen then enlarged Kant's theory of autonomy into the moral self-determination of society and humanity. The moral law has two meanings: "The idea of humanity and the idea of socialism."[35] These two ideas have no determinate content. They possess the character of "purpose." Humanity and socialism belong to the Ought, the world of ethical objectives; they exist as a mission for man's moral will.

Cohen's teleological idealism, reminiscent of Lotze's ethics, made an explicit place for the individual. Each person is a purpose in himself. The universal law of humanity is implanted in all men. Every man is an embodiment of ethical potentialities. This, said Cohen, is the new meaning of freedom; it does not require that man initiate a new act but that his conduct have an absolute purpose. As a bearer of purpose, man is an end in himself, never a means.[36] For Cohen, the integrity of persons and their purposeful role in the unfolding moral order constitute the essence of socialism. Society itself is a moral idea; it is the reforming and guiding principle of world history.[37] Therefore, the idea of socialism becomes a postulate of practical reason, indispensable to the coexistence of men in modern industrial society.[38] Only through the idea of socialism, Cohen and the Marburgers believed, could the discrepancy between social reality and moral existence of men as ends in themselves be overcome.

Cohen's philosophy of the state was the capstone of his ethical socialism. After he had denied that dialectical materialism and revolution were necessary to the socialist ideal, he rejected a third tenet of orthodox Marxism—the epiphenomenal character of the bourgeois state. The state is the self-legislating unity of individuals, and jurisprudence is the science that provides the necessary ethical foundation for this unity.[39] The state is, in fact, a juristic person exemplifying the idea of moral humanity.[40] There is no fundamental conflict between humanity and the state because the state-of-laws is no mere territorial or political entity; it is a cosmopolitan idea, carrying within itself the universal principles of humanity. Here, Cohen appealed to the cosmopolitan ideal of the classical epoch.[41] He rejected integral nationalism, even under the stress and patriotic pressures of the war. In 1914, even when his own students were being carried into cultural xenophobia by excessive patriotism, he expressed his conviction that the roots of German culture were deep in eighteenth-century humanism. There was no reason to suppose that cosmopolitanism was obsolete or that Germany could afford to dispense with the values of the Enlightenment.[42] When some of his closest associates were lending their prestige to anti-Western propaganda, Cohen was holding to his European commitment. This did not, however, prevent him from articulating a position fairly close to the "Ideas of 1914," with their often strident accent on the uniqueness of Germany and the cultural shallowness of the Western enemies.[43] Cohen's longstanding faith in the unity of Germanism and Judaism was expressed in strongly patriotic language. Yet at the same time he refused to join in xenophobic denigration of other national cultures. His commitment to the moral equivalence of German idealism and liberal Judaism, which he expressed in his response to Treitschke, had put him in a quandary. To prove the genuineness of this commitment and the compatibility of the two elements of his creed, he had to display his patriotism. His student Natorp put his finger on the dilemma when he criticized Cohen for being preoccupied with the Jewish side of the equation: Cohen believed that Kantian Jew equals good German.[44] It could not be fairly charged, however, that in the hysterical atmosphere of wartime, Cohen jettisoned his European convictions. His ineradicable humanism and universalism were doubtless, as one writer suggests, part of his Jewish heritage.[45] But non-Jewish intellectuals like Friedrich Meinecke, whom no one could accuse of lacking patriotism, were also warning against the exaggeration of Germany's spiritual distance from the West.

It is socialism, according to Cohen, that creates the bond between a people and their state. He objected to what he called the "romantic" idea of the state, with its notion of a "historically absolute community of the people."[46] The *völkisch* idea may provide a primitive form of unity, but it should be no more than a transitional stage. "Nations remain tribes until they are unified in the state." The state maintains the substance of ethical culture; therefore, without the state the *völkisch* principle is dangerous and barbaric.[47]

The state is also necessarily an expression of power. Without power it could not become a state-of-laws. Without power it would be unable to uphold the law equitably, irrespective of estates, classes, or special interests. The will of the state, which establishes the rule of law and guarantees that power will be used fairly, is expressed in universal suffrage. Political democracy makes the state a union of free wills. Democracy is the hallmark of liberty and the practical expression of freedom. Where democracy is deficient, as in Prussia with its three-class voting system, the state is only an implement of power and not the source of law.[48] Cohen did not accept the conventional liberal proviso that political education should precede enfranchisement of the masses. He believed the opposite, that democratic suffrage is the best means of political education.

Although Cohen was not an intellectual-in-politics like Lange, their political views were similar. Cohen agreed with Lange that the social inequities caused by large private ownership and unearned profits should be reduced by a steep inheritance tax.[49] Yet he favored stronger state authority, and his notion of the state as the guardian of justice and upholder of impartial laws put him closer to Lassalle than to Lange. Cohen was also more emphatic than Lange about the Kantian origin of socialist ethics. Lange was dissatisfied with Kant's arguments; his ethics was eudaemonistic, inclining him more toward English utilitarianism than Kant's ethical formalism. Cohen, on the other hand, saw Kant as "the true author of German socialism."[50] Industrialism had turned labor into a commodity, and man had become a "thing," deprived of his inherent dignity. Kant's categorical imperative was the appropriate moral antidote for this poisonous condition because it proclaimed that man is an end in himself, not merely a cog in the impersonal industrial process.[51] Cohen translated into Kantian terms the Marxist accusation of capitalistic exploitation as the alienation of the individual from his intrinsic moral worth.

Cohen believed that the restoration of human dignity required social reconciliation under the aegis of the democratic state. He wanted full integration of the laboring class into the life of the nation.[52] His socialism was moral, evolutionary, and parliamentary. He might still be classified as an intellectual liberal because his philosophy was based on an ethical individualism drawn from the middle-class philosophical tradition. But Kant's moral philosophy had been addressed to an illiberal society of princes and estates. It was Cohen who made Kantianism relevant to the predicament of the undereducated and unpropertied in the modern industrial state of the late nineteenth century.

Marburg Neo-Kantianism Extended: Natorp and Stammler

Hermann Cohen, by adding to the intellectual bequest of F.A. Lange, updated Marburg neo-Kantian ethics and democratic politics. His students Paul Natorp and Rudolf Stammler, beginning with his ethical idealism, extended the range of Marburg neo-Kantianism with their academic specialties. Natorp concentrated on the theory of education; Stammler applied neo-Kantian ethics to jurisprudence and became the legal philosopher of the Marburg movement.[53]

Marburg neo-Kantianism, until shortly before the war, was a coherent intellectual movement. Cohen and Natorp both taught at the university, where they jointly edited the *Philosophische Arbeiten*. At the university, Cohen's students studied transcendental criticism, each applying it to his special area of inquiry. The unity of the group was more in method than in doctrine, but the critical technique produced a relative homogeneity of ideas among them, especially in ethics. The main doctrines were the moral autonomy of persons, the social meaning of the categorical imperative, and the teleological reality of ethical values as the objects of moral will. In their social philosophy, the Marburg writers did not assign a special cultural and moral role to the middle class, as did conventional liberalism, but neither did they attribute an exclusive historical mission to the proletariat, as did the Marxists.[54] If modern democracy can be said to mean equality and social pluralism within a consensus on political fundamentals, rather than ineluctable conflict and victory of a particular social class, then the Marburgers represented a Western model of political democracy. But they were also fellow heirs of Marx, who was imbued with a strong sense of ethical idealism. His rage was directed at the alienation of man from his true worth by the incongruencies of modern production and ownership; therefore his vestigial ethical individualism, especially in his early thought, was of classical vintage. By stripping away Marx's dialectical interpretation of history and denying the primacy of economic relations, the Marburg socialist discovered the basic affinity between German socialism and the idealist heritage. The strength of the idealist tradition is perhaps one reason why orthodox Marxism never really triumphed in Germany. When the Social Democrats finally came to power, they were no longer a Marxist party.

But the economic materialism of Marxist philosophy was a point of irreconcilable opposition between most of the Marburgers and the guardians of orthodoxy in the Social Democratic party.[55] While recognizing economic variables in the study of social history, the neo-Kantians deplored Marx's monism—as earlier neo-Kantians had condemned Hegel for the same reason. Hegel and Marx had violated Kant's important formal separation of the Is from the Ought. By ignoring Kant's conceptual dualism, Marx allegedly suppressed the efficacy of human will in striving for ethical goals. Marxism was seen as a flat denial of moral freedom. To a Kantian, this was intolerable. Paradoxically, though, the Marburg socialists were so energetic in their emphasis on the reality of moral potentialities that they lapsed into a virtual metaphysics of moral values and lost sight of critical philosophy. Paul Natorp went farthest in this direction, exemplifying the return to metaphysics in the last stages of neo-Kantianism. The dissolution of Marburg philosophy as a critical, antimetaphysical movement can readily be detected in tracing his thought.

Natorp was Cohen's most important pupil, but for the last ten years of his life his thinking became almost totally alien to the spirit of Cohen's stringent epistemology. In fairness to Natorp it should be conceded that Cohen himself revealed in many ways the incipient abandonment of criticism. Before 1912, he had anticipated the resurgence of metaphysics in his effort to combine Platonic logic with transcendental philosophy.[56] After his retirement his interest in epistemology declined and he concerned himself almost exclusively with the articulation of a rational religion of pure morality based on the analogy between Judaism and German idealism. The hunger for a Weltanschauung, for a unified vision of the world appropriate to all the needs of the human spirit, became his consuming passion long before Natorp began his own odyssey beyond the frontiers of criticism and logic. The cleavage between Marburg principles and Natorp's philosophy was discernible although not as extensive as it sometimes appeared. In fact, both Cohen and Natorp have been associated with the Hegelian renaissance of the early twentieth century.[57]

Paul Natorp was born on August 17, 1854, in Düsseldorf. His great-grandfather Bernhard Christoph Ludwig Natorp had been a prominent educator during the Reform era, and was called by Wilhelm von Humboldt to the Ministry of the Interior as an expert on elementary education. At Humboldt's request in 1812, he drafted a master plan for the reorganization of Prussia's lower school system;[58] later, he was vice-general superintendent of schools in Münster. Paul Natorp's professional interest in educational theory may have been inspired by knowledge of his great-grandfather's work nearly a century before. Paul Natorp studied at the universities of Bonn and Strassburg. At Bonn he was a pupil of the philologist Hermann Usener, who was investigating the linguistic forms of mythological expression. Natorp believed that there is a typical, ideal spirit behind these forms, historically revealing itself in myth and religion. He wanted to find a method for bringing his theory into systematic clarity. While still at Strassburg, he heard from a friend at Marburg who enthusiastically described to him the critical method of Lange, Cohen, and "their Kant." The intellectual confusion that had beset Natorp was, as Cassirer tells us, promptly terminated by his discovery of Cohen's scientific philosophy;[59] in his first monograph, *Descartes Erkenntnistheorie. Eine Studie zur Vorgeschichte des Kritizismus* (1882), Natorp applied the newly acquired critical method. In 1881, Natorp went to Marburg as a *Privatdozent* and remained there the rest of his life. From 1885 to 1912, he held the chair in philosophy conjointly with Cohen; throughout their lives, the friendship between the two men was close and productive.

Natorp's conversion to Kantian criticism while engaged in his philological studies of myth created a permanent ambivalence in his thought. As a logician of the sciences, he was an unstinting adherent of Kant and Cohen, insisting on the limits of thought, but as a neo-Hegelian he was impelled toward metaphysics by his interest in the mythological expressions of the historical spirit. Eventually the logician was subordinated to the metaphysician of Logos. Natorp was also as much an heir of Fichte as of Kant and Hegel, shown by his concern for "moral education," which again was an indication of his kinship to Westphalian pietism, a part of his heritage from the Kügelgen family on his mother's side.[60] At first, Natorp was interested primarily in a pure system of scientific concepts, and he looked for the basic forms of knowledge in the logic of mathematics.[61] Only over a span of several decades did he slowly lose patience with pure methodology and begin his quest for the relationship of Logos and Life. Then, as one commentator aptly describes it, he went from "pure science to life, from rationalism to spirit, and from Kant ever nearer to Hegel."[62] Natorp can rightly be considered a neo-Kantian until about 1914; thereafter he began his search for a "metaphysics of concrete totality,"[63] which carried him away from critical philosophy.

Even before Natorp stepped beyond the pale of Marburg logic, there were significant differences between his and Cohen's ideas, particularly in the extension of ethics into social philosophy. Ethics for Cohen was the science of jurisprudence, which develops the moral fabric of the state. But Natorp's ethical philosophy was slanted toward the moral community rather than the state of laws. The various goals of practical ethics find their consummate expression in the unconditioned Idea of the Good. In working for this unconditioned Idea and in judging every empirical act according to it, individuals relate themselves to a community of wills. The self-willing individual finds his purpose in the community of the morally willing.[64] The difference between Cohen's state-of-laws, ordered by the unconditioned precepts of moral reason, and Natorp's community of moral wills is more than verbal. It reveals the conservative and voluntaristic drift in Natorp's thought, for in his community the volitional element exceeds the rational. Yet his "community" is not the historical or ethnic *Gemeinschaft;* it is an integral association of moral wills.

Natorp reduced Kant's pure moral will to natural impulse and then ennobled impulse by making it the servant of virtue. His quarrel with Kant was that in Kantian ethics there is no recognition of the concrete and actual. Natorp's moral will is still self-legislating and its values are found in the kingdom of Ought; however, its taproot is no longer in autonomous moral reason but in the empirical character of man.[65] If ethics ignores human nature, it can have nothing to say about contemporary social problems and will remain exactly where Kant had left it—a purely formal exercise in moral philosophy. The influence of Platonic ethics is just as evident here as in Natorp's inversion of Kant. Natorp was looking for a way to ascend from man's empirical condition, where moral values must be efficacious if they are to count at all, to the unconditioned, immutable world of the Ought. But for him the intelligible moral values of the Ought are no longer regulative ideas. Moral values become a sort of ethical nectar, the quintessence of good conduct, squeezed from arduous moral experience in the real world.

Although Natorp began with the conceptual dualism so pointedly elaborated by Cohen, he became increasingly inclined toward the modified eudaemonism of the early neo-Kantians. Perhaps this was because of his special interest in the philosophy of education. The "theory of social pedagogy" became the motif of his work. Because education is concerned with the empirical, or with the real rather than the theoretical man, the philosophy of education must remain practical. Yet the goal of all experience is the realization of moral ideals, not all of which can be reached within the bounds of experience itself. Natorp's definition of freedom is that "we are free to posit the objects of what ought to be without being limited to a posteriori values."[66] Our actions have no meaning without reference to these transcendent standards, but supraexperiential values are empty unless they can affect the actual relations of men in the moral community.

Natorp blurred the line between nature and ethical freedom by stressing that life is a process and, therefore, the dualism of nature and freedom is necessary only in the conceptual sense. The practical actions of men mediate their empirical and intelligible natures; therefore, dualism is dissolved by what Natorp called the *Aktcharkter* of values. At first this dissolution of dualism was only a secondary theme in Natorp's philosophy, but later it became pronounced. In his *Vorlesungen über Philosophie*, published posthumously in 1925 by his son, Natorp introduced a dialectics of knowledge similar to Hegel's. Theoretical and moral truths emerge dialectically in a three stage process: from possibility to necessity to reality.[67] In Natorp's terminology, Hegel's self-movement of concept reappears as the Act-Character of the Theoretical.[68] Thus, in the evolution of his own thought, Natorp roughly recapitulated the transition from Kant to Hegel by moving from an ethics of freedom to a dialectical ontology of spirit. Hegel had sacrificed the ethics of freedom to penetrate the logic of the immanent spirit. For Natorp too, Logos was an imperious deity.

Natorp's lectures on practical philosophy were the epitaph of Marburg neo-Kantianism. In his postwar writings, the neo-Kantian movement had come full circle. Kuno Fischer and Eduard Zeller, of first generation neo-Kantianism, began as Hegelians in their dialectical philosophy of spirit. They became Kantians in their advocacy of critical epistemology. Natorp made the same circuit but in reverse, beginning in pure criticism and ending with a phenomenology of the spirit. He was deeply affected by the war and spent the last years of his life in an atmosphere of spiritual crisis. To Natorp and many other German intellectuals, epistemology was an arid, useless occupation in the midst of moral chaos and political instability. The dulling of the critical edge in German philosophy after 1914 was largely the result of disorder and disillusionment in German life and the attendant desire for something more conducive to one's spiritual security than cold logic. Architectonic and all-encompassing systems such as Spengler's *Decline of the West* were, even if pessimistic, infinitely more satisfying than recondite critiques on the order of Kant and Cohen. The constructive skepticism of the neo-Kantian movement had little chance to survive in the hothouse climate of Weimar.

Yet Natorp deserves a permanent place in the history of prewar neo-Kantianism as the author of a "socialist" theory of education. His *Sozialpadogogik* was a neo-Kantian projection into the philosophy of education. It considerably widened the scope of middle-class thinking on education by proposing a democratic *Bildung,* that is, a cultural education for the entire national community. In the great *Bildung* debate, Natorp repudiated the exclusivity of the Wilhelmine intelligentsia and demanded a unified system of education accessible to all social classes. But he also saw a national program of education as a means of sustaining indigenous German values. His educational ideas thus naturally appealed to the prewar German Youth Movement, on which he had considerable influence—but he warned that racism and anti-Semitism were incompatible with its ideals. This position, and the clearly ethical nature of his social theory, resulted in his condemnation as an enemy of the people by conservative elements after the war. The intellectual pedigree of Natorp's pedagogy developed from the ethical idealism and educational program of Kant, Fichte, and Pestalozzi.

Natorp placed education at the apex of his philosophy, believing like Kant that it is the supreme vocation of man in society and the mainspring of human progress. Moral education cannot be understood exclusively as an individual process. It is possible only in human society.[69] Therefore, all education must be social education, the preparation of individual wills for life in the organic community where man finds his true nature. "Man becomes man only in the human community."[70] In the contractural society men are only externally related. Natorp's community is a moral rather than a merely legal entity. The individual does not lose his identity in it; neither does he have any significance outside of it; and without this organic relationship among individuals, true education is unthinkable.[71] In the parlance of Kantianism, Natorp hoped to find the conditions and laws of social education—the a priori forms of social learning. His "critique of pedagogical reason" developed the idea of a social consciousness which obeys laws of formation and synthesis just as the individual consciousness does. In short, he sought to create an epistemology for social education.[72]

Natorp's social theory is the matrix for his pedagogical program; it differs sharply from Cohen's idea of society as a juristic entity. The moral community of Natorp resembles Plato's *politeia*—an organic and spiritual polity in which the whole is greater than the sum of the parts. But Natorp clung to an irreducible element of individualism. Only if the individual retains his moral sovereignty and only if each individual is equal to every other and is free to attain full self-consciousness through the unlimited exchange of ideas will the moral community come to life.[73] His community was not the *Gemeinschaft* of National Socialist ideology in which the individual vanishes into the mystical union of the people, but it was a deviation from the uncompromised democratic individualism of Lange and Cohen. He shifted the emphasis from the individual to community, from law to social education. Society is no longer a juristic association following the prescriptions of moral reason. It is the organic community of wills created for the purpose of educating man as a social and cultural being. "Individual and community are necessarily one and the same," for the meaning of one passes into the other. Natorp praised Plato for having been the first to see that the laws of individual moral education are identical to those of the community.[74] Natorp's community is theoretically egalitarian, but the balance between the individual and the organic whole is precarious—the danger implicit in his educational theory.

The system of community education begins with the family at its center and extends to the larger concentric spheres of local, state, and national education, none of which can function without the others. Natorp, an avid disciple of Pestalozzi, attached great importance to the family and also felt that individuals must be free to develop spontaneously and naturally.[75] Socialism cannot be produced by fiat; it will emerge from the free development of the individual spirit through social education. *Bildung* is not the monopoly of a special elite; rather, it is the evolving moral nature of the organic community of which each individual is an integral part. Plainly Natorp was trying to socialize ethical idealism and to make the liberal ideal of *Bildung* something more than an undemocratic legitimation of cultural snobbery. The difficulty lay in his neglect of the liberal tenet that society is established to secure the liberty of the individual, whose intrinsic value is independent of his social relations. By hypostatizing the community—attributing to it a supraindividual reality—Natorp seriously compromised the moral individualism of the neo-Kantian tradition.

The insidiousness of Natorp's organic theory became apparent during the war in his collection of essays, *Der Tag des Deutschen.*In these ultrapatriotic outpourings there was little left of Marburg cosmopolitanism. He was sure that the war was a defense of German *Kultur* against its hereditary enemies: Slavic barbarism and Western materialism. The war had been forced on Germany—and he was one of many who believed this—therefore, there could be no turning back. Germany's universal cultural mission would be enhanced by the war, for war rejuvenates the entire nation. Natorp thus embraced one of the most common and certainly one of the most pernicious illusions of prenuclear man: the inevitability and desirability of national conflict. His wartime writings stridently emphasized Germany's cultural superiority to the West, proclaiming that Western democracy is alien to the Fatherland because the German idea of freedom is based on authority and on the moral organization of society through community education. Western democracy is based on a spurious individualism which denies the individual an integral place in the community. The nation-at-arms in 1914, he believed, was the moral community in its most militant and inspirational form.[76] Natorp's "metaphysics of the German essence" obviously grew from his prewar theory of the educative community and he became the self-styled Fichte of 1914, exhorting his countrymen to see the war as a continuation of Germany's special cultural vocation. In marked contrast to Cohen, Meinecke, Troeltsch, and other loyal Germans who nonetheless refused to repudiate Germany's debt to Western civilization, Natorp plunged into the vagaries of a mystical Germanism.

It is curious that the neo-Kantians most akin to Hegel in Weltanschauung, notably Zeller and Natorp, were those who became hortatory nationalists in times of patriotic excitement. It might be suspected that this was caused by the Hegelian historicizing of values and tendency to amplify the moral character of the nation-state. The result, however, made their country a surrogate for the absolute norms that have been relativized by the dialectics. Although old-fashioned national arrogance needs no metaphysics of history to encourage it, nevertheless one might reasonably suppose that Hegelian historicism creates a moral void which patriotic emotion seeks to fill.

Natorp appears in retrospect as a paradoxical figure in the fellowship of neo-Kantianism. Originally a proponent of pure logic and an enemy of speculative metaphysics, although greatly intrigued by the historical meaning of myths and symbols, he eventually put aside neo-Kantian criticism and, hoping to conquer the dualism of nature and spirit, ventured into the labyrinth of speculative metaphysics. He was much influenced by the new physics of Planck and Einstein, which also encouraged him to reject the dichotomies of Kantianism. The new quantum physics and the theory of relativity convinced him that Kant's fixed categories were no longer valid. He therefore tried to work out his own "open system" which would be compatible with contemporary science.[77] For example, in his later epistemology the opposition of subject and object is replaced by the *functions* of subjectivizing and objectivizing, a fluid process of knowing. His original Kantian theory of knowledge had, however, considerable influence among twentieth-century German philosophers, such as the phenomenologist Husserl, who borrowed freely from his 1887 essay, "The Objective and the Subjective

Foundations of Knowledge," in formulating his own critique of psychologism,[78] and also owed much to Natorp in his argument for the autonomy of logic.[79] The eventual split of the Marburg school into phenomenology and existence was already implicit in Natorp's work. Although he is no longer credited with having much influence on the history of modern German philosophy, nevertheless his philosophy at the time was an intellectual pivot, and his career anticipated the divergent strands of post-1918 German thought. His friend and colleague Rudolf Stammler remained much closer to the neo-Kantian tradition.

Stammler and the Rule of Right Law

Rudolf Stammler was one of the leading legal philosophers during the time of the empire and Weimar Republic. His reputation was international, for he was the best-known of the Marburg neo-Kantians outside Germany except for Cassirer, whose world stature came later. His application of Kantian criticism to jurisprudence inspired both respect and controversy in Europe and the United States.[80] Although he was noted for his careful and rigorous reasoning, he was also frequently reproved for being too formal and abstract. Certainly, he followed Kant's method of transcendental criticism almost to a fault, but his theory of right law emanated from a practical view of legal relationships. Behind Stammler's formalism is the idea of an ethical community founded on individual liberty and social justice, at the same time giving due recognition to the equitable reconciliation of material interests. But as one of his critics observed, Stammler created "not so much a philosophy of law as a logic for a philosophy of law"; his work was "a good prolegomenon to any possible philosophy of law but not the philosophy itself."[81]

Stammler lived from 1856 to 1938, long enough to see his legal principles defiled by National Socialism. He was born at Helsfeld in Hesse and educated at Giessen. Later, he studied at Leipzig where in 1880 he was appointed *Privatdozent* in Roman law; in 1882 he went to Marburg for two years, beginning his long association with Cohen and Natorp and coming under the influence of neo-Kantian epistemology. In 1884, he returned briefly to Giessen, going the following year to Halle, and in 1916 to Berlin. He lived in Wernigerode from 1923 until his death on April 25, 1938.[82]

As we have seen above, Cohen had developed the main thesis of Marburg socialism by broadening the categorical imperative into the fundamental rule of a society directed by moral reason and constituted under law. Natorp had gradually transformed Cohen's juristic society into a community of free-willing men who are integrally related to the organic whole. Stammler's social philosophy was a synthesis of Cohen's and Natorp's, but with a definitely stronger portion from the former. He appropriated Cohen's ethics and Natorp's idea of the voluntaristic community, and then proceeded independently to the philosophy of law, but the Cohen-Natorp pedigree was always in evidence.

Stammler's ethical philosophy begins with the Kantian notions of pure will and the conceptual separation of the Is and Ought. The goals of the Ought are no less real because they cannot be known in experience; they are set by pure will as a task. Even though these values cannot be comprehended by reason, they are comparable to the "polar star that guides the mariner."[83] This conceptual split does not mean that the goals and purposes of the Ought have no place in the course of human affairs. To be sure, man is a part of nature and must be studied by psychology as involved in causal relations; but as an agent of history, man must be seen as free and purposive. Freedom does not require the disruption of natural causality; it is the power to choose the means to a valued purpose. Intellectually, morally, and politically, man is self-determining. Only his physiological processes are subject to blind causality.[84] Stammler thus accepted Cohen's ethics with only slight verbal alterations. Clearly his ethics is not the same as right law but is propaedeutic to it; individuals in a just society must be "committed to the [ethical] Ought which is necessary for the realization of right law."[85] Conversely, ethics cannot become real without right law. Right law itself is, in Friedrich's description, "a standard for distinguishing what among all existing law is right law;" and, "law as a means in the service of human purposes requires for its justification the proof that it is a right means for a right purpose."[86]

Right law is offered by Stammler as a unitary method for achieving the "social ideal" in the form of a community of free-willing persons.[87] He used the expression *Gemeinschaft* but with a clear difference from Natorp's version. For Stammler, it is the final expression of unity under law.[88] The social ideal is a ceaseless task to be undertaken by moral reason with the aim of harmonizing the interests of free men while treating them as purposes in themselves, never as means. The social ideal is also the root of law, for "it is the only thing which belongs to all legal purposes in common."[89] Justice is the *ultima ratio* of right law and of the social ideal, but it is not to be confused with them; its nature is neither freedom nor equality nor welfare. Although these criteria are desirable, none of them can become a permanent standard. The only unchanging and universal element in all legal propositions is the "ad-

justment of individual purposes in accordance with the one final purpose of the community . . . the aim of the legal community can only be
the union of individuals so far as their volitions are ends in themselves."[90] In other words, the individual retains his moral sovereignty
but recognizes a universal obligation not to exercise his natural freedom so as to impair the moral sovereignty of others. Differences arising from conflicts of interest must be composed according to the social
ideal; otherwise, the individual will be submerged or society will disin-
tegrate. Stammler's social ideal is the power of law which strives to keep
centrifugal and centripetal forces in equilibrium. The purposes of the
community will often appear to be irreconcilable with the purposes of
the individual, but for Stammler the function of law is to adjust these
conflicts while respecting both the inviolability of persons and the ideal
goals of the community.

Stammler's socialism hewed to the lines laid down by Cohen. It was
idealistic, ethical, and evolutionary. His objections to Marxism, to its
economic monism and positivistic view of human society, were standard
criticisms from the neo-Kantian arsenal. The cardinal mistake of the
Marxists was to interpret the human condition causally rather than
teleologically.[91] Stammler's critique of Marxism and advocacy of ethical
and religious forces in history in *Wirtschaft und Recht* provoked the
Jovian wrath of Max Weber, who gave the book a scathing review. He
accused Stammler of logical inconsistency and of the most heinous
crime of all, in Weber's estimation, that of smuggling values into the
analysis of social history, an error which violated Weber's rule of value-
free inquiry.[92] But the argument was over method, not over Stammler's
substantive objections to Marxism.

Whatever Stammler's shortcomings as a sociologist may have been
according to Weber, his legal philosophy implied the possibility of social
reconciliation and renewed commitment to the universalism of the Enlightenment. His social ideal and principle of right law recognized no
class lines, and his critique of legal judgment was an explicit acknowledgment of universal norms in justice and equity. By the turn of
the century, German liberalism was showing signs of losing its already
attenuated sense of kinship to the eighteenth century and the West.
Romantic utterings about the special "inwardness" or the unplumbed
depths of the German soul were becoming more frequent.[93] Stammler's Kantian analysis of legal thought and his consequent opposition
to the national and historical schools of law were against the prevailing
beliefs of the prewar decade. His concept of right law was not a literal
return to eighteenth-century natural law, although he did defend nat-

ural law against the positivists.[94] A resemblance between the two was indeed indisputable, for Stammler tried to discover the universal forms of legal judgment—the logic of the law rather than its empirical content. He sought, as he put it, not the "law of nature" but the "nature of law." Natural law, Stammler said, is based on assumptions about the nature of man, but it "is impossible to prove that man has . . . certain a priori impulses guiding his conduct." "On the assumption of such impulses we can never arrive at an absolute and fundamental ideal of just social volition . . . . We must start from the idea of social co-operation as an object of a special kind . . . and by critical analysis discover the law immanent in it."[95]

Stammler withdrew all empirical content from law in order to find a legal consciousness as such, an a priori form of thought. This legal consciousness is a kind of social reason; it can be found only in legal thought which is about social relationships, because law is a "special subdivision of the formal conditions of social life."[96] The law of nature is doomed from the start because "the content of law has to do with the regulation of human social life, which aims to satisfy human wants. But everything that has reference to human wants and the matter of satisfying them is merely empirical and subject to constant change. . . . " "Our purpose," he concluded, "is to find merely a universally valid formal method, by means of which the necessarily changing material of empirically conditioned rules may be so worked out, judged and determined that it shall have the quality of objective justice."[97] Only in this manner, can we hope to attain a universal legal standard.[98] Some forms of juristic thought are unconditionally necessary for any legal content. The content of law changes, but its form persists.[99] If the jurist wants to discover a permanent, objective standard, he must look for it in the nature of law, not in the law of nature.

The search for pure forms of jurisprudence brought Stammler the rebuke of his critics for his allegedly sterile formalism and his attribution of real existence to legal concepts as Ideas of Reason. Erich Kaufmann argued that the only way Stammler could sustain the idea of the right law or apply it to life was to hypostatize it.[100] Philosophically, there is some justice in this charge, for it was a common practice of neo-Kantianism to separate normative from empirical Being, and then to attribute a different kind of Being to norms by playing semantic tricks with the terms *Sein* and *Dasein*. But the accusation that Kantian formalism cannot provide practical rules for real situations misconstrues the purpose of formal criticism. It is difficult to agree with Stammler's critic that the separation of the forms of experience from

their content, first attempted by Kant, was a complete break with Western philosophical traditions and contributed to Germany's increasing
intellectual isolation.[101] The main fault of this criticism is that it con-
fuses form with intention and thereby misses Kant's point. The common assumption in Western natural law from the Stoics through Aquinas and Locke is not that immutable laws can be found in the empirical
nature of man or that these laws are in harmony with the requirements
of human happiness, but that *human experience contains universal elements.*
Kant preserved this universal aspect from corrosive skepticism and
historicism by placing it in the various forms of reason rather than in
the shifting content of experience. The new sciences of nature and
society made the old natural law untenable, and it became even more
indefensible in the century after Kant. The neo-Kantians responded to
a similar challenge, defending the universal nature of reason in science,
ethics, and history by exploring the modes of thinking in those areas
which endure beneath temporal, geographic, and historical variations.
Stammler did not write laws and Heinrich Rickert did not write history;
both looked for the characteristic logic of their respective fields. Their
aim was to find the universal conditions of knowledge in law and history. Their common assumption was the universality of rational and
moral experience—which was also an indispensable assumption of natural law. But to the extent that they saw the development of freedom
and right as a historical task, as a struggling toward the regulative Ideas
of the moral Ought, the neo-Kantians like their master did away with
the complementary relationship between natural rights and phenomenal history.

Stammler was a true Kantian in both his critical method and his
ethical individualism. His final standard for right law was optimum
freedom for the individual in a free society.[102] He defined freedom as
the "objectivity of determination of ends," a somewhat stilted way of
saying that the individual sets goals which are not exclusively determined by his finite personal interests but which are "universally valid
for any man placed in the same situation."[103] Thus, the highest attainment for a society is to become a community of free-willing men.[104]

The war was a severe test for neo-Kantian humanism. The intellectuals could either give an example of cosmopolitan moderation or suc-
cumb to chauvinistic hysteria. They did not have to act seditiously or
embrace pacifism to demonstrate their allegiance to European civilization—this would have required a courage and saintliness too rare to be
expected—but only to speak out against the tribal passions that were
exploding all over the civilized world. To Stammler's credit, he man-

aged to appear loyal without joining his friend Natorp in his vaporous *Deutschtums Metaphysik*. Stammler was convinced, as were most Germans early in the war, that the Russians had attacked. Few Germans knew about the ultimatum to Belgium but many were aroused by rumors of French air raids on southern German towns. Stammler thought that his country was fighting a just war, but he felt that in the transitory intoxication of national unity it should not be forgotten that wider unity "in common bond with all the nations of the earth" would be of more lasting achievement than military victory.[105] He accepted Natorp's notion that war had galvanized the national spirit, but for him the will to victory must not be permitted to threaten the principles of right law and humanity. All Germans should remember the famous dictum of Clausewitz that war is a continuation of politics by other means and not an end in itself. Force should be used responsibly, according to rational political considerations. Stammler reminded his readers of the psalmist who said: "The law must always be the law." In the same context, he cited the German proverb: "Misfortune comes when power prevails, but law brings fame to the king and blessings to the land."[106]

In 1915, Stammler gave several public addresses during the centenary celebration of Bismarck's birthday. Under the circumstances, purple oratory must have been a temptation, but Stammler kept his tone moderate. He spoke of Germany's "overflowing" gratitude to Bismarck for bringing political unity to a divided people, adding that full social unity was still unachieved. Social reconciliation within the nation must be built on justice and the recognition of every German as a participant in the national community. Bismarck had created a formidable structure, but inside it was still incomplete. The completion of the task, the integration of all Germans into the national community, demanded an answer to the social question.[107] Stammler and other progressives used the democratizing effects of the war effort to justify democratic reform and to urge the abolition of such political anachronisms as the three-class suffrage in Prussia—they had, of course, been preaching social democracy for several decades.

The Marburg socialists and the revisionists of the Social Democrats shared the same vision of a nonrevolutionary melioration of German life, inspired by ethical idealism in politics and guided by a theory of social change that did not ipso facto exclude the possibility of class cooperation.[108] Eduard Bernstein tried to make this the credo of the Social Democratic party, but he was defeated by Karl Kautsky, a moderate but strictly orthodox Marxist who won the backing of Bebel, Liebknecht, and the party leadership.[109] The anathematizing of Bernstein's ethical socialism did much to ruin the embryonic alliance between neo-Kantianism and the working-class movement. Marburg Socialism was confined thereafter to the lecture halls and academic journals. Its greatest effect, ironically, was to foment theoretical squabbling and consequently weaken the Social Democrats at a time when the party needed all the strength it could muster.

It would be unfair to place the entire blame for the failure of social integration on the German bourgeoisie. The sages of the proletariat were often just as narrow and class-bound in their way, as their peremptory rejection of Marburg ethical socialism demonstrates. When Kautsky closed his mind to the pragmatic advantages of revisionism, another opportunity was lost for finding a political modus vivendi. As long as the working class professed to follow revolutionary Marxism, regardless of its actual behavior, a major part of the middle class would continue to be an apprehensive, intransigent, and sometimes paranoic enemy of socialism in all its manifestations. Marburg socialism hoped to be a nondoctrinaire congealment. Instead, it became a source of intramural inflammation. It must also be conceded that, given the refeudalization of the German middle class and the organization of commerce, industry, and agriculture into powerful pressure groups, as well as the unrepresentative character of Prussian politics, the proposed alliance between evolutionary socialism and democratic liberalism had little chance of success.

6

The Southwestern School

The Will to Truth: Windelband, Rickert, and Baden Neo-Kantianism

Wilhelm Windelband once said, "All we nineteenth-century philosophers are Kantians." There is much truth to this, since Kantian criticism had become the basis of philosophical training in the universities: "The Kantian critique was so generally taught as a point of departure for all philosophical thinking that it influenced many scholars who were not professional philosophers. Kant's position affected almost every aspect of German learning on some level of theoretical coherence,"[1] influencing many nineteenth-century German philosophers to some degree. For some, he was the philosopher of empirical science; for others, the enemy of dogmatic metaphysics; and for still others, the rescuer of morality and religion from skepticism. The neo-Kantians themselves, ostensibly the true legatees of Kant, did not always agree on what facet of Kant's philosophy to emphasize. Yet there were two points of concord between the Marburg and Baden or Southwestern schools: The imperative need to criticize and examine the foundations of knowledge itself, and the superior claim of practical over theoretical reason.

Richard Kroner, a product of the Baden school, says that the "two great cultural powers at the very foundation of Kantian philosophy are natural science and moral life."[2] The Baden philosophers were more concerned with the "fundamental moral questions which Kant's critical philosophy attempted to answer"[3] than the Marburg philosophers, who went back to Kant's epistemological criticism. Yet this customary division of neo-Kantianism into epistemological and moral sections is misleading. The Marburg neo-Kantians were first logicians, but eventually turned to Kant's ethics and the social implications of the categorical imperative. Windelband and Rickert of the Baden school were also interested in logic, but in the logic of the humanities, especially history. Thus, they differed from the Cohen group in their greater interest in a critical philosophy of values for the understanding of history rather than in the logical structure of the natural sciences, but agreed that there was a conceptual division of reality and purpose, or Being and Values, and that reality and purpose unite in moral action. They also agreed on "the primacy of the willing subject over all knowledge and all speculative constructions of reality."[4]

Moral questions were important to the Baden philosophers only in the theoretical sense. Their interest in social problems and practical politics, as compared to that of Cohen, Natorp, and Stammler, was minuscule. Windelband and Rickert used their theory of values to explore logical problems and to delineate the boundary between natural science and the humanities. In this respect they were less concerned with the practical implications of Kant's ethics than the Marburg school; both seemed to have admired Fichte more than Kant as a political thinker. Some years after the war Rickert published an article expressing his belief that any future political science on idealist lines would have to follow in form Fichte's *The Closed Commercial State*.[5] The primacy Rickert gave to theoretical over practical problems in political thought has been criticized as typically mandarin and implicitly nonliberal.[6] Liberalism of the Western tradition focuses on concrete issues and the resolution of healthy competing interests. The politics of idealism is conceptual rather than practical; it scorns interest politics and searches for permanent harmony.[7] If one is ready to accept Ralf Dahrendorf's liberal criteria as paradigmatic, then the Baden sages clearly were deficient in their liberal idealism[8] But their cultural philosophy had characteristics which implied humanism of an undeniably Western provenance and scope. And thus a Baden Weltanschauung developed. Although there were many quarrels between Baden and Marburg, congruency of outlook arose, nevertheless, from their common Kantian lineage.[9] The Baden Weltanschauung believed in a world under the order of rational moral precepts, a historical process infused with the ideal purposes of men, and a cultural life measured by enduring, universal standards of value. As opponents of historicism and relativism, Windelband and Rickert sought the universal nature of values, while Stammler looked for the universal nature of law. This was a return to the mode, not the substance, of natural law thinking characteristic of eighteenth-century Enlightenment. The Baden philosophers wrote extensively on the significance of individuality in history—a trait of Romantic historiography—but basically they were rationalists. They wanted to find the universal value represented in each unique historical event; therefore, Baden neo-Kantianism was inherently humanistic and universal.

In one of those historical ironies that frequently overtake intellectual movements, neo-Kantianism sometimes gave rise to its opposite—irrationalism. The neo-Kantians tried to retrieve consciousness and reason from irrationalism and determinism, which by the latter part of the century had formed an alliance with positivism. But a sort of irrational backlash resulted from the neo-Kantian emphasis on the subjective observer and from the tendency to suggest that scientific judgments are problematic.[10] Hans Vaihinger's philosophy of fictions, for example, could easily lead to the antithesis of Baden neo-Kantianism—the relativity and subjectivity of truth. If the study of science, society, or history employs purely arbitrary constructs, then the universal and necessary character of knowledge maintained by Kant dissolves into subjectivity. In his philosophy of norms, Windelband aimed at defeating just such an arbitrary notion of truth.

Yet the great strength of idealism as represented by Windelband and the neo-Kantians, that is, its determination to establish permanent values, was at the same time its greatest weakness. Neo-Kantian idealism tended to dissolve real problems into spiritual and moral categories, thereby, as Ringer observes: "The analysis of political realities was neglected, and relatively little attention was paid to questions of political technique. These matters were generally felt to be trivial."[11] That neo-Kantianism had some practical content was shown by Cohen and his group. But Windelband and Rickert were consistently engaged at a very high level of abstraction, and their preoccupation with cultural values doubtless drew their attention away from everyday issues. In style, tone, and temperament the Baden writers seem separate and certainly more conservative than the Marburg writers. Cohen was at heart an optimist who welcomed what he saw as the progressive forces in modern life. Windelband and Rickert were more typically "mandarin"; Windelband, particularly, harbored Burckhardtian apprehensions about the future and feared for the survival of culture in a technological age.[12]

Wilhelm Windelband: Philosophy as the Science of Values

Wilhelm Windelband, like Cohen, was personally linked to early neo-Kantianism. He was a pupil of Lotze and Fischer, and a personal friend of Liebmann, author of *Kant und die Epigonen*. Born on May 11, 1848, the year of revolutions, he first attended the Potsdam gymnasium and then went to Jena, Berlin, and Göttingen. In 1870 he completed his doctoral thesis, "Ueber Lehren vom Zufall," under Lotze's direction at Göttingen. That year he volunteered for military service and received his commission in time to serve in the Franco-Prussian war.[13] In 1873, with the acceptance of his typically Kantian doctoral thesis, he became a *Privatdozent*. In 1876, he was called to Zurich, four years after Lange's departure, and a year later he went to Freiburg im Breisgau, then to Strassburg in 1882. In 1903, he replaced the retiring Kuno Fischer at Heidelberg, soon to be the center of Baden neo-Kantianism, and died there on October 22, 1915. His successor was Heinrich Rickert, his student and protégé.

Windelband inherited Fischer's mantle as the neo-Kantian historian of philosophy. At Freiburg he began his *Die Geschichte der neueren Philosophie*, an admirable survey and commentary, which is still read with interest today.[14] Ten years later Windelband brought out his *Geschichte der Alten Philosophie*, and his general compendium, *Geschichte der Philosophie*, in 1892.[15] He wanted to illustrate historically the connection between philosophy and the general culture. Going beyond Fischer, and closer to Dilthey, he was concerned with the psychological necessities which produce different types of philosophical thought. In his *Lehrbuch der Geschichte der Philosophie*, Windelband states that the historian should ask: "Through what impulses of thought in the course of historical movement are the principles, which we use today to understand and judge man and his world scientifically, brought to consciousness and improved?"[16] He believed that the history of philosophy unfolds according to psychological necessities rather than according to the laws of the Hegelian Logos. Windelband was much closer to Dilthey's "understanding" method than Fischer's dialectics of the spirit. But he was opposed to any doctrinaire approach, for he believed that the history of thought should be studied from a variety of viewpoints—psychological, causal, pragmatic, and teleological. He displayed none of the methodological dogmatism sometimes attributed to the neo-Kantians.[17] His major service to Baden philosophy was his development of Lotze's embryonic value theory. If any single enterprise typifies Baden philosophy, it is the theory of value. Windelband's value theory was to become the fulcrum of Rickert's more elaborate studies in the logic of history.

Windelband often repeated his favorite motto: *"Kant verstehen heisst über ihn hinausgehen,"* (to understand Kant is to go beyond him).[18] In this he was most successful, continuing into a form of post-Kantian idealism very close to Fichte's. The value setting or universal normative consciousness of Windelband is the descendant of Fichte's Absolute Ego, the voluntaristic mainspring of all knowledge and culture. In his essay "Normen und Naturgesetze," he tried to reconcile the perennial antinomies: causality and values, necessity and freedom. On one level, he resorted to Fischer's definition of freedom as being aware that we are responsible for our actions because they flow necessarily from our character. Freedom, in other words, is related to the mere recognition that we cannot act otherwise because, tautologically, we are what we are. We are morally free to accept responsibility for actions that emerge, according to causal laws, from our character. Windelband's dissatisfaction with this notion of freedom is revealed by his second definition.[19] In moral decisions, he said, we become conscious of a norm—a standard of right action. Consciousness of this norm enables us to choose among several causal series. The norm of the good is thus in some way able to infuse itself into the causal sequence of behavior. Freedom becomes the ability to determine actions according to a norm. Yet Windelband insisted that freedom does not mean the capacity to interfere with causality or to initiate a new chain of events. He recognized the paradox that practical action requires the axiom of causality—we must assume that our actions will produce predictable consequences—but moral responsibility requires the assumption of freedom.

He did not think that Kant's doctrine of intelligible freedom was a satisfactory resolution of the dilemma. His theory of objective norms was an attempt to dispense with Kant's dualism. The norms are ideal standards or rules of the true, the good, and the beautiful.[20] These normative values have nothing to do with explaining events theoretically—that is, according to natural laws. Norms are "rules of judgment," which can be used to evaluate causal events. There is, according to Windelband, a normative consciousness that is capable of recognizing the relationship of an event to objective values. The normative consciousness makes teleological judgments; it decides whether things measure up to what they ought to be, as determined by an ideal standard. Normative judgment is not subjective or personal. Norms in the Kantian sense are objective, in the same way that the laws of the understanding are objective.[21] The normative consciousness is an aspect of man's universal character, hence it overcomes relativism in man's theoretical, moral, and aesthetic judgments. But Windelband's objective norms were a socialized version of Kantian regulative Ideas. Placing norms in the actual process of history where they may have an impact on events, he maintained that moral law can become a form of causal motivation itself, once the individual becomes conscious of it.[22] He tried to conquer formalism by putting freedom, as the normative choice among causal alternatives, over empirical consciousness. Freedom becomes the power to select a course of action from several causal possibilities.[23] This was in harmony with Kant's doctrine that man must gradually moralize himself through history in order to become worthy of his humanity. He formulated his answer to the freedom problem in such a way that efficacy of freedom in phenomenal history was stressed, but his concern was wholly theoretical. He gave little attention to the immediate issue: How can the actual freedom of real people in the existing world of arbitrary authorities and privileged interests be insured?

The Logic of the Historical Sciences

The rational will is the crux of Baden philosophy. Indeed, volition is a strong undercurrent in all neo-Kantian thought, and it comes to the surface in Windelband's normative theory. Every experience, he believed, is accompanied by a "thou shalt." Every act carries a theoretical, moral, or aesthetic imperative which commands "judge me according to a universal norm." All man's transactions are measured by his Will according to transcendent norms or values of the true, the good, the beautiful. For Windelband, Plato's ideas and Kant's regulative ideas are norms. Normative consciousness then enters the stream of experience when rational will commands a judgment. Man in all his cultural activities, Windelband argued, is bound to norms.[24] Although the volitional element is strong, and truth becomes that which is judged by rational will to be true, Windelband was not a voluntarist in the sense of making will the supreme cosmic principle. The conceptual content of normative consciousness is reason, and freedom in this context is obedience to reason.[25] The autonomous individual makes universal norms the maxims of his activity; therefore, will is guided by theoretical, moral, and aesthetic reason. The willing individual is unquestionably primary, but his volition does not run riot. Reason employs will as a power in the service of transcendent norms. Reason presides over man's three main cultural enterprises—scientific, moral, and aesthetic—and in each sphere there is a permanent, perfect standard to which he can refer. Hence, despite the unsolved difficulties in Windelband's theory of freedom, his consistent rationalism and antirelativism were cut from genuine neo-Kantian cloth.

Windelband's philosophy of norms was most expressly stated in his 1894 Strassburg rectorial lecture, "Geschichte und Naturwissenschaft," which became a touchstone in the debate over the difference between the physical sciences and the humanities.[26] In that lecture he argued that consciousness of value, apart from the value of pure theoretical truth, attaches only to single, individual things. Although other things may have a price, only the single or unique has intrinsic worth.[27] This proposal was to become an important contribution toward freeing the humanities from methodological servitude to science, but it was by no means the first.

Wilhelm Dilthey, in his *Einleitung in die Geisteswissenschaften* (1883), proposed a distinct methodology for the humanities.[28] He strenuously objected to the mutilation of historical reality by trimming it to fit the methods of the natural sciences. The positivist treatment of history, he argued, created truncated experience rather than a full, unfragmented presentation of reality. Dilthey believed that the methodology of history first required, in the Kantian sense, a critique of consciousness. But he tossed aside Kant's transcendental consciousness and Hegel's objective spirit as metaphysical abstractions. Consciousness is a moment of living experience determined by all the faculties, and in this moment, full identity of subject and object takes place. Expressions of these living experiences or articulations of the whole individual are the stuff of history. History can be understood by a living individual because he knows from his own experience "the process by which life tends to objectify itself in expressions."[29] An "understanding" psychology was required, according to Dilthey's earlier theory, to unlock history in its fullness and wholeness.

Dilthey is frequently numbered among the neo-Kantians, and his views have some important similarities with Baden philosophy.[30] Both he and the Baden philosophers believed that the historian seeks "meaning" and "significance" in the events he studies rather than general laws. For Dilthey, as Hajo Holborn noted, "meaning is the fundamental category of historical thinking;"[31] for Windelband and Rickert, "valuing" is the fundamental category. There is, however, little difference. Dilthey differed from the Baden neo-Kantians in his broader definition of the humanities and his rejection of the Baden tenet that history is exclusively an "individualizing" treatment of reality. Steeped in the

Hegelian writings of the Tübingen school, he was interested more in how the human spirit manifests itself in the wholeness and variety of culture than in pure methodology. But he displayed the typical neo-Kantian animus for the hegemony of positivism and he helped inaugurate the search for a distinctive historical method. His critique of historical reason was conceived as a special kind of psychology, while the Baden critique was based on logic and epistemology. Dilthey's was also a *Lebensphilosophie*; he saw the mental expressions of experience as originally rising from the stream of life, a vitalistic notion alien to the rationalistic spirit of Baden thought.

Windelband's rectorial lecture developed the main idea of neo-Kantian historical logic—that history would be distinguished from natural science by its methods rather than by its special content. He rejected the old cliché that the humanities deal with spiritual or psychic life while natural science studies the corporeal. In which category does psychology belong, Windelband asked, if the distinction is between the physical and spiritual? Since psychology is concerned with the relation of physical and psychic processes, is it science or humanity? Windelband resolves the difficulty by using method rather than subject for his distinguishing criterion. Psychology does indeed belong to the natural sciences because it generalizes on the basis of facts. Each datum of psychology is treated as the instance of a general law. The hallmark of all natural sciences is their method and intention—to discover and formulate general laws. On the other hand, a division of the humanities such as history does not look for general laws, but instead is directed toward bringing

> single, non-recurring realities limited in time to full and exhaustive expression . . . according to their particularity. The principle of separation is the formal character of their [natural science and history] epistemological goals. The one seeks universal laws, the other particular historical facts. In the language of formal logic, the aim of the one is general, apodictic judgment, that of the other, the singular assertive statement.[32]

Windelband then made the distinction in his lecture that has ever since been associated with him: The natural sciences are "nomothetic," and the humanities are "idiographic."[33] Historical facts are not only singular and unique; they are teleological. They always relate to a meaning or purpose, because as single, never recurring events they possess inherent value. If historical facts embody values, then they must ultimately be judged by the normative consciousness. But Windel-

band did not enlarge upon the integral relationship between his ideographic theory of historical method and his axiological theory of values. The two are complementary, but it was not elaborated upon until
his student Heinrich Rickert saw the connection and made it the basis
of his historical logic. Rickert, it could be said, built his career on the
modest outline presented by Windelband in his 1894 lecture.

Heinrich Rickert: Permanent Values in the Flux of History

Heinrich Rickert fitted perfectly the professorial stereotype. Large
and prepossessing in appearance, with a tendency toward loquacious-
ness, he had the reputation among his students for toughness and
intolerance of dissent, a "regular academic autocrat" (*Schulhaupt*); but
to at least one observer, he was not as formidable as had been anticipated—"no Matterhorn, but perhaps a Mont Blanc." This was the
man who, in the words of a scholar, rigorously "systematized the
Logos"[34] of Wilhelmine philosophy. Rickert, to a greater extent than
the Marburgers or Windelband, was a pure methodologist, who came
closer to creating a true critique of historical reason. He wrote no
history or social theory, and only considered ethics tangentially as part
of his epistemology. His writings as a whole are devoted to the problem of formulating a logic of history which defeats relativism but at
the same time remains scientific by suppressing personal subjectivity.
Today Rickert is usually mentioned only because of his influence on
historians and philosophers of greater breadth and versatility than
himself, such as Weber, Troeltsch, Meinecke, and the giants of Germany's late nineteenth-century intellectual renaissance. He rarely re-
ceives separate consideration. Yet his pioneer studies in the nature of
historical logic were germinal in the blossoming of German historical
and social thought which began around the last decade of the century.
The intellectual character of this vital epoch cannot be understood
without reference to him.

Rickert grew up in an exciting political and intellectual milieu. He was
born on May 25, 1863, the year after Meinecke and the year before
Weber. His father, Heinrich Rickert, Sr., was a Danzig journalist, politician, and later deputy to the Prussian Diet and German Reichstag, where
he was frequently the protagonist of Bismarck's political nightmares.[35]
In addition he was a member of the *Nationalverein* and, as a Danziger
with expertise in maritime matters, became its special authority on naval
affairs. Shortly after being returned to the Reichstag in 1874, he was
made reporter on naval policies for the budget committee. He also be-

came one of the leaders of the left wing in the National Liberal party—
altogether a very controversial figure. To Bismarck the father was an
ambitious intriguer, scheming to place himself and Albrecht von Stosch,
chief of the admiralty, at the head of a new cabinet with the accession of
Frederick III, the "liberal" kaiser. Apparently there was no such plot,
but Rickert found himself repeatedly opposing the chancellor's policies
in the late seventies, especially after Bismarck began his shift toward
tariffs and paternalism.[36] Rickert was a liberal of the Manchester mold,
professing free trade, laissez-faire, and responsible parliamentary government. His social policy was, however, quite advanced, as his concern
for the Danzig dockworkers illustrates. In 1881, Rickert, Sr., was at the
head of a group of secessionists from the National Liberal party, their
defection caused primarily by Bismarck's trade policies. These secessionists in 1884 joined a group of dissident liberals who had broken away
from the party in 1886. Together they formed the Libertarian party
(*Freisinnige Partei*), an uneasy alliance of left-wing liberal factions. Bismarck, who seems to have greatly overestimated the threat,[37] hoped to
bring about about Rickert's political downfall by having him denounced
in the official press, but was unsuccessful..

Heinrich Rickert, Jr., grew up in the midst of this political vortex.
Many of the great and powerful of that era came, at one time or
another, to his father's home; Rudolf von Bennigsen, Ludwig Wind-
thorst, Theodor Mommsen, Georg von Siemens, and a host of other
Wilhelmine notables were frequent guests. But he was apparently
never tempted by the blandishments of power or intoxicated by the
political excitement in his home. There is an interesting resemblance
between his family history and that of the Buddenbrooks in Mann's
novel: His grandfather was a wealthy, cosmopolitan merchant of Scot-
tish descent; his father a public official and politician; and his mother a
cultivated woman who fostered her son's taste for poetry.

At first, Rickert seemed destined for journalism, writing while still a
gymnasium student theater, book, and art reviews for his father's news-
paper, *Danziger Zeitung*. He attended Wilhelm Scherer's lectures on
German literature at the University of Berlin, but was repelled by
Scherer's positivist method, especially in his presentation of Goethe's
Faust. He also attended the lectures of Friedrich Paulsen, biographer of
Kant and author of a history of German universities, whose course on
British empiricism focused on Hume. For a time Rickert adapted to the
positivist climate, studying at Zurich under Richard Avenarius, a pro-
ponent of empirico-criticism, and later under Ernst Laas at Strassburg.
Gradually he was drawn toward philosophy as a vocation, but he soon

rebelled against the positivist approach. Although acknowledging that scientific method was competent to trace the causal workings of nature, he found that positivism was unable to account for meaning and value in human experience. While at Zurich he also came into contact with Russian Marxism and read socialist books then proscribed in Germany. The materialist interpretation of history espoused by the socialists he found as repugnant as Scherer's naturalistic interpretation of *Faust*.[38] Under Windelband's wing at Strassburg, Rickert discarded positivism completely and turned toward Kant's critical idealism. His doctoral thesis of 1888, *Zur Lehre von der Definition*, in which he made his initial exploration of critical epistemology, was a capsule preview of his mature philosophy.

In 1891, Rickert settled at Freiburg where he renewed his friendship with Max Weber. Rickert became something of a trailblazer by permitting Weber's wife to attend his lectures in the early nineties, before the admission of German women to sacred male academic precincts was generally practiced. Rickert was upholding a family tradition and returning a favor: much earlier his father, an advocate of women's rights, had arranged for Weber's mother to attend university lectures at Berlin; and when Alois Riehl left Freiburg, Weber had smoothed the way for his appointment to Riehl's chair.[39] Weber and Rickert had much in common, particularly their similar family backgrounds. The intellectual relationship was important to Weber's work, for in his sociology, he brought Rickert's theory of knowledge to its full meaning. But only Marianne Weber has adequately acknowledged Rickert's strong influence on her husband.

Rickert remained at Freiburg until 1915, when he succeeded Windelband at Heidelberg; he taught there until his death in 1936. His career covered almost half a century—from 1888 when he received his doctorate, the year of the three emperors, to the witnessing of Hitler's dramatic gamble in the Rhineland in March 1936. Thus, his professional life began in the same year the hopes of German liberalism were most optimistic; they soon sank to the depths with the accession and death of the "99 day Kaiser"; when he died German liberalism seemed no longer viable. How Rickert reacted to the apparent demise of liberalism is difficult to determine, but we do know that in illness and old age he accepted the Third Reich.

Rickert's immediate background was conducive to progressive politics. His father was a left-wing liberal who opposed Bismarck and suspected him of dictatorial ambitions. In the 1890s, however, Rickert, Sr., became more militantly nationalist, supporting large army budgets and the expansion of the German navy.[40] He died in 1902, before the armaments race was under full swing, but his son had become friends with Alfred Hugenberg, who at that time was on the commission for the resettlement of German farmers in the eastern provinces, and from 1909 to 1918, was on the Krupp directorate. Eventually he built a communications combine, of newspapers, film companies, and public information services. He emerged as leader of the Nationalist party during Weimar and was made economic minister in Hitler's first coalition cabinet.[41] His conservative monarchism and tolerance of the National Socialists may have influenced Rickert according to his pupil August Faust who says that he became a strong nationalist, rejecting the idea of humanity as a pale abstraction and enunciating "the concept of the national type."[42] Rickert was planning at the time of his death a book on Fichte which "would have developed his idea of the nation." There is some evidence that he became sympathetic to National Socialism, but in the last years of his life his health declined to the point where his mind became clouded. Plagued for many years by extreme claustrophobia, Rickert's personal appearances at Heidelberg gatherings became increasingly rare. By the 1930s, he rarely attended meetings of the university senate.[43]

Since Rickert succumbed to the narrow specialism frequently generated by the neo-Kantian movement, he is somewhat vulnerable to criticism. Lacking Max Weber's keen political sensitivity and awareness of the ominous conflict in Germany between power and moral responsibility, Rickert did not confront the dilemmas of his era—at least not in his work. Neither was he granted the deep historical consciousness of Meinecke, on whom he had an important influence. Measured alongside such contemporaries, Rickert seems a pedant, his vision constricted by academic blinders. His pre-1914 writings were almost exclusively epistemological from his *Gegenstand der Erkenntnis* in 1892 to his *Die Grenzen der naturwissenschaftlichen Begriffsbildung* ten years later.[44] After the war Rickert continued, in his writings and Heidelberg lectures, his crusade against popular *Lebensphilosophie,* which he considered irrational and unsystematic. He also wrote books on Kant, Goethe, and the Heidelberg tradition in German philosophy.[45] His interests had expanded well beyond his prewar concentration on historical epistemology, but his philosophical position remained essentially the same. He was determined to defend the rational and critical tradition against the onslaught of irrational decisionism which he discerned not only in popular philosophy but in the literature of early Weimar as well. However, his reputation today rests on his books about historical epistemology, in which he broke new ground and inspired further enterprises by men now better remembered than he.

Rickert's Critique of Historical Method

Kant, says Karl Jaspers, "provides no doctrine of the metaphysical world, but a critique of the reason that aspires to know it."[46] A similar statement can be made about Rickert. He provided no doctrine of the historical world, but a critique of the reason that aspires to make valid judgments about it. His historical logic was spun from the threads of his general theory of knowledge. When he was at Freiburg he expounded the rudiments of his epistemology in *Der Gegenstand der Erkenntnis*. In this small book was the nucleus of his entire philosophy, in which he followed the customary dualism of neo-Kantian thought, making practical reason even more potent. The true object of knowledge, Rickert said, is the Ought, not Being. His position as explained by Aliotta is:

> All human judgments may be mistaken. There is only one which can never be false—the judgment that there exists a value of absolute truth. It is impossible to doubt the transcendent Ought as an object of knowledge . . . because it is the necessary condition of all affirmations, even those of a skeptical order.[47]

Thus, absolute truth cannot be denied without contradiction, for such a denial is itself asserted with absolute certainty. The will to truth or the imperative to judge according to a norm of truth is a necessary function of thought. Rickert thus inverted the ontological question and made it dependent on judgment. A judgment is not valid because it says what *is*; on the contrary, reality owes its status to judgment. Only that which is *judged to be,* really *is*.[48] If judgments had to be brought into agreement with reality, Rickert argued, we would require, prior to judgment, a full knowledge of Being. This is putting the ontological cart before the epistemological horse. First we judge, and then we know what is—not the reverse. Judgment itself is not directed toward Being but toward the Ought, from whence comes the command that representations shall be judged by a transcendent norm of truth.[49] Practical reason is king, theoretical reason its compliant vassal. Nothing exists except in judgment. The same rules apply in Rickert's logic of historical method.

Rickert's volitional epistemology, his practical will to truth, has the ring of subjectivism, but the exact opposite was his intention. He agreed with Windelband that "truth is in all cases that which ought to be affirmed."[50] They both believed that the teleological Ought, which is the transcendent object of normative consciousness, is the only secure port beyond the sea of experience. Truth is not the agreement of the object to our concept of it, but the correspondence of the concept to the transcendental norm of truth. If we see a green tree, for instance, we are justified in affirming that "the tree is green" not because tree and green happen to go together in our representation, but because we recognize a demand to affirm the represented connection of tree and green.[51] Cognition is therefore a practical activity motivated by the will to truth and validated by a transcendent norm. Objects exist only in judgment and facts are such only so far as they are recognized.[52]

Rickert thus makes theoretical reason entirely dependent on pure practical reason. Reality is affirmed by the necessity to judge.[53] In other words, even cognitive knowledge is based on a categorical imperative. "Every act of cognition presupposes an autonomous will capable of conforming to an ideal norm."[54] The primacy of practical reason and its corollary, the necessity of judgment, are the cardinal doctrines of Rickert's epistemology, and they become the operative principles of his historical logic. Here was a sharp contrast to Marburg philosophy. Marburg epistemology proceeds from the theory of experience rather than from the nature of judgment. Cohen and his followers did not integrate practical and theoretical reason as thoroughly as Rickert.

The Conquest of "Historismus"

Before Rickert became Windelband's protégé, he described himself as " a student deeply stuck in the morass of positivism."[55] Then he learned from Windelband that philosophy is the science of universal and necessary values.[56] History, therefore, becomes an urgent subject of study for philosophers because it is where universal values are realized in consciousness.[57] Thus, it is necessary to have a critical philosophy of historical judgment. Before this can be achieved, however, historical method must be distinguished from that of the physical sciences, whose concern is causality not value. Rickert followed the main idea of Windelband's 1894 lecture, "Geschichte und Naturwissenschaft," in affixing the line of demarcation between history and science. He looked for that universal element in historical judgments which makes valid statements possible without impairing historical individuality. In effect, Rickert was attempting a synthesis of *Historismus* and rationalism. Expanding on Windelband's thesis, he maintained that history considers reality under an entirely different viewpoint from science. Science generalizes; individual events are merely instances of a universal law. But history seeks the particular, for "the single event is the only thing that really happens."[58] The behavior of particles according to Newton's law is not an event in the historical sense, but the Puritan revolution, a unique, nonrecurring individuality, is historical. "Everything we know that happened in definite loci of time and space is history, and if this knowledge is scientific, we call it historical science."[59] Yet if historical knowledge aims at the individual and eschews the universal, what guarantee is there of its validity? His whole philosophy was devoted to answering this question.

Rickert wanted to free history from naturalism.[60] He began by trying to establish the limitations of scientific concepts, that is, by showing how much of reality escapes scientific generalization and must therefore be captured by history. In a preliminary article on the nature of scientific logic,[61] and later in his epistemological opus *Die Grenzen,* his theme was the same as Lotze's—the poverty of conceptual thought. The term *concept,* Rickert complained, has been used carelessly. It had come to signify both the most simple elements in the logical process and the most complex form of thought. In the natural sciences, concepts are used to organize our understanding of the physical world. Scientific concepts are not representations of facts immediate to the mind. The physical world is an incomprehensible manifold of individual forms and processes. Scientific concepts can never grasp the physical world in its fullness and multiplicity, but they do serve knowledge.[62] Concepts bring reality into a form we can understand. Scientific concepts are abstractions employed to organize the unconquerable welter of data from experience. But as indispensable as these constructs are to science, much is lost in the conceptualizing process. The individuality and richness of facts are ignored when they are organized according to their common qualities. "The true nature of a scientific concept," Rickert said, "is simplification of the physical world." In this process of simplification, individuality is squeezed out. The two characteristics of reality are continuity and heterogeneity. Neither can be reduced to a concept. Those who insist that science reproduces reality are faced with the impotence of conceptual thought.[63]

Scientific concepts, unlike historical judgments, must have no spatial or temporal limitations. Boyle's law must be valid not only in the seventeenth century but in the nineteenth as well. It must hold true in both Tibet and London. Scientific concepts, according to Rickert, are "unconditioned universal judgments that say something about the physical world."[64] Science constructs the necessary relations among things. If the logical connection of elements is necessary—that is, demanded by the transcendent norms—then the concept is true. Hence, the scientist generalizes and the rich individuality of reality slips through his fingers. Science to Rickert is, as R.G. Collingwood says, "a network of generalizations and formulae built up by the human intellect."[65]

History rather than physics is the true science of reality, for it does not aspire to formulate universal laws. Although it employs causal explanation, the object of history is the individual. As far as possible, history gives full justice to difference and diversity. In accord with Kant and Windelband, Rickert believed that only the nonrecurring individuality possesses intrinsic value. Therefore, if history is the science of individualities, it is also ipso facto concerned with values. Here is where the universal element comes in. Values must be necessary and universal; even though the historian seeks to grasp individuality, his criteria are the universal values to which he relates his data. This is what Ernst Troeltsch meant when he said that Windelband and Rickert were hoping to reach "the reflective-universal from the historical individual."[66]

Rickert did not adopt the traditional terms used to distinguish the domains of natural science and the humanities. He believed that human studies, with its implication of a purely spiritual or psychic content, was misleading. History is assuredly among the human studies but it is an empirical discipline, by no means confined to the realm of spirit as opposed to physical reality. "I think," Rickert said, "that the term *cultural science* best designates this concept. And therefore we want to ask ourselves: What is cultural science and in what relation does it stand to natural science?"[67] He admitted that the two categories, nature and culture, were only the polar extremes and often overlap. Yet he has been criticized for overlooking the ambiguous character of some disciplines which employ both generalizing and individualizing methods, although he was well aware of methodological overlapping.[68] Rickert's concept of nature followed Kant's definition that nature means the existence of things insofar as they are determined according to universal law.[69] The cultural sciences, he maintained, needed an equally appropriate concept; they lacked the firm foundation Kant had given to natural science. He made the nonrecurring event, in its individuality and particularity, the fundamental concept of the cultural sciences, that is, the formal principle which distinguishes them from natural science.

There is a "material" principle of distinction as well. Every cultural phenomenon embodies some value recognized by man.[70] All cultural products are valuable entities, whereas the products of nature are devoid of value, or simply value-neutral.[71] The products of nature "grow freely of the earth," but the products of culture "are brought forth directly by man according to valued ends."[72] "The presence or absence of relevance to *values* can thus serve as a reliable criterion for distinguishing between two kinds of scientific objects."[73] Rickert's definition of cultural values is based on Windelband's theory of normative judgment:

> In regard to values considered in themselves, one cannot ask whether they are *real*, but only whether they are *valid*. A cultural value is either actually accepted as valid by all men, or its validity . . . is at least postulated by some civilized human being. Furthermore, civilization, or culture in the highest sense, must be concerned not with the values attaching to the objects of mere desire, but with excellences which . . . we feel ourselves more or less "obligated" to esteem and cultivate for the sake of the society in which we live or for some other concomitant reason.[74]

Rickert's view of cultural values resembled Lotze's as transmitted to Rickert by Windelband. Rickert, like Lotze, assumed a common core of cultural values on which all or at least most civilized men could agree. This is an assumption of great importance, for it infers the universality of cultural experience and does not limit the idea of culture to a specially endowed people or nation. Rickert's theory of culture, in keeping with pre-1914 neo-Kantian traditions, was cosmopolitan. "It suffices," he said, "that, in general, the value be connected with the idea of a norm or of some good that ought to be actualized."[75] Values have, therefore, a teleological rather than a eudaemonistic basis, and they are related to universal norms of the good, the true, and the beautiful. His examples of cultural values are:

> Religion, church, law and the state; custom, science, language, literature, art, economy and the technical means necessary for their preservation are—at any rate in certain stages of their evolution—cultural objects or goods precisely in the sense that either the value attaching to them is acknowledged by all members of a community or its acknowledgment is expected of them.[76]

Religion, church, law, and so forth are, to be sure, contingent empirical values, but they are oriented toward and measured by transcendent values of a universal order. Anthropological values merely reflect universal values of an ethical and obligatory nature.

Values and Objectivity in Historical Judgment

When Rickert said that the historian uses an individualizing, valuing method, he did not mean subjective judgment. This would be to impart bias deliberately. The historian's valuations have nothing to do with his personal approval or disapproval. The valuing of an individual historical event is relating it to an objective value or norm. When the historian confronts his material, he finds it necessary to separate the essential from the nonessential. He has the criteria of selection at his disposal, for within Western European civilization there is a modest body of commonly accepted values. Yet the objectivity of these values is still historically limited. If history possesses merely contingent value and no absolute truth, standards of worth would come and go "like waves in the sea." To extricate himself from this relativistic snare, Rickert asked: "Must we not presuppose the validity of transhistorical values to which factually derived cultural values are at least proximate or distant? Is this not the only way to place historical objectivity on a par with scientific objectivity?"[77] Rickert's defense of historical objectivity is thus based on an apparently gratuitous assumption. He must assume the existence of absolute values—those undemonstrable but perfect standards to which all empirical values are accountable. But viewed in the framework of his full epistemology, this assumption is not as baseless as it appears. Rickert argued that reality is confirmed in judgment. Every act of cognition presupposes an autonomous will capable of conforming to an ideal norm. Therefore, the will to truth or the primacy of pure practical reason over the theoretical—the sovereignty of Ought— asserts the objectivity of Rickert's transcendental values. His value theory is often misunderstood because ontological arguments are confused with epistemological arguments. He did not try to justify values ontologically. This would be a violation of Kantian dualism. Because he was a firm believer, like Kant, in the finitude of pure reason, he placed universal values in the teleological kingdom of Ought rather than in our cognition of Being. But these transcendent values are not thereby inaccessible. They are mediated to experience through pure practical will which obeys the categorical command of reason to judge truthfully.

Rickert had a further criterion of selection for the historian. If he possesses values of cultural derivation and assumes the existence of a transcendental system of values, to what province of experience does he then turn? Only to those objects, Rickert answered, "which possess communal or social interest." Man as a social being is the chief object of historical research, for he is participating in the realization of social values. The name of the process through which these values materialize is culture. Hence, the task of history must be to represent a part or the whole of human cultural life.[78] He proposed three kinds of criteria to which historians would refer in the process of selection which is an integral part of their work: Social values pertaining to man's development as a social being; general cultural values representing civilized man's commonly accepted standards; and transcendental ideals toward which the first two should be oriented. The objectivity of historical judgment depends on the assumption of transcendental values. Rickert believed that he had already demonstrated the necessity of this assumption in his *Gegenstand der Erkenntnis*. His attempt to defeat historicism in his works on historical method hinged on the teleological idealism he had propounded in 1892. However, he admitted that the timeless standards demanded by this assumption were yet to be established; they remain in the future as a task or goal for the philosopher of values. And it should be underscored in passing that his first criterion of selection, "values pertaining to man's development as a social being," would lead any historian following his precepts to social realities, not exclusively to the empyrean of culture. Taken together, Rickert's general theory of knowledge and his studies in historical logic transferred Kant's question to history and attempted to answer his query: "How is objective experience possible?"[79]

Rickert's logic was designed to refute the two underlying propositions of historicism: That no statement can be considered true or false without reference to its place in historical time; and that all historical judgments are "value-charged" and therefore cannot be objectively valid. Historicism, however, is put to flight "if it could be shown that the interests of the subject which guide the historian's interpretations are universal and necessarily valid recognitions of some transcendent cultural values."[80] This is exactly what Rickert hoped to accomplish, but the success of his venture has been controversial.

R.G. Collingwood criticized Rickert's logic severely. Although a neo-idealist, Collingwood was Hegelian by way of Benedetto Croce, the Italian philosopher of history. He accused the Baden school of making history a branch of ethics and of remaining unwittingly within empiricism.[81]

> Rickert regards nature, . . . as cut up into separate facts and he goes on to deform history by regarding it in a similar way as an assemblage of individual facts supposed to differ from the facts of nature only in being vehicles of value. But the essence of history

lies not in its consisting of individual facts, however plausible these facts may be, but in the process or development leading from one to another.[82]

Collingwood found Rickert faulty in his understanding of how the past relates to the historian's mind: "Rickert fails to see that the peculiarity of historical thought is the way in which the historian's mind, as the mind of the present day, apprehends the process by which this mind itself has come into existence through the mental development of the past."[83] In short, Collingwood criticized Rickert for not having anticipated his own view that the past is encapsulated in the mind of the present. He believed that Rickert had disregarded the presence of the past in historical consciousness. But what are Rickert's cultural values, if not the accumulated cultural experience of the past mediated through history to the mind of the present? Collingwood did not recognize that his own thesis was already implicit in Rickert's notion of common cultural norms. He could have assailed Rickert's teleological theory of transcendent values—a far more vulnerable point.

In his study of values and the philosophy of history, Alfred Stern criticizes the very heart of Rickert's theory—the objective values themselves.[84] For if Rickert's value theory is untenable, his conquest of historicism is unsuccessful. Stern doubts that Rickert's conception of universal values "constitutes the protection against relativism" which he claimed:

> Who are those he calls "all" (those for whom acceptance of cultural values is necessary)? They are the members of a cultural community confined to a certain space and a certain time. Perhaps it is the German cultural community of this epoch, perhaps the European or Occidental cultural community of the twentieth century . . . .
> Since they are themselves products of history, cultural values cannot escape historical relativity.[85]

Rickert, as Stern admits, did not mean cultural evaluations that arise from the historian's personal background. He believed that values such as the state, art, and religion are ascertainable facts. The historian discovers that certain values were appreciated by certain societies, but he does not judge these values himself. Rickert used the French Revolution as an example. The historian does not decide whether the revolution was beneficial or detrimental to Europe. He cannot doubt, however, that this event has been significant for the cultural development of France and Europe. Therefore, the French Revolution is an essential part of European history.[86] Yet Stern maintains that terms like *significant* and *essential* are not, as Rickert implied, entirely free of the historian's personal evaluations. This is indeed a valid objection to his "theoretical relating to values," which he thought was an objective process.

Rickert's final values, though, are on a level above the historian's theoretical connecting of events to the significant and essential. Even so, Stern argues that Rickert's cultural values are not universal but collective, for "they depend on the collective peculiarities of the group which affirms them, and their validity is restricted to this group. He suggests that Rickert wanted to universalize the cultural values of nineteenth-century Germany.[87] If Stern is correct, then Rickert was heading for the sort of "German cultural metaphysics" that captivated Natorp after 1914. Natorp universalized German culture and equated it with humanity. Culture became Germany's historic vocation. But Rickert, as Stern recognizes, confessed that his own cultural values were empirical and therefore did not meet the requirement of universality. He said that historical objectivity ultimately rests on immutable, formal values. The task of finding them is paradoxically both necessary and insoluble.[88] At this point Stern's critique goes astray. He asks, "What can we know about a metaphysical reality which could be the presupposition of transcendent values, serving as standards for judging the cultural values of history?"[89] Rickert did not try to establish his values metaphysically. He knew that metaphysical grounds are problematic, at least so far as the historian is concerned. Rather, he argued for the epistemological indispensability and teleological necessity of transcendent ideals. By insisting that Rickert prove the ontological reality of values, Stern misses the guiding principle of neo-Kantian value theory—the primacy of practical over theoretical reason. Rickert's transcendental values are postulates of historical reason.[90] As such they do not require the presupposition of "a metaphysical reality." They must be seen to manifest not "Being" but "validity."

Rickert's philosophy of value raises numerous philosophical issues which are still argued today. The continuing debate testifies to the seminal quality of his work. But the controvertible character of his theory should not obscure the underlying intention. Like Wilhelm von Humboldt and Ranke, Rickert believed that in every individuality "an idea shines through."[91] And like Kant, he believed that there is more in human intelligence than the senses feed it. There is a universal element in historical experience and there are imperative forms of judgment which presuppose universal ideals. Kant's critical philosophy is the antithesis of the historicist spirit, for it upholds the immutable and suprahistorical status of reason. Rickert's value theory, true to the spirit rather than the exact writ of Kant, is equally inimical to historicism because it proposes universal standards of historical judgment.

As an anti-Romantic, anti-historicist program for finding historical norms in the values of Western European culture and ultimately seeking them in the universal character of teleological judgment, Rickert's philosophy descended directly from Kant's moral and cosmopolitan scheme of history, and indirectly from Ranke's belief that the historian can detect the universal significance of each individual moment in the historical process. His work was a coda on the idealist tradition in historical thought, a mighty effort to confound the nihilistic implications he perceived in the doctrine of historical relativism.

7

Individuality, Society, and Humanity: The Consequences of Neo-Kantianism

Two open questions in Gemany before 1914 were: Would the German intelligentsia overcome its ambivalence toward the West and, at the same time, would the German nation develop an authentic constitutional democracy which would reasonably accommodate the interests of all classes? The revival of Kant's ethics and theory of knowledge, in spite of many ambiguities, contained an affirmative answer to both questions. Neo-Kantianism, although contributing to the new ferment in German thought from around 1890, attempted to deal constructively with the most divisive issues of society and state. The relationship between philosophy and politics in Germany has always been remarkably intimate, perhaps because philosophy was known among Germans before there was a nation. Germany's philosophers were her conscience, for good or ill, long before the "belated nation" came into existence. Because the study of philosophy preceded the nation-state, the problems of national life were intellectualized before they became realities. Therefore, German intellectual history as a whole, particularly after 1849, has been a tortuous effort to reconcile philosophical presuppositions with rapidly changing political situations. After 1849, the inescapable fact of bourgeois political impotence and Prussia's temporary renunciation of national leadership undermined the confident, grandiose rationalism of the orthodox Hegelians who had looked to Prussia for both power *and* liberalism. Immanent Reason, which the pre-March liberals had believed would reveal itself in the progressive Prussian state, could no longer inspire faith.

After Bismarck's consolidation of the empire around Prussia (unification is a misnomer), the liberal plight was reversed—actual power rather than national impotence became the unassimilable datum for liberal philosophy. How could the moral and ethical absolutes of German idealism be preserved in a world of amoral power, with its sometimes demonic and always compromising expediencies? Only by the apotheosizing of the German nation and culture as infallible moral agents. Many neo-Kantians were convinced of the permanent conflict between might and right to such a degree that they could not resort to such a Treitschkean sophistry. Adherents of neo-Kantianism usually had a keener and more universal sense of ethical priorities than their contemporaries.

The German liberals had hardly regained their perspective after the heady experience of the founding period when an equally urgent challenge appeared in the form of industrial labor and the concomitant spread of Marxism. The new power state and the political awakening of the masses caused severe strain within German liberalism; those two developments would compel liberals to decide if their creed would function as a progressive force in German life or would become, as their Marxist opponents charged, a mere ideology for the propertied and privileged middle class. The traditional liberal theory of the state was essentially an ethical teleology—the state as an agent of moral values—which was difficult to harmonize with *Realpolitik*. And the conventional, liberal, social philosophy was intellectually and culturally aristocratic; there was little room in it for the uneducated wage earners or the ambitious entrepreneurs who seemed a threat to cultural refinement and social stability. German liberalism entered the new age ill-equipped to react responsibly to power politics, big business and the urban masses. Ultimately, the failure of the German middle class to cultivate both a sense of responsibility and restraint in national politics and an attitude of fair play and toleration toward social issues led to the catastrophic destruction of liberal values in the 1930s. But history is an open-ended process, and this tragic outcome was not predetermined. The liberal intellectuals were in a position to encourage a sense of proportion and perform an inestimable service by warning against the risks of provocative imperialism and by imparting new breadth to bourgeois social attitudes. Some did try, but they were too few in number, too academic in style to attract public attention, and, when war came in 1914, too distracted by the anguish of conflicting values to speak out unequivocally against the purblindness of their own government.

Neo-Kantianism became, in the early 1900s, the strongest current within intellectual liberalism; it contained bright possibilities for freeing liberal thought from the confines of class ideology. The neo-Kantians looked to the Enlightenment for their cultural standards. Since they were fundamentally "European," they could form a counterweight to the chauvinists. Marburg neo-Kantianism was social democratic; therefore, it was an alternative to narrow intellectual liberalism. In spite of the weaknesses and inconsistencies in the movement, its underlying character was ethical, democratic, and cosmopolitan. The neo-Kantians no more wanted their country to emulate English or French democracy than they desired a literal revival of eighteenth-century rationalism, but they recognized that Germany's spiritual estrangement was a dangerous trend. The most gifted and perceptive among those who were affected by neo-Kantianism, Weber, Meinecke, Troeltsch, and Cassirer, did not feel compelled to renounce their love of indigenous German culture, although they realized that Germany was drifting toward irresponsibility and national hubris. On the contrary, their neo-Kantian background deepened their reverence for the enduring qualities of German civilization and sharpened their awareness of the disturbing antinomies in national life. Both the potentialities and limits of neo-Kantianism are found in these four men. Meinecke, Weber and Troeltsch were disciples of Baden philosophy, but their interests were wider than their teachers Windelband and Rickert, while Cassirer was the protégé of Hermann Cohen at Marburg.

The proliferation of Kant scholarship, beginning in the 1890s, can be seen by a glance at the rolls of the Kant Society which show how many incongruous and opposing points of view were brought together in a common enthusiasm for Kantiana. The Kant Society, formed in 1904 by Hans Vaihinger of Halle, had a membership of more than 400 by 1912.[1] Its official journal *Kant-Studien*, first published in 1896, was devoted to shedding light on the "dark places in Kant," to interpretation and textual criticism, and to the general interests of philosophy.[2] Although the early contributors were usually from the Marburg group (Vorländer, Stadler, Kinkel, Natorp, and others), the society did not represent any particular sect of neo-Kantianism and articles by authors from other neo-Kantian schools were soon published in the journal. The Baden philosophers had also started their own journal, called

Logos, with Meinecke as one of the original coeditors. Membership in the Kant Society included nearly all the Wilhelmine intellectual spectrum, from Ernst Cassirer to Elisabeth Förster-Nietzsche. Werner von Siemens, baron of Germany's electrical industry, held a lifetime membership. Kantianism had not become the new public philosophy, but the number of prominent people interested enough to support the society's work suggests its great prestige and reflects educated Germany's veneration of a philosopher widely admired but frequently misunderstood. Apparently some Germans read Kant's moral law as an injunction to mindless bureaucratic or military obedience, regardless of the principles served. The most recent and heinous instance of this was Adolf Eichmann's invocation of the categorical imperative at his trial in Jerusalem.[3] More books and articles on Kant did not mean that he was being better understood or that his ethical humanism was transforming the German psyche, but the spread of interest beyond the universities indicates that neo-Kantianism was capable of more than it ultimately achieved. The prewar generation was thirsting for fresh values and ideals; much depended on those ideas that would eventually quench this thirst.

Troeltsch, Weber, Meinecke, and the Response to Baden Neo-Kantianism

The spiritual crisis of the late Wilhelmine era was poignantly exemplified by Ernst Troeltsch, Max Weber, and Friedrich Meinecke. All three were significantly influenced by Baden neo-Kantianism; if they owed to it few specific doctrines, they were still indebted to Windelband and Rickert who had raised the right questions and continued the critique of historical reason begun by Dilthey. They were haunted by the typical antinomies of neo-Kantian thought: between cognitive finitude and the quest for intellectual certainty, between historicism and universal values, and between power and right. The tension of unresolved Kantian dualism in their work was a source of both strength and frustration, but they never took refuge in an uncritical metaphysics or an atavistic "decisionism." The monism of immanent Spirit was just as repugnant to them as the idea of an ineluctable sequence of material causality. Troeltsch, Weber, and Meinecke were skeptical about moral absolutes and uneasy about the implications of their skepticism. They knew that at least problematic truth was indispensable to life and thought, but permanent and perfect truth in the metaphysical sense was unattainable. Thus they remained, as H. Stuart Hughes says of

Weber, suspended in a twilight zone between relativism and universal values.[4]

Troeltsch recognized that the problem of ethics was an expression of changing social and religious situations. He could not accept Rickert's argument for the ultimate objectivity of values. Meinecke, embedded in the Rankean tradition, was an avowed historicist and, for most of his life, a proponent of the national idea. Weber used historicist suppositions in exploring the effects of religious ideals on economic attitudes and believed that the categories of sociological thought were useful fictions constructed for their heuristic value. But none of them evaded the dilemmas generated by the conflict between a skeptical view of knowledge and their own spiritual predilections. In probing the serious intellectual and moral questions raised by historicism, they began with the epistemology of Baden neo-Kantianism, but found parts of it inadequate. A full analysis of their work cannot be undertaken here, but their response to the theories of Windelband and Rickert should be considered in order to measure the historical importance of Baden philosophy.

Troeltsch, Weber, and Meinecke spent their careers in the universities of Strassburg, Freiburg, and Heidelberg where, as students and then as rising young scholars, they were closely associated with each other and with Windelband and Rickert. Troeltsch lived for a while with the Webers in Heidelberg. Troeltsch and Meinecke were frequent companions after their return to Berlin in 1915, taking long walks in the Grunewald and discussing philosophy and politics.[5] This distinguished trio were thus, at one time or another, linked in their common exposure to neo-Kantian thought. They had also lived and studied in southwestern Germany where French and German culture are contiguous and therefore where the problem of Germany's relationship to Western Europe was particularly visible and acute.

Troeltsch, like his neo-idealist contemporaries, was seeking an alternative to positivism without at the same time rejecting the standards of scientific inquiry. He had found positivism unsatisfactory for the same reason as Rickert: It could provide no cultural or moral values. In the introduction to his *Social Teachings of the Christian Churches*, largely inspired by Weber's study of the Protestant ethic, Troeltsch said, "In point of fact the science of society cannot create ultimate values and standards from within."[6] The historical and sociological approaches to human experience could not repair all the defects of positivism but they can make room for the workings of the human spirit by denying that man is completely enmeshed in the natural mechanism. In the

actual writing of history, which is often a better test of the historian's
assumptions than his theoretical expositions, Troeltsch made his historicism explicit. The Christian churches are contingent institutions;
they are "at all points conditioned by the past."[7] Here Troeltsch's problem is painfully clear. As a theologian he was committed to universal
and timeless Christian principles, but as a historian he was forced to
concede that Christianity has been affected substantively by its manifold and evolving historical context. As a social scientist, he was just as
conscientious about objectivity and "value-neutrality" as Weber. He
tried to keep the moral and religious dilemmas from intruding upon
scientific judgment. But like Meinecke and Weber, he was imbued with
the conscience of German Protestantism and its fixed categories of
good and evil—also its consciousness of man's insuperable finitude. His
crisis of spirit reached its peak during the war and it was finally overcome by a kind of humanistic fideism. For him as for Weber and
Meinecke, Baden philosophy was the point of departure in the ensuing
struggle with *Historismus*.

Troeltsch devoted the last years of his life to the foundling Weimar
Republic and to the challenge of historicism. While he was writing the
famous *Spektatorbriefe,* appealing to his countrymen to comprehend
their defeat and to accept the regime born of it, he was preparing his
major study of historicism and its critics from Kant to Croce. The result
was *Historismus und seine Probleme,* published in 1922. In *Historismus,*
Troeltsch explored the Windelband-Rickert solution to the problem of
historical relativism at some length.[8] He characterized their effort as
the search for a principle of Parmenides to preserve historical judgment from the Heraclitean flux of reality, but he thought they had not
succeeded. Rickert had tried to prove that scientific history was possible
without sacrificing the historicist idea of individuality, which sees history as "ideographic" as opposed to generalizing in the natural sciences.
Meinecke once aptly summed up the problem of historicism in the
words of Heraclitus and Archimedes: "Everything flows. Give me a
place where I can stand."[9] Rickert found his place to stand in a teleological system of values, but Troeltsch was not convinced. Rickert had
failed to show the connection between historical individualities and
objective values. His values came from outside history rather than from
inside. Troeltsch also found Rickert's theory oblivious to the spirit of
empathy, the subject-object immersion that occurs when the historian
contemplates his topic. Rickert had not duly considered Dilthey's notion of reexperiencing as part of the psychological process of interpret-
ing the past. Consequently, Rickert's philosophy of historical knowl-

edge struck Troeltsch as being static, dualistic, and without a means of explaining historical development. In spite of his admiration for Rickert's attempt to solve the problem, Troeltsch felt that he had failed. He had permitted his reverence for historical individualities to be smothered by his rationalism.[10] Troeltsch believed that Rickert had, in fact, attempted to square the circle. There was no definitive solution: "The indispensable relativism of historical-genetic thought seems to be in hopeless and deep-rooted opposition to every notion of a universally valid, absolute goal of history."[11] He was sure that the criteria of historical interpretation were, owing to the Kantian limits of empirical knowledge, necessarily immanent ones; therefore, he could not accept Rickert's transcendental grounds for historical judgment. He admired Rickert's consistent, if somewhat equivocal respect for the concrete and individual in history, and praised him for avoiding the "complete rationalism and anti-historicism of Kant,"[12] but he felt he had gone astray in using historical individualities "merely as an arsenal of examples for the value theory."[13]

Troeltsch's affection for the individual and indigenous in German history began to lose some of its ardor during the war, although in the beginning he was still an advocate of the German idea of freedom. Yet even before 1914, he had written on Western natural law and its emergence in the Stoic-Christian eras.[14] Only after the German collapse did he return to this theme and emphasize the universal dimension in his view of history. He deplored, as Meinecke says, the nationalistic simplifications of war propaganda and the consequent sharpening of the contrast between Germany and the West. "His inclination was too universal and European." Hence, he defended the indestructible and living unity of Western civilization.[15] Although his wartime essays were not entirely free of hostility toward Western democratic egalitarianism, gradually his antagonism diminished and the proponent of German cultural uniqueness shifted toward the "reflective-universal" quality he found in neo-Kantian philosophy. His published essays and speeches from this period, *Deutscher Geist und Westeuropa,* document his attitude during the war.[16] His patriotism was moderate but his historicism continued unabated. Dissociating himself from the "super-idealists," he did not see the war as a conflict of ideas between totally inimical cultures. "We Germans originally came from the culture of European liberalism," he wrote, but "we now occupy a special place within it."[17] German institutions have assumed special characteristics which set them apart from the artificialities of Western democracy. The greatest threat of the war is that the distinctiveness of German life will be obliterated. The

German idea of freedom is different from Western liberalism, which Troeltsch ponderously defined as:

> The unity of an independent and conscious affirmation of the supra-individual community spirit, united with lively participation in it; the freedom of voluntary obligation to the whole and of an inviolable identity of the individual within the whole; the freedom of public spirit and discipline, both depending on personal recognition of these ideas and therefore closely tied to our entire ethical-religious character, which differs deeply from the English and French.[18]

Although Troeltsch believed that German values were in danger, he saw the war itself as caused by "imperialistic tensions" having little to do with the contrasting philosophies of Germany and the Entente. He differed from Natorp and other adherents of the "Ideas of 1914" who preached that the war was an ideological Armageddon. Yet he still feared that the special virtues of German life would be destroyed. As a barrier against alien political ideas from East and West, he recommended a voluntary central European federation consisting of Germany, the Danubian monarchy, and its satellites.[19] The concept of a federated Middle Europe had been a recurring dream since the early nineteenth century, but its immediate source was the former Lutheran pastor Friedrich Naumann, with whom Troeltsch, Weber, and Meinecke were closely associated in the founding of the German Democratic party in 1919.[20] Naumann's social and political ideas had found great favor among the intellectuals of Troeltsch's generation who hoped to combine social democracy at home with power in Germany's external affairs.[21] This free association of Germanic peoples would be, according to Troeltsch, a bulwark against the incursion of "Russo-Asiatic imperialism." He also considered it imperative for Central Europe to protect itself against the Western "giant monopoly" states of the Entente, Britain and France, whose spirit was embodied in that "Baptist Lloyd George and the Freemason Briand."[22] Although Troeltsch had often acknowledged the common origin of German and Western culture and their continuing points of contact, during the war his veneration for indigenous German values, a natural corollary to the historicist fetish for cultural individuality, impaired his sense of proportion.

In one of his postwar lectures, Troeltsch underscored the need for a "universal-historical" viewpoint in Germany to counteract the ill effects of historicism.[23] In the age of Kant and the Enlightenment, the orientation of German thought had been universal, but the post-Kantian age

conceived the idea of individuality as the essence of history and culture—a brilliant achievement but dangerous:

> This same idea of individuality has also produced some conse-
> quences which may well give us pause. In its permanent effects, it
> has been altogether disastrous to universal history. It dissolved and
> disintegrated that conception; it enslaved it to notions of "relati-
> vity": it transmuted it either into specialization, buttressed by
> "method," or pure national introspection. . . . All these causes
> turned most of historiography into the paths of materialism or
> complete relativity.[24]

This bitter indictment of a historical philosophy which Troeltsch sub-
scribed to most of his life reveals the extent of his disillusionment. As a
remedy, he proposed a universal philosophy of history, one which
would include the notion of goals and purposes: "True history, we may
say, is teleological history."[25] The most urgent task of the day was to
explore the possibility of such a teleological theory. Here Troeltsch was
apparently accepting the transcendental value theory of Rickert, but
even at that, his devotion to the unique and original was ineradicable.[26]
He agreed with Meinecke that the idea of individuality had been Germany's special contribution to historical thought. Although he recognized the deleterious effects of historicism, he did not believe that its
ideographic postulate led necessarily to relativism. The relativity of
values is a result of the interaction of the Is with the Ought, the famous
conceptual twins of Kantian dualism. But value-relativity merely points
to the gap between reality and unfulfilled ideals which will be realized
in man's future universal history. Moral relativism is not a logical consequence of incomplete historical values. At the same time, however,
the objectivity and universality of moral values were undemonstrable,
leaving Troeltsch to turn to the Divine as the ultimate ground of moral
truth.[27] He thus ended in fideism since he had denied the possibility of
universal values derived from history or based on postulates of practical reason. The irony of Troeltsch's unrelenting historicism was, as
Meinecke said, that its scientific virtue was its ethical vice.[28]

Max Weber also investigated the antinomies of German thought; for
him they were freedom and causality, ethics and political power. He
admired Rickert's *Der Gegenstand der Erkenntnis,* and thought that he
had found help in the Baden philosopher's epistemology. The exchange of ideas between Weber and Rickert was made natural and easy
when the two families became friends.[29] After his appointment to the
Heidelberg chair, Weber turned to the problem of methodology in the

social sciences. After reading Rickert's *Die Grenzen der Naturwissenschaft-lichen Begriffsbildung*, he told his wife that, except for certain reservations about Rickert's terminology, he was fundamentally in agreement with him.[30] Soon thereafter Weber applied Baden conceptual theory to economic history. In a series of essays on Wilhelm Roscher and Karl Knies, founders of the "historical school," he developed his own critique of methodology in the mold of Rickert's logic.[31] In these essays is found the clearest expression of Weber's debt to Rickert. He began by acknowledging his reliance on the nomothetic-ideographic distinction between the generalizing and individualizing methods of natural science and history. He cited Windelband, Simmel, and especially Rickert, as his sources.[32] "I believe I have been faithful to the meaning of Rickert's historical viewpoint." One of his aims was "to test the usefulness of this author for the methodology of our own discipline."[33] Weber then formulated his own version of Rickert's logic: "The epistemology of history confirms and analyzes the meaning of 'relating to values' for historical knowledge, but for its own part does not establish the validity of values."[34]

The Roscher-Knies essays were written in 1902. Two years later Weber joined Werner Sombart and Edgar Jaffé on the editorial board of the *Archiv für Sozialwissenschaft,* which soon became the leading journal of German social science. In its first issue under the new editorship, Weber described the position of the *Archiv* on the methods of social science:[35] Heinrich Rickert's logic would be the touchstone of its views on methodology.[36] Weber wrote in the preface, "Those who know the work of the modern logicians—I cite only Windelband, Simmel, and for our purposes, particularly Heinrich Rickert—will immediately notice that everything of importance in this essay is bound up with their work."[37] Weber's description of sociological method suggests the extent of Rickert's influence: "Wherever causal explanation of a 'cultural phenomenon' or 'historical individual' is under consideration, the knowledge of causal *laws* is not the end of the investigation but only a means. . . . But the more general and abstract the laws, the less they can contribute to . . . the understanding of the significance of cultural events."[38] Following Rickert closely, Weber explained that the social scientist is concerned with individual events possessing cultural significance which he relates to values but does not judge the values themselves. This is what Weber meant by his celebrated standard of value-neutrality.[39] The student of history may relate the Crimean War to a number of historical concepts, political, military, even medical, for it was certainly an event of significant and farreaching consequences, but he must not judge moral qualities or decide whether it was right or wrong for Britain and France to fight Russia. This example (which Weber did not use) or that of any major episode taken at random reveals to anyone who has ever read or written history that the idea of merely "relating to values" without judging is a difficult one and probably unattainable for mortal historians. It could also be argued that value-neutrality is an undesirable standard, for by excluding moral judgments from history, individuals are exempted from moral accountability for their actions. The modern search for objective history beginning with Ranke has not avoided the pitfalls of self-deception and ethical insensitivity. But in his own work on bureaucracy, rationalization, and charismatic leadership, Weber did not hesitate to draw decidedly moral conclusions.

In this same essay, Weber also explained the relationship between "ideal types" and value judgments: "Ideal types have nothing to do with judging values."[40] The goal of the ideal-typical concept-construction is always to make clearly explicit not the class or average character but rather the unique individual character of cultural phenomena."[41] His ideal types are unquestionably the progeny of Rickert's "theoretical relating to values." Weber stated again the importance of Rickert's theory in an article on the logic of the cultural sciences: The popular misunderstanding that objective cultural science must be a simple reproduction of facts "has been dealt with adequately by Rickert and Simmel."[42]

In 1917, Weber again turned to the question of value judgments in social science, which by that time had assumed serious political implications. The neo-Kantian journal *Logos* published his essay, "The Meaning of 'Ethical Neutrality' in Sociology and Economics."[43] He repeated his thesis that the social scientist eschews "practical evaluations of the unsatisfactory or satisfactory character of phenomena subject to our influence."[44] "What is really at issue," he argued, "is the intrinsically simple demand that the investigator and teacher could keep unconditionally separate the establishment of empirical facts (including the value-oriented conduct of the empirical individual whom he is investigating) and his own practical evaluations, that is, his evaluation of these facts as satisfactory or unsatisfactory."[45] He said it more succinctly: "I hold that a lecture is different from a speech." Relevance to values does not mean related to the personal predilections of the scientist. "Concerning the significance of this expression I refer to my earlier writings and above all to the works of Heinrich Rickert."[46] Weber's clarification of value free inquiry and his denunciation of personal bias were aimed at the prophets of the "Ideas of 1914," which were produced "by dilet-tantes."[47] He was, of course, referring to Paul Natorp and other ultra-nationalistic intellectuals who were using a warped interpretation of history to preach Germany's cultural mission from their academic pul-pits. Their lectures had become speeches; therefore, they had betrayed science and abused their positions of academic eminence.

Weber's views on the proper procedure for history and social science were thus an extension of Baden neo-Kantianism. His attitude toward Germany's social problems was similar to Marburg neo-Kantianism. He would have agreed with Hermann Cohen's statement that the real mea-sure of liberal idealism is the breadth of its social philosophy.[48] In his inaugural lecture at Freiburg, Weber called "social unification" the most urgent goal of politics; the laboring class must be made a full participant in the state.[49] Unlike the conventional liberals, he saw noth-ing to fear in the philistine Social Democratic party. The middle class had been living in fear of the socialists' millennarian "earthly paradise," but from what Weber had seen of the Social Democratic party in opera-tion, he doubted that this bourgeois anxiety complex was justified.[50] He hoped that the socialists and left-wing liberals would learn to cooperate, and he encouraged Social Democratic party intellectuals to contribute to the *Archiv*. A close friend of Weber was his former student Robert Michels, the political scientist who had been denied a teaching position in Germany because he was a socialist. Although Weber was skeptical about the chance for adequate social integration in the near future, he favored the kind of intellectual rapprochement represented by Mar-burg neo-Kantianism, a tradition of which he was aware. He once twit-ted Michels for "having forgotten his Cohen."[51]

Weber was alert to the danger lurking in Germany's slow and incom-plete accomodation of the industrial class. He warned that disaster would follow if Wilhelmine Germany failed to foster a workable polity in which social democracy would enjoy greater opportunity "for posi-tive participation in the state . . . instead of being stigmatized by the phrase, an enemy of the Reich."[52] His prognosis was correct. It would be National Socialism which would, as Walter Simon has observed, finally give the German proletariat a sense of full, if spurious integra-tion into the Reich under the aegis of the German Labor Front in 1933.[53] Although Weber accurately interpreted the situation, he ig-nored the economic side of integration. When the opportunity came in 1919, and he could put his principles into practice as a member of the Socialization Commission, he backed away. As an old-fashioned liberal who supported capitalism and economic individualism, he opposed nationalization of basic industries and the concept of labor-management councils for large factories. Hence, he resigned from the commission in disgust—a futile gesture, for very little was done toward creating a socialist economy.[54] Weber's sympathy for socialism was political and ethical; it did not extend to economics.

On the question of German power Weber remained a National Liberal and a reserve lieutenant. He did not consider the state an absolute, but he insisted that power was the essence of it. A constant struggle exists between the intrinsic necessities of the power-state and private ethics: "The genius or demon of politics lives in an inner tension with the god of love, as well as with the Christian God as expressed by the Church. This tension can at any time lead to an irreconcilable conflict."[55] The man who chooses politics as a vocation must learn to live with ethical paradoxes: "He must know that he is responsible for what may become of himself under the impact of these paradoxes . . . he lets himself in for the diabolic forces lurking in all violence."[56] Weber then made his famous distinction between what he called the ethics of ultimate ends and the "ethics of responsibility." The former is the morality of universal values; the latter, the ethics of the rational statesman. He made the schism between the real and the moral utterly unbridgeable. He did not share the ethical optimism of the Marburg socialists that politics could gradually be imbued with moral values but instead took a tragic view of politics as an expression of the human hunger for power—the ineffaceable mark of Adam, the permanent stigma of man's imperfectibility.

Weber deepened the Baden dichotomy between reality and value but did not span the separation as Rickert had with an overarching, transcendental ethics. For him, the splitting of the Is from the Ought found its correlate in the severance of politics from ethics. Consequently, "in Max Weber's personality and fate are symbolically expressed the greatness and deficiency of German intellectual liberalism around 1900, the penetrating insight, the genuine will to truth, and the incapacity to translate knowledge into action."[57]

Friedrich Meinecke lived through the "icy winter" predicted by Weber not long before his death in 1922. Meinecke's views on history and politics were similar to Weber's, but Meinecke, who lived much longer, was able to observe the ultimate effects of historicism and cultural nationalism on German life, and to modify his views accordingly. His odyssey ended in cosmopolitan humanism, which he had early regarded as a prelude to national consciousness. Before 1914, he shared Weber's view that power is not only essentially diabolic but also indispensable for the moral and cultural tasks of the national state. Meinecke, who also agreed with the main ideas of Baden historical logic, did not accept the ethical optimism of Marburg philosophy nor did he find the teleological ethics of Cohen compatible with his tragic view of the human situation. An intellectual descendant of Ranke by way of Droysen, he believed that the nation is the most intelligible unit of historical study, yet he was critical of Prussian historiography for its moral apotheosizing of power politics. In *Weltbürgertum und National-staat,* he argued that the nation-state is not the embodiment of moral-ity; rather, the state must be willing to subordinate universal ethical values before it can transform itself from a cultural to a political na-tion.[58] The essence of the state is power not morality.

Events, however, gradually altered his thinking. At first he welcomed World War I as a vivification of national unity, but he later opposed the annexationists and the declaration of unrestricted submarine warfare. After the first flush of impassioned patriotism, he began to reconsider the implications of historicism and the consequent doctrine of cultural peculiarity; still, his confidence in the central assumption of historicism seemed undiminished. He looked upon his country as a unique histori-cal phenomenon with intrinsic qualities that distinguished it from the West. In his essay on German freedom, a typical excursus on the spe-cial nature of German liberty, he traced the German idea of freedom back to Kant and Fichte. Their theory of freedom "raised the inner-most voice of the individual over . . . universal law. . . . From this flows not only voluntary submission to national duty but also practical liberty and the demand for freedom."[59] This statement expressed the philo-sophical paradox that lies at the root of German liberalism. The Ger-man idea of freedom is an unstable fusion of personal autonomy, po-litical order, and universal moral law. In practice, moral law is often equated with national duty. Thus it becomes the obligation of the self-legislating individual to realize his freedom through obedience to laws he has, hypothetically, imposed on himself. The main problems found in the German theory of freedom are its ambivalence toward authority and personal liberty and its failure to stipulate the moral criteria which limit legitimate authority. Is duty to be determined by the universal prescriptions of moral reason in the Kantian sense, or by the contin-gent and often faulty prescriptions of the historical state? At that time, Meinecke did not have an unequivocal answer. His historicist presup-positions confirmed his reverence for the German nation as an inimi-table historical individuality worthy of respect and obedience, but he denied that any nation-state represents the supreme ethical value.[60]

Meinecke's historicism, increasingly hedged by qualifications, did not lead him into integral nationalism. He conceded that Western ideas had contributed to early German liberalism in the age of Kant, Stein, and Boyen. But German freedom must not be confused with the eighteenth-century ideal of egalitarian freedom. In this connection he cited Troeltsch's formula for German liberty: "German freedom wants cultural individualism united with state socialism."[61] In other words, the cultural aristocracy must extend political and social justice to the masses through the state. By Meinecke's time, intellectual liberalism had acquired a sense of noblesse oblige but still resisted the leveling implications of Western democracy.

In the first chapter of *Weltbürgertum*, Meinecke distinguished the two kinds of individualism—egalitarian and aristocratic. The latter is both the individualism of the cultivated man[62] and the individualism of German freedom[63]—clearly an elitist notion of liberty. His philosophy of freedom was a logical correlate of historicism; his doctrine of historical and cultural individuality found epistemological support in the writings of Rickert, whose emphasis on universal values Meinecke at first seemed to ignore.

Consonant with his approval of Troeltsch's appeal for the union of individualism and socialism, Meinecke supported the growing demand in wartime Germany for social democracy. In keeping with the humanistic ideals of Goethe and German classicism, he urged greater freedom and mobility for the gifted and energetic irrespective of social background. He believed that "careers open to talent" had been unduly impeded by the military, bureaucratic nature of the state and by the disproportionate influence of the Junkers in German life. All social and political barriers must be removed.[64] The masses are a reservoir of talent and rejuvenating energy. To incorporate them into the political life of the nation, the suffrage must be made fully democratic. The popularly elected assembly in the German parliament, however, should be balanced by an upper chamber based on vocations and corporations. Corporatism was Meinecke's conservative counterweight to popular sovereignty, a necessary equipoise because, in his opinion, the Western parliamentary system gave too much power to the potentially tyrannical majority. "The popular will is not the same as the majority will."[65] Like Lotze, he looked upon monarchy as a stabilizer, standing above the conflicting interests and passions of the political arena. In 1917, he still hoped that a "social monarchy" could successfully integrate the masses into national life without introducing the mechanical parliamentarianism of Western democracy. Meinecke's advocacy of social reconciliation brought him closer to Marburg neo-Kantianism, but his major theme remained the ideal of intellectual liberalism which kept him considerably to the right of Marburg social democracy. It was the more conservative Baden tradition which had the greatest influence on Meinecke.

Unmitigated *Realpolitik* gave way to moderate raison d'état in his next work, *Machiavellism*, [66] in which he put the problem of political realism in the larger perspective of European history since the Renaissance. Only after his spiritual ordeal under National Socialism did he return to the cosmopolitan humanism of his first historical work, the biography of Boyen. [67] In *The German Catastrophe*, written after the defeat of the Third Reich, Meinecke speculated on the causes of the disaster and proposed a return to the generous and anational humanism of Goethe's era. [68] His social philosophy had broadened measurably, but it revealed an impractical nostalgia for the apolitical cosmopolitanism of the classical period: "To be a socialist and socialist-minded today," he wrote, "and to act accordingly means nothing else but the following of a general humane ideal. It means applying the concept of humanity in a concrete way in modern society—and this humanity is to benefit not only one's own country but also the human community in general."[69]

Meinecke did not foresake the historicist idea of individuality but instead tried to restore the element of universality that was always an important, if secondary, part of it. The great figures of the classical epoch, he said, " strove for and to a large degree realized the ideal of a personal and wholly individual culture. This culture was thought of as having at the same time a universal meaning and content."[70] Here Meinecke was expressing the "universal-reflective" dimension as found in Baden philosophy and discussed by Troeltsch in his lecture of 1920 on natural law. Baden theory holds that the historical individual is a moment embodying universal values. This tenet can serve to correct a narrow political interpretation of cultural individuality. The knotty matter of universality in the historical individual had already been raised by Meinecke in *Weltbürgertum*, where he referred to the state as the concrete "trans-individual personality."[71] Such a description comes perilously close to the sometimes mystical personifications of the state by the romantic historicists. But Meinecke argued that nationalism was a natural and not incompatible product of the cosmopolitan background. Genuine nationalism contains "within itself the cosmopolitan ideal of a supranational humanity."[72] In support of this Fichtean thesis, he cited Zeller's essay on "Nationality and Humanity," which proposed the same paradoxical idea.[73] The notion that the universal is immanent in the historically concrete phenomenon was a remnant of Hegelianism which had never been entirely expunged from neo-Kantian thought, and can be traced from the South German Hegelians through Zeller and Fischer, to Windelband and Rickert, and then to Meinecke. The neo-Kantians had eliminated the dialectical *deus ex machina* and revived Kant's dualism to replace Hegel's principle of identity. The Baden theory of universal values reflected by historical individualities was Hegel's objective spirit deprived of its ontological immanence and made transcendent. The result could be described as Platonic ontology synthesized with the voluntaristic ethics of Kant, that is, the world of eternal forms is reflected in the phenomenal world of individualities. The transcendent forms are recognized and applied to phenomenal reality by, as Windelband phrased it, the normative will to truth. The will to truth, a self-evident category of judgment, presupposes the transcendental validity of perfect norms, even though these norms cannot be known empirically any more than the moral law can be known in phenomenal experience. Meinecke took a dim view of historians who philosophize, believing that abstract speculation vitiates the historian's sense of the concrete.[74] Yet in his own ruminations on historical method he gave due credit to Baden philosophy and revealed a profound disquiet over the ethical and political implications of *Historismus*.

Meinecke first met Rickert at Freiburg.[75] Although the intellectual influence seems at first to have been negligible, years later Meinecke commented at length on Rickert's logic in his essay, "Causalities and Values":[76] "Behind all investigations of causality stands . . . the search for values, after that which is called culture in the highest sense, that is, breakthroughs and revelations of the spirit within the natural network of causality."[77] He agreed with Rickert that the historian selects his subject from a multitude of historical events, and this selection is keyed to "major cultural values."[78] He did not accept Rickert's argument that the historian's "relating to values" is unaffected by his personal values. For Meinecke, the standard of objectivity was unattainable and, in a sense, not even desirable.[79] In a long footnote, he questioned Rickert's "separation of values from the logical essence of history." Value-neutral history would be a soulless accumulation of facts, a dull rehearsal of events without life-giving interpretation. It is the very subjectivity of the historian, the animating spirit of his own temperament, that makes history colorful and lively. Even if the historian tries, he cannot entirely suppress his own valuations, and so much the better. Otherwise, his work would be spineless. As an example of what history should be, Meinecke extolled the "monumental historical researches of Max Weber," the advocate of value-neutrality! Selecting and arranging facts according to values is also a process of value judging.[80] This did not mean that Meinecke was absolving the historian of his duty to ascertain the accuracy of his information and to judge it fairly.

Meinecke thus found Rickert's criteria of individuality and value congenial to his own thinking, but he did not go so far as to agree with Rickert's transcendentalism or his belief in the possibility of objective valuation. In *Die Entstehung des Historismus,* Meinecke restated the ideographic character of history: "The kernel of historicism resides in supplanting a generalizing interpretation of human-historical forces with an individualizing interpretation."[81] The alleged objectivity of relating facts to values and the teleological argument for transcendent norms did not seem to Meinecke a credible defense against historical relativism.[82] In his philosophy of history, he remained an acolyte of *Historismus* and a votary of the nation-state almost to the end of his life. Yet, as Richard Sterling in his study of Meinecke writes: "That he was able to combine such parochial concerns with an authentic cosmopolitanism is one of those human paradoxes with which Meinecke so often dealt."[83]

From Baden to Marburg Politics: Intellectual Liberalism to Social Democracy

Neo-Kantian politics started slightly to the left of center on the Wilhelmine spectrum; the basis was Kantian ethics but thereafter neo-Kantianism split into divergent traditions. The Baden neo-Kantians and the neo-idealists influenced by them tried to balance their historical nationalism with the cosmopolitan perspective of Kant and classical idealism. They were careful to distinguish the German national idea from raw nationalism, the excesses of which they were well aware.[84] The German idea of freedom was a native value not to be confused with the *egalité* of revolutionary France or with the historic rights of lords, yeomen, and shopkeepers in England. German liberty, to its proponents, was both more philosophical and more historical: It was the voice of conscience prescribing duty, or the autonomous person imposing law upon himself and thereby expressing his freedom and at the same time constituting order. This was the venerable German juxtaposition of spiritual freedom and external constraint and was intended to foster freedom for mobility in a meritocracy rather than the homogenizing equality of Jacobin democracy.

The conservative neo-idealists did not make German cultural and political values absolute in the style of the Treitschkean school; they maintained, in the spirit of Schiller and Fichte, that the unique qualities of German life contributed to the enrichment of universal human culture. The principal theme in their politics was the idea of cultural individuality, which is also the hallmark of historicism. Despite Rickert's theory of universal values, the emphasis was on the ideographic nature of historical statements. From this it follows that the German nation as an important cultural phenomenon should be studied *sui generis* and only secondarily in its universal context. The nation is a conveyance of universal values, but it remains essentially a unique historical entity. Baden philosophy contained a rationale for both patriotic politics and authentic cosmopolitanism, but the two values were in constant tension, with the former generally exerting the stronger pull.

Troeltsch, Weber, and Meinecke moved beyond conventional liberalism in their social thinking but not nearly so far as the authentic social democrats of the Marburg school. Weber was more interested in the creation of a new political class in Germany. He saw the Weimar assembly as the training academy for a new political elite rather than the forum for a sovereign people. Like many liberals before him, he distrusted the masses. What he feared most was the progressive rationalization of society through impersonal, egalitarian democracy, and the concomitant disappearance of the true cultural aristocrat. Weber and other intellectual liberals of the Baden school remained aristocratic liberals in the tradition of De Tocqueville, Burckhardt, and Ortega, for the fear of bureaucracy and democracy as potential agents of barbarism was not a trait of German liberalism alone. Yet, in Germany, this variant of elitism was especially debilitating because it was one of the prejudices that prevented the middle class from joining forces with industrial labor to reform the authoritarian state.

The widest and most promising deviation from liberal norms was the neo-Kantian social democracy of Hermann Cohen and his students at Marburg. The politics of Marburg philosophy were wholly democratic, if still implicitly elitist, and recognized the need for social as well as political democracy. And Marburg cultural values were, at least as far as Cohen was concerned, solidly Western European. The fact that he was a Jew did not, in his emphatic opinion, make him less a German; however, he was primarily a European.

Cohen's most distinguished pupil was Ernst Cassirer, whose work was a summa of Marburg scholarship. He was concerned with the logic of all sciences, tracing them historically and describing the development of their methods; he extended the scope of Marburg philosophy to include the whole of man's cultural experience as expressed in symbol and myth; and late in life, in the United States during World War II, he delved into the most potent myth of them all—the myth of the state.[85] In the febrile atmosphere of the "Ideas of 1914," Cassirer decried the superheated Germanism of Natorp and the metaphysicians of the German soul. His book *Freiheit und Form,* written during the war, was an evocation of Germany's classical heritage, in which he turned to the question of his country's cultural peculiarity, the principal thesis of Germany's patriotic intellectuals. He made clear his intention "not to conceal or weaken the connections which exist between German intellectual history and the other great European nations."[86] Looking back to the Enlightenment, he saw the Age of Reason culminating in Goethe in whom, he wrote, "all the preceding tendencies of German intellectual history attained fulfillment and completion."[87] Every educated German undoubtedly knew what Goethe's attitude had been during the Napoleonic era; hence, Cassirer's allusion to the cosmopolitan sage of Weimar left little doubt where he stood in 1916. When Hitler came to power, Cassirer left Germany, first going to the University of Oxford, then Göteborg in Sweden, and finally Yale and Columbia universities in the United States. The blatant, vulgar, and inhumane Third Reich was the antithesis of Cassirer's irenic spirit and mellow humanism. He was the most gifted and universal figure to emerge from the neo-Kantian ferment.

Cassirer was born in 1874 and studied at Berlin, Leipzig and Heidelberg; but the culmination of his education was in 1894 when he attended Georg Simmel's lectures on Kant in Berlin. Simmel was informally associated with the Baden school and had written a monograph on historical logic in the genre of Windelband and Rickert.[88] One day he told his students that "undoubtedly, the best books on Kant are written by Hermann Cohen, but I must confess that I do not understand them."[89] By this admission he put his finger on one of the serious limitations of neo-Kantianism—its abstruse, technical style. Cassirer, however, immediately purchased Cohen's books and two years later, in 1896, he first heard Cohen lecture in Marburg. Although he soon became Cohen's protégé, he was hesitant about pursuing an academic career. After the success of his *Erkenntnisproblem,* the first volume of which was published in 1906, he decided to teach if he could find a position in Berlin. His appointment was opposed by two powerful members of the university faculty, but Wilhelm Dilthey, then professor emeritus, intervened, saying, "I would not like to be a man of whom posterity will say that he rejected Ernst Cassirer."[90] Cassirer was given the appointment.

It might seem that Cassirer was an apolitical, timeless spirit like Erasmus and Goethe, but actually he was a student of the most ominous political problem of his age—the subrational plane of politics as embodied in the central myths and symbols of history. The Marne and its aftermath had badly shaken the faith of European intellectuals in the capacity of reason to order human affairs. Cassirer saw that the theory of knowlege developed by Kant and Cohen was incomplete and that in Gawronsky's words: "It is not true that only human reason opens the door which leads to the understanding of reality, it is rather the whole of the human mind, with all its functions and impulses, all it potencies of imagination, feeling, volition and logical thinking which builds the bridge between man's soul and reality."[91] Cassirer, in elaborating on this proposition, moved toward his philosophy of symbolic forms.[92]

Yet his comprehension of irrational forces in history did not destroy his faith in the values of Western civilization produced by reason. In his *Individual and Cosmos in the Philosophy of the Renaissance* (1927) and *The Platonic Renaissance in England* (1932), he appraised the beginnings of modern secular thought and then turned to the eighteenth century in *The Philosophy of the Enlightenment,* shortly before he left Germany. There, he examined what he called the "universal process of philosophizing;" he was interested in the total European movement of thought, not solely the German Enlightenment. His personal credo was: "Man can participate in a higher order of human life only through the realization of the perennial forms of human thought."[93] Patently, this was the opposite of *Historismus.*

In his inquiries Cassirer went beyond Marburg philosophy in originality and range, and always remained true to the universal humanism of Cohen.[94] In his search for an organon for the understanding of human culture, he also followed Cohen. He did not believe that there were two sciences, one for nature and one for history. He specifically rejected the logic of Windelband and Rickert: "It is not possible to separate the two moments of universality and particularity in this abstract and artificial way. A judgment is always the synthetic unity for both moments."[95] Here, Cassirer's Marburg lineage is clear. Cohen and Natorp had done some preliminary research on symbolic forms in their precritical work on folk psychology and mythological expression. Cassirer had little in common with Baden philosophy except his adherence to the tradition of critical idealism.

Although Cassirer remained European in his values during the war, other students of Cohen did not. Paul Natorp, albeit an extreme case, is proof that neo-Kantian precepts did not guarantee immunity against chauvinism and xenophobia. It might be that his theory of the voluntaristic, organic community predisposed him during the war toward a narrow Germanism. After 1914, he was closer to Fichte than Kant. Rudolf Stammler was also swayed by the crisis, but not to the same extent as Natorp. He had been one of the principal critics of the German historical school of law. Had he followed the political implications of his legal philosophy—which was rational and universalistic—his war nationalism might have been even more temperate. But Stammler did not swerve from his ethical socialism or from his conviction that justice can be served only in a free society. His teacher Cohen argued that the law must be paramount even in wartime, and he continued to call for electoral reform in Prussia.

The deviations of Natorp and Stammler notwithstanding, Marburg neo-Kantianism created a philosophical foundation for evolutionary socialism and parliamentary democracy. These principles brought the middle-class intellectuals of Marburg into contact with Eduard Bernstein, Eduard David, and other revisionists of the Social Democratic party. In fact, Marburg socialism and revisionism closely resembled what orthodox German social democracy had actually become in practice.

The great historical possibility of Marburg neo-Kantianism was that it would bring middle-class philosophy to a comprehension of working-class politics. As Carl Landauer explains, "the victory of gradualism within the socialist movement, aside from other presuppositions, [was encouraged by] the influx of ideas which were not affected by dialectical philosophy."[96] The infusion of nondialectical ideas was largely the work of neo-Kantians, or of socialist intellectuals who had been influenced by them. In neo-Kantian social theory, Hegel's dialectical monism is replaced by Kant's ethics of freedom, a substitution which was in accord with the ethical, evolutionary character of revisionism. Therefore, revisionists like Bernstein, who had actually been hostile to Kantian philosophy, were drawn to Marburg socialism because it gave theoretical force to their demand for an updating of Marxism. The neo-Kantian socialists themselves, as Peter Gay says, "rarely went beyond bourgeois reformism, [but] their ethical philosophy made them sympathetic to the political Left."[97]

The principal intermediary between the socialist ideologues and the educated public was Karl Vorländer, a student and associate of Cohen and Natorp. After taking his philosophy degree at Marburg, Vorländer was a gymnasium teacher at Solingen, Neuweid, and München-Gladbach. In 1919, he went to Münster where he worked as a secondary school administrator and taught philosophy at the university. It is significant that he originally taught in secondary schools. This gave him an opportunity to extend neo-Kantian influence beyond narrow university circles and to experience the gigantic problem of educating the German public to democracy. He was not able to join the Social Democratic party formally before the war without sacrificing his career, but in 1919 he became a regular member. He was elected to the Westphalian Diet and was also a member of the Prussian State Council. He continued to take part in party politics and to write for socialist periodicals until his death on December 6, 1928.[98]

Vorländer was aware that his philosophical and political creed suffered a great handicap. It was philosophy for trained philosophers and, therefore, too esoteric to attract many readers. In the second volume of his Kant biography, he wrote: "I wanted to produce a book not only for the academicians but also to present to my contemporaries the great philosophers as both men and thinkers. . . . Kant must once again become a real power in our lives."[99] In his history of German thought and in his studies of Kant, Vorländer tried to make his subjects understandable without descending to banal popularization. Had more of Marburg philosophy achieved such a balance between scholarship and intelligibility, it might have exerted a stronger influence on German politics.

The conjuncture of Marburg socialism and revisionism occurred between 1898 and 1901, when Bernstein was causing dismay among orthodox Marxists by proposing that Marxism was, in many respects, obsolete. He first used the slogan "Back to Kant" in 1898, in an article for *Die Neue Zeit*.[100] In a letter to Vorländer, he explained that he first became interested in neo-Kantianism by Ellissen's biography of F.A. Lange. As a result, Bernstein had written a series of articles for *Die Neue Zeit* in 1892, entitled "Zur Würdigung F.A. Langes."[101] Six years later, he proclaimed that the neo-Kantian movement had "a certain validity for socialism."[102] He was not alone in his discovery of Kantianism. In 1896, Ludwig Woltmann and Conrad Schmidt suggested a synthesis of Kant's epistemology and Marxism, which provoked a counterattack from the Russian Marxist Plekanov, who later denounced Bernstein's invocation of Kant.[103] But Schmidt and Woltmann had too little influence in the party to cause more than a ripple.[104] With Bernstein it was a more serious matter. He was one of the leading Social Democratic party theoreticians and after years in exile, he was something of a hero in the socialist movement. His espousal of Kantian ethics was, as Bebel and Karl Kautsky recognized, a threat to unity.

Bernstein argued that Kant was a far greater realist than the apostles of scientific materialsism.[105] Critical idealism was needed to cure socialism of its ideological anachronisms. He chided the scientific materialists for their neglect of ideals and moral purposes, and their relegation of them to the "superstructure." When Bebel asked him to clarify his views, he responded with *Voraussetzungen des Sozialismus* in 1899, which contained little of Kant and much on the anomalies of Marxism. But the last chapter carried the motto, *Kant wider Cant*. Here Bernstein maintained that without criticism and without idealism there can be no socialism, but he was not suggesting a literal adoption of Kant's episte-mology and ethics.[106] "Back to Kant" was intended as an appeal for critical appraisal of cherished dogmas in light of new realities. It also was meant to symbolize the need for a new moral leaven in socialist theory. Bernstein was not, as his biographer rightly observes, a neo-Kantian in the strict philosophical sense. Yet he had discovered an affinity between revisionism and Marburg neo-Kantianism which offered the possibility of a timely convergence of bourgeois reformism with the working-class movement.

Although such an intellectual alliance failed to mature for several reasons, it was mainly because Bernstein's proposals seemed to jeopar-dize party solidarity. Bebel's reaction was typical of the party leaders: "I doubt very much whether people in the party will be grateful to you. This continuous opening of new discussions creates bitterness in our ranks. . . . You have done a disservice to the party with this talk."[107] Another characteristic response came from Lily Braun after hearing Bernstein speak in 1901: "We had expected a prophet of a new truth, and instead we saw before us a doubter."[108] Other socialists were suspi-cious that neo-Kantianism was a middle-class stalking-horse used by the revisionists to distract the party with bourgeois ideas. "Neo-Kantianism," said Plekanov, "is an intellectual weapon of the middle class in the struggle for existence," and he accused the liberal intellectuals of trying to drug the proletariat with Kantian reformism.[109] At this time, Pleka-nov was a "very paragon of orthodoxy."[110] Ironically, in 1916 he used Kantian ethics to support the national defense of his own country.[111] But during the revisionist controversy, he was a firebrand of straight Marx-ism. A detente between the left wing of the bourgeoisie and socialism had little chance in such an atmosphere of suspicion and hostility. As Lily Braun implied in her disillusioned comment on Bernstein, his thinking was disturbing because it was inspired by the constructive skep-ticism of neo-Kantian logic; therefore, it was a menace to scientific certi-tude and to the credibility of sacred doctrines. He was fomenting a "crisis of faith in the foundations of international Marxism."[112]

Marburg neo-Kantianism finally and fatefully entered the arena of political action in the person of Cohen's student, Kurt Eisner, who led the Bavarian revolution in 1918.[113] Eisner was a middle-class intellectual who had converted to socialism before he went to Marburg. He was neither a social liberal like Cohen nor a democratic revisionist like Bernstein, but a revolutionary idealist who thought that Marx and Kant were compatible. When he arrived at Marburg in 1893, he was prepared to study Cohen's teachings and to go far beyond them.[114] His presidency of the first revolutionary regime in Bavaria was a fitting climax to a stormy career. After graduating from the prestigious Askanische Gymnasium in Berlin in 1886, and then attending the Friedrich Wilhelm for eight terms, Eisner became a journalist—a more appropriate vocation for his polemical and satirical talents than the academic world. His gift of satire landed him in Plotzensee prison in 1897 for lese majesty against the kaiser, an episode that made him known to the socialist hierarchy in Berlin. After his release in August 1898, he was made coeditor of *Vorwärts* with Franz Mehring. In the barrage of diatribes that shook German socialism during the revisionist conflict, Eisner was in an uncomfortable predicament. Although he sympathized with Bernstein's campaign to infuse socialism with a Kantian moral sense, he had no faith in the efficacy of gradual reform.[115] He was closer to Kautsky than Bernstein, but this did not prevent their rupture in 1904 and Eisner's subsequent dismissal from the *Vorwärts* staff.[116] Before Eisner fell from grace he used *Vorwärts* to articulate his particular brand of neo-Kantianism. He did not accept Bernstein's version of Kant's place in the socialist movement, but he agreed that Kant's ethics constituted an indispensable ideal. "Kant's moral law is the task which sets the direction for mankind."[117] Kantian morality stands above all concrete social orders and demands no particular kind of society, but any community which claims to be civilized must measure itself by this moral law.[118] Yet under existing circumstances, Eisner concluded, the Kantian ideal can be achieved solely through socialism:[119] the liberal descendants of Kant can find refuge only in the socialist movement.

In 1905, Eisner aggravated his already deteriorating relations with the staff of *Vorwärts* by quarreling with Kautsky over the relative importance of ethics and economics in history.[120] He saw no need for the dispute between the ethical and economic interpretations, and he criticized Kautsky for underrating moral forces. "The proletariat does not want only to understand history but to make it."[121] Ethics sets the direction of history; economics explains the actual process. A knowledge of purposes and ideal goals and faith in moral effort are the requisites of success for socialism. He ended his argument with the admonition, "More idealism—that is the rousing cry of the day—more idealism, and that means—Kautsky don't turn pale—more ethics."[122]

Eisner failed to convert his colleagues to Hermann Cohen's ethical socialism. Franz Mehring, who was a prolific but even-tempered defender of orthodoxy, was typical of the negative reaction to Eisner's ethical crusade. Although more open-minded than most of his fellow Marxists, he believed that Eisner's moral, teleological theory of historical causation "carried about as much weight as a small cirrus cloud floating about in ether."[123] In the same vein, he criticized Cohen for asking the socialists to give up historical materialism—this was like asking an army to discard its most powerful weapon. However, Mehring did not conceal his respect for some of the neo-Kantian writers, especially Vorländer, whom he considered a genuine, if patently bourgeois friend of socialism. Vorländer's attempt to make Kant's categorical imperative and its corollary the moral thesis of socialism was admirable, but its influence on the party had not "amounted to a grain of sand."[124] Since Kantian ethics had caused much consternation and commanded much attention in the socialist journals, Mehring was certainly engaging in understatement. To him, and to the other pundits of orthodoxy, Kantianism was a bourgeois conjuring trick. The return to Kant would be a "fatal leap backward."[125]

Eisner was better at evocative writing than searching analysis. His effectiveness was as a polemicist, not as a theoretician. Yet he might have become a powerful agent for ethical socialism within the Social Democratic party had the guardians of orthodoxy been less fearful that the vague Kantianism of Bernstein and Eisner would be a dangerous opening toward bourgeois reformism—a method acceptable for tactics but inadmissible as ultimate strategy. Eisner's life ended in a manner presaging the political and racial violence of Hitler's Germany. On February 21, 1919, he was shot by Count Arco, a nationalist fanatic. His memory was later reviled by the Bavarian Nazis who vilified him as the typical "Marxist-Jew" and found him a convenient scapegoat in their anti-Bolshevik and anti-Semitic propaganda. His fate bears witness to the terrible social and racial fissures that were beginning to open on the already scarified surface of German life.

Conclusion

Marburg neo-Kantianism was politically important because it held out the possibility of an intellectual alliance between liberal reformism and working-class socialism; obstinate prejudices on both sides, however, stood in the way. Prestigious liberal reformers would have had to discard their bias against the proletariat because of its lack of education and to assuage the bourgeois fear of social revolution. The working-class socialists, on the other hand, would have had to suppress revolutionary cant and to abandon the doctrine of class irreconcilability. By the turn of the century, revolutionary dialectics had become strictly *pro forma*. Party liturgy bore little resemblance to actual tactics. But when Kautsky applied the theoretical scourge to Bernstein's revisionism and Eisner's ethical idealism, he turned down an opportunity to bring philosophy more into line with practice and to secure an ally in the struggle against a much more reactionary enemy than middle-class capitalism—the authoritarian Wilhelmine state. This alliance eventually formed, beginning with the peace resolution of 1917 and culminating in the first Weimar coalition, but under unpropitious conditions. The turmoil of 1919 forced the socialists to invoke the physical power of their principal adversary, the military elite, to restore order. This was a fatal compromise, for it prevented them from destroying the main prop of the Wilhelmine regime. This expedient, in spite of the provisions of Versailles, left intact the prestige and the internal structure of the very institution that helped to clear the way to Hitler's chancellorship in 1933. Had a viable popular front been created before 1914, the coalition parties might have been better prepared for responsibility in 1919, and perhaps if the Weimar coalition had been the product of evolution under normal conditions rather than the congenitally damaged offspring of defeat and revolution, its later deterioration would have been prevented. But given the harsh realities of Wilhelmine politics, these are very large ifs.

This is not to argue that the general acceptance of Marburg neo-Kantianism alone would have altered the course of German history. However, it offered a possible *via media* for the two social classes which

179

must accommodate one another if democracy was to survive the tensions of industrialization and power politics. Marburg politics were descended from the bourgeois liberalism and ethical individualism of Kant. Marburg neo-Kantianism was rooted in middle-class idealism but extended beyond it into social democracy; therefore, it also spoke to the working class. But the enduring suspicions of both groups, followed by war and revolution, prevented a positive integration of attitudes and seriously impaired the short-lived democratic consensus of early Weimar.

The problem was partly within neo-Kantianism itself, an intellectual movement so various and complex that it scarcely bears designation in the singular, although there was an underlying unity at that. Kurt Eisner, the revolutionary idealist, was far from the austere logician Rickert, but running between the two extremes was a strong common tendency toward individual freedom, social justice, and cosmopolitan values. The motif of neo-Kantian politics is well expressed in the Fifth Proposition of Kant's *Idea of a Universal History*: "The greatest practical problem for the human race . . . is the establishment of a civil society, universally administering right according to law."[1] The lawgiving mandate, Kant said, can come only from the united will of the people.[2]

Even abstruse Baden philosophy had practical implications. Weber's dictum that all questions are essentially political could be applied to neo-Kantian logic, despite the ostensibly epistemological character of Baden theory.[3] The normative philosophy of Windelband and the transcendental values of Rickert were conceived to unite historical individuality with conceptual generality and ethical universality. These Baden philosophers influenced some of Wilhelmine Germany's most prominent intellectuals in their attitude toward their country's place in the Western cultural community and in their search for stable values. Neo-Kantianism grew from the reaction against Hegelian monism, naturalism, and relativism.[4] In Meinecke's words, the neo-idealists believed that to exorcise relativism and "to attain once more to the faith that there exists some absolute, are necessary in both a theoretical and a practical sense."[5]

The quest for universality in all areas of human experience was characteristic of neo-Kantianism. Rejecting Hegel's immanentism, the neo-Kantians sought teleological values in the intelligible world suggested by Kant. There was little agreement on the relationship between the noumenal world of values and the phenomenal world of experience, but both ethical freedom and universal standards of right were considered indispensable as regulative ideas for practical life. Although acknowledging the limits of cognitive reason, they stressed the moral necessity of certain absolutes, but they did not hide from this essential paradox of the human situation. Unlike absolute idealists of the Hegelian persuasion, they did not try to think the thoughts of God.[6] Translated into practical terms, neo-Kantianism meant individual liberty, toleration, and cosmopolitan pride in European civilization. Social antagonism and national hubris were not entirely expunged in the neo-Kantian movement, but its principal aim was in the opposite direction.

Yet there remained among the neo-Kantians a fundamental problem—one of orientation. Their intellectual energies were directed toward the realization of moral ends in all man's activities, from historical research to social reform. This was wholly admirable in itself, for moral values should form an integral part of any fully rounded and humane political philosophy. But there was a serious imbalance between theory and praxis. The neo-Kantians had achieved a commendably moral perspective on the world but lacked the means to change it. Neo-Kantianism, at least in the case of Cohen and his followers, suggested some concrete ideas for the creation of social democracy in Germany, but failed to recognize sufficiently the huge social and political barriers between means and ends. A poignant instance of this lack of realism is found in Meinecke's suggestion in *The German Catastrophe* that political attitudes in his country could be changed by starting Goethe discussion groups throughout the land. By overvaluing the power of mind, the idealists consistently undervalued the force of circumstances. Their faith in noumenal freedom, always tempered in Kant by his awareness of human frailty, soared beyond their understanding of the phenomenal obstacles in their path.

Still, the heirs of Kant should be given their due. The neo-Kantians were concerned about the fate of freedom and reason in an increasingly unbalanced, power oriented society. They rightly believed that these values were in jeopardy.[7] The forces that were threatening reason and freedom in Germany could not have been defeated by Kant's doctrines alone; far more was required than a philosophical conversion. But Kant's admonition, "Have the courage to use your own reason," would have been a good place to begin. "Enlightenment," Kant said, "is man's release from his self-incurred tutelage."[8] Neo-Kantianism was an attempt to liberate German philosophy and politics from tutelage to intellectual confusion, social narrowness, and cultural vanity.

Notes

Works cited briefly have full bibliographical details in bibliography. Translations from the German are by the author.

Chapter 1

1. This characterization of the sixteenth century is found in A.J.P. Taylor, *The Course of German History* (New York: Oxford Galaxy Books, 1962), p.17.

2. Franz Schnabel, *Deutsche Geschichte im neuenzehnten Jahrhundert*, 3: v.

3. See Theodore Hamerow, *Restoration, Revolution, Reaction*, pp. 1–95; Franz F. Wurm, *Wirtschaft und Gesellschaft in Deutschland, 1848–1948* (Opladen: C.W. Leske, 1969); and Heinrich Bechtel, *Wirtschaftsgeschichte Deutschlands im 19. und 20. Jahrhundert*, 3 vols. (Munich: Georg W. Calleway, 1956), 3: 147–251.

4. This is the argument in Donald G. Rohr, *The Origins of Social Liberalism in Germany*.

5. Hamerow, p. 151. Hamerow stresses the identification of 1848 liberalism with middle–class economic interests. Rohr maintains that Hamerow has misunderstood liberalism by overlooking the wide range of liberal opinion on social issues (pp. 9 ff.). While there was undeniably a literature of social liberalism before 1848, during the revolution the differences between the liberal bourgeoisie and workers (mainly the still dominant handicraft laborers) proved "too profound to be adjusted" (Hamerow, p. 153).

6. Hamerow, p. 154.

7. Leonore O'Boyle, "The Middle Class in Western Europe, 1815–1848," *American Historical Review* 71 (1966): 826–46. Theodore Hamerow, *The Social Foundations of German Unification, 1858–1871*, pp. 64–65, gives a useful description: "What held its [the middle class] members together was an economic dependence on manufacture, commerce, or the learned professions, a generally intermediate position within the social order, a common minimum level of income and education, and a pervasive hostility to the hierarchical structure of authority."

8. The literature on the humanistic theory of *Bildung* is, extensive. See especially Hans–Georg Gadamer, *Wahrheit und Methode*, 3d ed. (Tübingen: J.C.B. Mohr, 1960), pp.1–9; W.H. Bruford, *The German Tradition of Self–Cultivation: Bildung from Humboldt to Thomas Mann* (London, New York: Cambridge University Press, 1975); I. Schaarschmidt, *Der Bedeutungswandel der Worte "bilden" und "Bildung" in der Literaturepoche von Gottsched bis Herder* (Ph.D. diss., University of Königsberg, 1931); Joseph Speck, Gerhard Wehle, *Handbuch Pädagogischer Grundbegriffe*, 2 vols. (Munich: Kösel, 1970), 1: 134–85: Johannes von den Driesch, Josef Esterhues, *Geschichte der Erziehung und Bildung*, 5th ed. 2 vols. (Paderborn: Ferdinand Schöningh, 1960); H. Ritter von Srbik, *Geist und Geschichte vom deutschen Humanismus*, 2 vols. (Munich: F. Bruckmann, 1950–64); Ernst Lichtenstein, *Zur Entwicklung des Bildungsbegriffs von Meister Eckhart bis Hegel* (Heidelberg: Quelle and Meyer, 1964); Schnabel, *Deutsche Geschichte*, 3: 252–87.

9. *Wanderungen durch die Mark Brandenburg*, quoted in Joachim Remak, *The Gentle*

Critic. Theodor Fontane and German Politics, 1848–1898 (New York: Syracuse University Press, 1964), p. 39.

10. See *Sämtliche Werke,* ed. H. Glockner, 20 vols. (Stuttgart: Frommann, 1927–30), vol.7, *Grundlinien der Philosophie des Rechts,* pp. 282–83, where Hegel identifies the middle class with the spirit of rational order and freedom.

11. On the social and ideological implications of middle–class humanism and idealism, see R.H. Thomas, *Liberalism, Nationalism and the German Intellectuals, 1822–1847,* where, for example, he observes that classical humanism "was beginning to serve as a defense of the culture of the property–owning middle–class," p.80. See also Georg G. Iggers, *The German Conception of History;* Fritz K. Ringer, *The Decline of the Mandarins,* esp. pp. 81–128; Hajo Holborn, "Die deutsche Idealismus in sozialgeschichtlicher Beleuchtung," *Historische Zeitschrift* 174 (1952): 359–417.

12. Quoted by Thomas, *Liberalism, Nationalism,* p.6. For Hansemann's views, see Rohr, *Social Liberalism,* pp. 92–96.

13. See Eugene N. Anderson, *The Social and Political Conflict in Prussia,* pp. 382–443; Hajo Holborn, *A History of Modern Germany,* 3: 99–173; Ludwig Bergsträsser, *Geschichte der politischen Parteien in Deutschland,* pp. 94–143.

14. For an analysis of social forces in Germany under Bismarck and his attitude toward the middle class, see Arthur Rosenberg, *Imperial Germany,* pp.1–33.

15. Johannes Ziekursch, *Politische Geschichte des neuen deutschen Kaiserreichs,* 1: 188.

16. As Rosenberg says, "The military power placed in the hands of the Emperor afforded the capitalist middle class the best defence against the danger of a proletarian revolution." *Imperial Germany,* p. 7. From this perspective, acceptance of Bismarck's solution was not a surrender of principles by the middle class; it was consistent with their desire for national unity and with their perception of the radical threat. On the complexity of the liberal situation in 1866 and the dangers of applying a narrow Western standard of liberal conduct, see Heinrich A. Winkler, "Bürgerliche Emanzipation und nationale Einigung. Zur Entstehung des Nationalliberalismus in Preussen," in *Probleme der Reichsgründung,* ed. H. Boehme (Cologne and Berlin: Kiepenheuer and Witsch, 1968), pp. 226–37.

17. Ziekursch, *Politische Geschichte* 1: 192.

18. Gustav Mayer, "Die Trennung der proletarischen von der bürgerlichen Demokratie in Deutschland (1863–1870)," *Archiv für die Geschichte des Sozialismus und der Arbeiterbewegung* 2 (1912): 2.

19. Ziekursch, *Politische Geschichte* 1:113–14. See also Roger Morgan, *The German Social Democrats and the First International, 1864–1872* (Cambridge: Cambridge University Press, 1965), pp. 1–30.

20. Mayer, "Die Trennung," p.7. The editor was Heinrich Rickert, father of the Baden philosopher and a prominent figure in the left wing of the Progressive party.

21. Ibid., p. 11.

22. Bebel and Liebknecht, unreconciled, founded a democratic People's party in Saxony along with a number of workingmen's educational associations and sought ties with the South German People's party of Eckhardt and Sonnemann. Mayer, p.1, and Ziekursch, *Politische Geschichte* 1: 243–49.

23. See Carl Landauer, *European Socialism,* 1: 135–39.

24. Hamerow, *Social Foundations,* pp. 49–98.

25. F.C. Sell defines intellectual liberalism as the tendency in German culture which is based on the conscious and proud freedom of the "thinking I," a tradition going back to Kant, Schiller, and Goethe. According to Sell, whereas political liberalism was weak after

1871, intellectual liberalism was potent; it became a fillip for imperialism, largely in the form of Friedrich Naumann's National Socialism. Sell's definition is useful but his historical treatment one–dimensional. See his *Die Tragödie des deutschen Liberalismus*, pp. 299–300. For a critical opinion of Sell and the view that liberalism was not unitary but multilayered, see Walter Bussmann, "Zur Geschichte des deutschen Liberalismus im 19. Jahrhundert," in H. Böhme, *Probleme der Reichsgründerzeit*, pp. 85–103. Another pluralistic approach to German liberalism is Heinrich Heffter, *Die deutsche Selbstverwaltung im 19. Jahrhundert. Geschichte der Ideen und Institutionen* (Stuttgart: K.F. Koehler, 1950). See also Leonard Krieger, *The German Idea of Freedom*; Hermann Lübbe, *Politische Philosophie in Deutschland*; Hajo Holborn, "Die deutsche Idealismus;" Karl Lütgert, *Die Religion des deutschen Idealismus*, vol. 3; and Schnabel, *Deutsche Geschichte* 2: 90–214.

26. See chap. 7, and Peter Gay, *The Dilemma of Democratic Socialism*, in which the importance of neo–Kantianism to the revisionists is minimized; also, Allan Mitchell's study of Eisner, *Revolution in Bavaria, 1918–1919*, pp. 34–75.

27. See George L. Mosse, *Germans and Jews*, p. 5, for the thesis that neo–Kantian socialism was part of the search for a "Third Force" in German life, an alternative to both capitalism and Marxism, an "idealistic commitment that stood above and beyond present reality."

28. Rosenberg, *Imperial Germany*, pp. 48–49. Liberal–socialist cooperation occurred first and with more enduring results in the southern states, particularly in Baden where a Grand Coalition of the Left became "a model opposition to Wilhelm II, " p. 49.

29. "Wert—Wert Problem," *Wörterbuch der philosophischen Begriffe*, ed. Rudolf Eisler (Berlin, 1884), 2: 725–32; *Encyclopedia of Religion and Ethics*, s.v. "Value."

30. *Essays in the Sociology of Culture* (London: Kegan Paul, 1956), p. 94.

31. Ibid., p. 123.

32. Theobald Ziegler, *Die geistigen und sozialen Strömungen des 19. Jahrhundert*, p. 352.

33. On the permutations of Hegelianism, see Karl Löwith, *From Hegel to Nietzsche*, trans. D.E. Green Garden City, N.Y.: Anchor Doubleday, 1967); Sidney Hook, *From Hegel to Marx* (London: Victor Gollancz, 1936); Willy Moog, *Hegel und die Hegelische Schule* (Munich: E. Reinhardt, 1930); and a recent critical view of previous accounts, William J. Brazill, *The Young Hegelians* (New Haven: Yale University Press, 1970).

34. The divergence of German philosophy from politics is the thesis in Lübbe, *Politische Philosophie*. Ziegler suggested earlier the same problem in his *Die geistigen und sozialen Strömungen*, p. 354.

35. William Cecil Dampier, *A History of Science and Its Relations with Philosophy and Religion*, 4th ed. (Cambridge: Cambridge University Press, 1948), p. 289.

36. Ibid., quoted by Dampier.

37. Friedrich Lilge, *The Abuse of Learning*, p. 59.

38. Karl Löwith, *From Hegel to Nietzsche*, p. 113.

39. Dampier, p. 202.

40. Lilge, p. 78. This analogy was, like most of the stock ideas of the materialists, not original. In J.H. Randall, *The Career of Philosophy*, 2 vols. (New York: Columbia University Press, 1965), 2: 376, it is attributed to Cabanis.

41. Lilge, pp. 78, 177n.

42. Ziegler, p. 317; Ernst Cassirer, *The Problem of Knowledge* (New Haven: Yale University Press), p. 11.

43. From *Popular Lectures on Scientific Subjects*, quoted by Dampier, p. 291. Helmholtz's prefiguratively neo–Kantian essays on epistemology are found in *Wissenschaftliche Abhandlungen*, 2 vols. (Leipzig, 1883), 2: 591–663.

44. Dampier, *History of Science,* p. 292.

45. Ziegler, p. 319.

46. See *Allgemeine Deutsche Biographie,* s.v. "Vogt, Karl." Hereafter cited as ADB.

47. Bruford, *German Tradition of Self–Cultivation,* pp. 164–90.

48. Lübbe, pp. 41–77; Brazill, pp. 1–25.

49. Holborn, *History of Modern Germany* 2: 516.

50. See E.M. Butler, *The Saint–Simonian Religion in Germany: a Study of the Young German Movement* (Cambridge: Cambridge University Press, 1926), and Walter Simon, *European Positivism in the Nineteenth Century* (Ithaca: Cornell University Press, 1963), pp. 238–64.

51. Randall, *Career of Philosophy* 2: 362.

52. Heine to Varnhagen von Ense, 27 June, 1831, in *Briefe von Stagemann, Metternich, Heine und Bettina von Arnim* (Leipzig, 1865), p. 232.

53. Lübbe, p. 25.

54. Otto Pflanze, *Bismarck and the Development of Germany: The Period of Unification, 1815–1871* (Princeton: Princeton University Press, 1963), p. 47.

55. Lübbe, pp. 25, 78. Holborn, *History of Modern Germany* 3: 121, qualifies the conventional judgment that the post–revolutionary decade was one of resigned pessimism: "It was not Schopenhauer's general pessimism that the members of this generation cherished most; on the contrary they applied all their energies to the practical tasks of this world. But they no longer conceived of their activities as direct contributions to the political future of the country."

56. Haym, *Hegel und seine Zeit* (Berlin, 1857). Although renowned as a liberal enemy of conservative Hegelianism, Haym's political attitude foreshadowed the anti–democratic liberalism of the late sixties and after. In a letter to Hansemann in 1848, he said that there must be no lack of energy in "driving back the brutality of the masses with all possible violence." Quoted in R. H. Thomas, *Liberalism, Nationalism,* p. 138.

57. See Rosenkranz, *Georg W. F. Hegels Leben* (Berlin, 1844), and his *Apologie Hegels gegen R. Haym* (Berlin, 1858).

58. Herbert Marcuse, *Reason and Revolution: Hegel and the Rise of Social Theory* (Boston: Beacon Press, 1960), pp. 10–12. The *locus classicus* of this expression is Hegel's *Grundlinien der Philosophie des Rechts,* ed. Glockner, 7: 33. "Was vernünftig ist, das ist wirklich, und was wirklich ist, vernünftig."

59. Quoted in Sell, p. 302.

60. Marcuse, p. 15.

61. Schnabel, 3: 9.

62. Krieger, *German Idea of Freedom,* p. 88.

63. Ibid., p. 87. On the unresolved difficulties in Kant's ethics, see Krieger's entire chapter, pp. 86–124. Also, Lewis White Beck's introduction to *Kant's Critique of Practical Reason and Other Writings in Moral Philosophy.*

64. On Kant as demolisher of the natural law, see Leonard Krieger, "Kant and the Crisis in Natural Law," *Journal of the History of Ideas* 26 (April–June, 1965): 191–211. Leo Strauss similarly interprets the Kantian element in Max Weber, in his *Natural Right and History,* pp. 41 ff. Walter Simon has written that Kant revived the Lutheran separation of inner from outer life. For Kant, freedom has "little if any political content," *Germany: A Brief History* (New York: Random House, 1966), p. 71. Koppel Pinson concludes his encomium of Kant's humanism with the serious reservation: "Kantian ethics . . . created the fatal dichotomy of the realm of morality and legality," *Modern Germany, Its History and Civilization* (New York: Macmillan Company, 1954), p. 19. The above are samples of a long-established canon. On the other hand, Kant has found eloquent defense, for ex-

ample, in George Armstrong Kelly, *Idealism, Politics and History,* pp. 75–181, and Hans Reiss, ed., *Kant's Political Writings* (Cambridge: Cambridge University Press, 1970), pp. 1–37. Hans Saner, *Kant's Political Thought. Its Origins and Development,* trans. E.B. Ashton (Chicago: University of Chicago Press, 1973), is an indictment of those who have minimized the relevance and importance of Kant's politics.

65. Pflanze, p. 25.

66. Krieger, *German Idea of Freedom,* p. 124.

67. Wilhelm Metzger, *Gesellschaft und Recht in der Ethik des deutschen Idealismus,* ed. Ernst Bergmann (Heidelberg, 1917), p. 110.

68. *Foundations of the Metaphysics of Morals,* ed. L. W. Beck, p. 52.

69. Karl Jaspers, *The Great Philosophers,* trans. Hannah Arendt and Ralph Manheim, 2 vols. (New York: Harcourt, Brace and World, 1962), 1: 293.

70. Strauss, *Natural Right,* p. 279.

71. Kant, *Foundations of the Metaphysics of Morals,* p. 90.

72. Vorländer, *Der Formalismus der Kantischen Ethik in seiner Notwendigkeit und Fruchtbarkeit.* Inaugural dissertation (Marburg, 1893), pp. 23–24.

73. Ibid., p. 24.

74. Jaspers, *Great Philosophers* 1: 346.

75. Krieger, "Kant and the Crisis in Natural Law," p. 195. John H. Hallowell, *The Decline of Liberalism,* deals with the same question but argues that natural law liberalism contained contradictory premises from the beginning, that is, the notion of universal absolute principles, and the positivist belief that laws are inherent in the nature of things. He blames the rise of scientific positivism for the severance of the two premises because the positivists reduced values to subjective preferences or feelings, pp. 1, 77–78, 86, 90, 111–12.

76. Strauss, p. 52n22.

77. Krieger, "Kant and the Crisis in Natural Law," p. 194.

78. Ibid., p. 195.

79. "Natural Law and Humanity," in Otto Gierke, *Natural Law and the Theory of Society,* trans. Ernest Barker (Boston: Beacon Press), pp. 201–2.

80. Krieger, "Kant and the Crisis in Natural Law," p. 196.

81. Pp. 11–12.

82. Kant, *Groundwork for the Metaphysic of Morals,* trans. H. J. Paton (London: Hutchison University Press, 1961), preface, p. 7.

83. Ibid., p. 57.

84. Strauss, p. 28.

85. *Foundations of the Metaphysics of Morals,* p. 52. Schnabel, 2: 107, argues that the liberal theory of right *demands* a dualistic position. The aim of liberal ethics is the victory of morality over nature and history, that is, over experience. Therefore, the true *Rechtsstaat* can be built only on standards that transcend historical experience, which itself can produce only mutable values.

86. Krieger, "Kant and the Crisis in Natural Law," p. 205.

87. The secular version of the *jus naturale* has been defined as "the law imposed on mankind by common human nature, that is, by reason in response to human needs and instincts," De Zulueta, *Legacy of Rome,* p. 201, quoted by Barker in Gierke, *Natural Law,* p. vi. But Kant rejected any heteronomous standard derived from human needs or utility, hence he remained within the Christian natural law tradition of the Thomists who were essentially dualistic. "Catholic writers on Natural Law . . . continue to speak in terms which go back to St. Thomas, and indeed beyond St. Thomas—terms of divine dispensa-

tion: terms which make Natural Law appear as an objective scheme of divinely constituted realities and rules.... " Barker, p. xli. Although Kant did not believe that this "objective scheme" was a demonstrable foundation for law, in the sense of possible rational cognition in the phenomenal world, he would place it in the realm of regulative ideas, or postulates of practical reason. St. Thomas and Kant were anti–eudaemonistic, both propounding an autonomous theory of the Good. See *Summa Contra Gentiles*, bk.3, chap. 27–38, in *Basic Writings of St. Thomas Aquinas*, Anton C. Pegis, ed. (New York: Random House, 1945), 2: 51–62. In St. Thomas, the Good is beatitude, or the pure contemplation of God. In Kant, the Good is obedience to the Moral Law within. Kant, it is argued here, represents a rationalistic variant of Christian ethics and natural law.

88. *Foundations of the Metaphysics of Morals*, p. 71.

89. Robert Tucker, *Philosophy and Myth in Karl Marx* (Cambridge: Cambridge University Press, 1961), argues that Marx is a culmination of the tendency toward self–deification in the tradition from Kant through Hegel. It is difficult to agree with Tucker's inclusion of Kant in this evolution. "We find in Kant a conception of morality as the expression of a compulsion in man to achieve absolute moral perfection," p. 33. The term *compulsion* implies a pathological condition and in Kant's case is gratuitous. Tucker diminishes the importance of Kant's skeptical view of the possibility of human perfectibility. He is aware that Kant denied the possibility of absolute knowledge.

90. Quoted in Schnabel, 1: 290.

91. Ibid., pp. 210 ff. See also Ernst Cassirer, *Freiheit und Form*; Eduard Spranger, *Wilhelm von Humboldt und die Humanitätsidee*, 2d ed. (Berlin, 1928); and n. 8 above.

92. *Philosophische Strömungen der Gegenwart*, pp. 4–5. In Ueberweg–Heinze, *Grundriss der Geschichte der Philosophie* 4: 417, T. K. Oesterreich lists seven varieties of neo–Kantianism or *Neukritizismus*: (1) physiological (Helmholtz, Lange); (2) metaphysical (Liebmann, Volkelt); (3) realistic (Riehl); (4) logical (Cohen, Natorp, Cassirer); (5) criticism of value theory (Windelband, Rickert, Munsterberg, and the Baden School); (6) the relativistic transformation of criticism (Simmel); and (7) psychological (adherents of Fries such as Nelson). These categories, though not entirely apt, suggest the diversity of neo–Kantianism but obscure many underlying affinities, for example, between Lange and the Marburg School.

93. I. M. Bochenski, *Contemporary European Philosophy*, pp. 88–93.

94. Kelly, *Idealism, Politics and History*, pp. 4–5.

95. *Schriften zum Metaphysik*, in *Sämtliche Werke*, ed. G. Hartenstein, 4 vols. (Leipzig, 1851), 3: 64.

96. (Stuttgart, 1847), p. 20.

97. (Leipzig, 1847).

98. *Hegel und seine Zeit*, pp. 468–69.

Chapter 2

1. G.S. Hall, *Founders of Modern Psychology* (New York: D. Appleton and Company, 1912), pp. 68–69.

2. E. E. Thomas, "Lotze's Relation to Idealism," *Mind* 24 (1915) : 496–97.

3. T. M. Lindsay, "Hermann Lotze," *Mind* 1 (1876): 363.

4. Hall, p. 71.

5. Merz, *History of European Thought*, 2d ed., 4 vols. (London and Edinburgh: William Blackwood and Sons, 1914), 4: 599, 773.

6. Paul Grimley Kuntz, introduction to *Lotze's System of Philosophy*, by George Santayana, pp. 3–12.

7. Ibid., p. 48.

8. Merz, 4: 601.

9. For a biography of Lotze, see Max Wentscher, *Hermann Lotze, Leben und Werke*. See also ADB, s.v. "Lotze, R. H."; R. Falckenberg, *Lotzes Leben*, based largely on his correspondence; and the comparative study by Falckenberg, *Fechner und Lotze*, in *Geschichte der Philosophie in Einzeldarstellungen*.

10. Wentscher, *Hermann Lotze*, p. 5; for a description of Lotze's novel, pp. 7–8.

11. On the social character of German idealism, see especially Holborn, "Die deutsche Idealismus in sozialgeschichtlicher Beleuchtung," pp. 360–61, and Ringer, *Decline of the German Mandarins*, pp. 81–128.

12. Philip Devaux, *Lotze et son influence sur la philosophie anglo-saxonne* (Brussels, 1932), quoted by Kuntz, introduction to *Lotze's System*, by Santayana, p. 50. Kuntz's introductory essay is indispensable for an appreciation of Lotze's impact outside Germany.

13. John Passmore, *A Hundred Years of Philosophy*, p. 49.

14. Lotze took from Spinoza the idea of an underlying spiritual substance as the ground of unity, and borrowed from Leibniz the notion of interacting spiritual entities.

15. Wentscher, p. 25.

16. Ueberweg–Heinze, *Grundriss der Geschichte der Philosophie*, 11th ed., 4 vols. (Berlin, 1907), 4: 181, 227.

17. Wentscher, pp. 101–2.

18. Kuntz, p. 13.

19. Wentscher, pp. 106–7; R. Falckenberg, "Aus Hermann Lotzes Briefen an Theodor und Clara Fechner," *Zeitschrift für Philosophie und Philosophische Kritik* 3 (1897): 178.

20. See F. C. Sell, *Die Tragödie*, p. 129.

21. Wentscher, pp. 114–15.

22. Falckenberg, *Lotzes Leben*, pp. 30–31, and his "Aus Lotzes Briefen," p. 185.

23. Falckenberg, *Lotzes Leben*, p. 13.

24. Ibid.

25. Ibid., p. 34.

26. Ibid., p. 36.

27. Karl Lütgert, *Die Religion des deutschen Idealismus* 3: 252 ff., and Ziegler, *Die geistigen und sozialen Strömungen*, pp. 317 ff.

28. In Helmholtz's *Vorträge und Reden* (Braunschweig, 1896).

29. Hall, pp. 94–95n.

30. Falckenberg, *Lotzes Leben*, p. 65.

31. Ibid., p. 77.

32. Ibid.

33. Ibid., pp. 77–78.

34. Ibid., p. 106.

35. Wentscher, p. 116.

36. Falckenberg, *Lotzes Leben*, p. 94.

37. For the correspondence about Lotze's decision, see Falckenberg, "Aus Lotzes Briefen," pp.131–32, and on earlier offers, Falckenberg, "Zwei Briefe von Hermann Lotze und R. Seydel und E. Arnoldt," in W. Windelband, B. Erdmann, and H. Rickert, eds., *Sigwart–Festschrift*, Philosophische Abhandlungen (Tübingen, 1900).

38. Kuntz, p. 54.

39. Wentscher, p. 56.

40. *Metaphysik*, p. 604.

41. Ibid., p. 65; Wentscher, p. 56.

42. Henry Jones, *A Critical Account of the Philosophy of Lotze,* p. ix. See also George Santayana, "Lotze's Moral Idealism," *Mind* 15 (1890): 191–212.

43. *Microcosmus,* pp. 355–56.

44. A. Eastwood, "Lotze's Antithesis between Thought and Things," *Mind,* n.s. 1 (1892): 307.

45. Jones, p. x.

46. *Metaphysik,* pp. 5, 8.

47. *Microcosmus,* pp. 286–87.

48. *Metaphysic* 1: 16.

49. H. Høffding, *History of Modern Philosophy* 2: 519.

50. Jones, p. x.

51. *Microcosmus,* pp. 396–97.

52. Merz, 4: 666–67.

53. *Microcosmus,* p. 356.

54. Ibid., pp. 539–40. For more on the Hegelian theory of value see *Logik,* p. 13.

55. *Microcosmus,* pp. 539–40.

56. Ibid.

57. On Lotze's philosophy of history, see A. Schroeder, *Geschichtsphilosophie bei Lotze.* Lotze believed that progress in history was possible only through conflict (p.40), and that mankind's greatest achievements were the work of heroic individuals. He did not, however, subscribe to Darwinian theory, the popular extension of which he saw as a mockery of human ideals. Kuntz, p. 31; *Metaphysic* 2: 145–50.

58. Thomas, p. 489.

59. *Microcosmus,* p. 325.

60. Eastwood, p. 488.

61. *The Philosophie of "as if," a System of the Theoretical, Practical and Religious Fictions of Mankind,* trans. K. Ogden (London, 1924).

62. Kuntz, pp. 49–50; Otto Kraushaar, "What James's Philosophical Orientation Owed to Lotze," *Philosophical Review* 47 (1938): 517–26.

63. *Praktische Philosophie,* pp. 5–7.

64. F. Chelius, *Lotzes Wertlehre,* p. 25.

65. *Mikrokosmus,* 2d German ed., 2: 313, 398.

66. *Praktische Philosophie,* p. 28. Kant would not have accepted the idea of a normative consciousness. In the *Critique of Practical Reason* (Beck, ed.) he said, "I need not mention that universality of assent does not prove the objective validity of a judgment," p. 127.

67. *Praktische Philosophie,* p. 1.

68. Ibid.

69. Ibid., pp. 3–4.

70. Ibid., p.6.

71. Ibid., pp. 12, 31.

72. Ibid., p. 18.

73. Ibid., p. 19.

74. Ibid., p. 26.

75. Ibid., p. 31.

76. Ibid., p. 4.

77. Quoted in W. Bruford, *Germany in the Eighteenth Century* (Cambridge: Cambridge University Press, 1935), p. 229.

78. *Microcosmus,* p. 548.

79. Ibid., p. 59.

80. Ibid., p. 97.
81. *Praktische Philosophie*, p. 84.
82. Ibid., p. 11.
83. Ibid.
84. *Microcosmus*, p. 539.
85. *Praktische Philosophie*, pp. 73–74.
86. Ibid., p. 54.
87. Ibid., pp. 58–59.
88. *Microcosmus*, p. 515.
89. Ibid., pp. 263–64.
90. *Praktische Philosophie*, p. 63.
91. Ibid., p. 65.
92. Ibid., p. 77.
93. Ibid., pp. 76–78.
94. Ibid., p. 82.
95. W. Windelband, *Lehrbuch der Geschichte der Philosophie*, p. 527.
96. Kuntz, pp. 48–49.
97. Ibid., p. 49; Passmore, p. 51.
98. *History of European Thought* 4: 393.

Chapter 3

1. Fischer's first publication was his thesis on aesthetics, *Diotima, Die Idee des Schönen* (Pforzheim, 1849). A major theoretical work appeared three years later: *System der Logik und Metaphysik oder Wissenschaftslehre* (Stuttgart, 1852). His monumental *Geschichte der neueren Philosophie* began with a volume on Descartes in 1854, but his signal contribution to the rise of neo–Kantianism was his two–volume work on Kant, the first edition of which appeared as *Kants Leben und die Grundlagen seine Lehre* (Mannheim, 1860).

2. Fischer's most prominent antagonist was the Aristotelian, Adolf Trendelenburg, an opponent of Hegelian philosophy and professor at the University of Berlin from 1833 to 1872. He was also anti–Kantian in that he argued for the objectivity of space and time against the Kantian position that they are subjective intuitions. See his critique, *Kuno Fischer und sein Kant*. Fischer replied in his *Anti–Trendelenburg*. Hermann Cohen, later the major figure in Marburg neo–Kantianism, was inspired by the Fischer–Trendelenburg controversy to begin his own examination of Kant. See chapter 5.

3. There is no biography of Fischer. The best sources are Hugo Falckenheim's sketch in *Biographisches Jahrbuch und deutscher Nekrolog*, s.v. "Fischer, Kuno." Hereafter cited as BJ. *Badische Biographien*, s.v. "Fischer, Kuno." Hereafter cited as BB.

4. Quoted in BB 6: 520.

5. BJ 12: 257.

6. BB 6: 520; BJ 12: 527.

7. BB 6: 521.

8. For example, his *Lessing als Reformator der deutschen Literatur; Goethe–Schriften; Goethes Faust* (Stuttgart, 1893); *Schiller als Philosoph* (Heidelberg, 1891).

9. BJ 12: 257.

10. BJ 12: 259. The envy of Fischer's colleagues may have been aggravated by his legendary arrogance. According to an anecdote related to me by the late Hajo Holborn, Fischer once threatened some workers outside his home that he would accept an offer from another university unless they ceased the racket they were making. A description of Fischer's "free lecture" method is found in draft form in the Heidelberg Universitäts-

bibliothek manuscript section, under HS 2603, a bound copy of draft and proofs for his *Logik und Metaphysik oder Wissenschaftslehre*. Fischer subtitled this manuscript "Lehrbuch für Akademische Vorlesungen" (published Stuttgart, 1852).

11. BB 6: 521.

12. Fischer's rebuttal was *Das Interdict meiner Vorlesungen und die Anklage des Herrn Schenkel*. Schenkel answered in his *Abfertigung für Herrn Kuno Fischer* (Mannheim, 1854). Fischer's final response was *Die Apologie meine Lehre*.

13. BJ 12: 260.

14. Ibid., and in his *Geschichte der neureren Philosophie* 1: 3–15. Hereafter cited as *Geschichte*.

15. BB 6: 552.

16. BJ 12: 262.

17. Ziegler, *Die geistigen und sozialen Strömungen*, pp. 342–46.

18. BJ 12: 263.

19. BB 6: 523.

20. BJ 12: 272.

21. For example, Karl Vorländer, *Geschichte der Philosophie* 2: 418; Ludwig Stein, *Philosophische Strömungen*, pp. 271–72; Hans Meyer, *Geschichte der abendländischen Weltanschauung* 5: 114.

22. Windelband, *Kuno Fischer*, pp. 24–25.

23. Ibid., pp. 30–31.

24. *Geschichte* 1: 3.

25. Ibid., 1: 11.

26. Ibid., 1: 3–4.

27. Windelband, *Kuno Fischer*, p. 34.

28. *Geschichte* 1: 32.

29. Ibid., 1: 7–8.

30. Ibid., 1: 14.

31. Holborn, *Modern Germany* 2: 308.

32. Fischer, "Ueber die menschliche Freiheit," *Kleine Schriften* 1: 1–46.

33. Ibid., p. 45.

34. Ibid., p. 12.

35. Ibid., p. 13.

36. Ibid., p. 37.

37. Ibid., p. 38.

38. Ibid., p. 39.

39. Ibid., p. 41.

40. Ziegler, pp. 330–31.

41. Schopenhauer, *The World as Will and Representation*, trans. E. F. J. Payne, 2 vols. (Indian Hills, Colo.: The Falcon's Wing Press, 1958), 1: 416.

42. Ibid., 1: xxiii.

43. *Geschichte* 5: 541.

44. Ibid., pp. 551–52.

45. Ibid.

46. Ibid.

47. *German Idea of Freedom*, p. 101.

48. H. J. Paton, *Kant's Groundwork for the Metaphysic of Morals*, trans. H. J. Paton (London, 1961), p. 7.

49. *Geschichte* 5: vi.

50. Karl Löwith, *From Hegel to Nietzsche,* p. 119: "The return to Kant, in the way it took place, shows a retreat behind the limit of questioning which the Young Hegelians had reached in religious, social and political matters." George Lichtheim, *Marxism: A Historical and Critical Study* (London: Kegan Paul, 1961), p. 291, tends toward the same view, but concedes that neo–Kantianism was a genuine effort to revitalize German liberalism after the ascendancy of positivism and scientism in the 1850s and 1860s. "The school . . . was neo–liberal as well as neo–Kantian and, insofar as it was neo–liberal, critical of the existing state of affairs."

51. BJ 13: 47.

52. See Zeller, *David Friedrich Strauss in seinem Leben und seinem Schriften,* and *D. F. Strauss Ausgewählte Briefe,* ed. E. Zeller (Bonn, 1895).

53. BJ 13: 48. On Zeller's Tübingen background, see Wilhelm Dilthey, "Aus Eduard Zellers Jugendjahren," *Gesammelte Schriften.* 8 vols. (Stuttgart, 1959), 4: 433–51.

54. BJ 13: 48.

55. Hermann Diels, *Gedächtnisrede auf Eduard Zeller,* p. 14.

56. Ibid., p. 16.

57. Ibid.

58. Ibid., p. 22. The first German edition of Zeller's history of Greek thought is *Die Philosophie der Griechen in ihrer Entwicklung,* 3 vols. (Leipzig, 1845–52).

59. Diels, p. 23.

60. Ibid., p. 25; BJ 13: 50.

61. Diels, p. 25.

62. Ibid., p. 26; BJ 13: 51.

63. Diels, p. 29.

64. Ibid., pp. 27–30.

65. See Zeller, *Staat und Kirche.*

66. Diels, p. 30; BJ 13: 50.

67. "Ueber die Freiheit des menschlichen Willens, das Böse und die moralische Weltordnung," *Theologische Jahrbücher* 5 (1846–47), no.1: 28–89; no 2: 191–258.

68. (Berlin, 1886).

69. In 1888, Zeller assisted his student Ludwig Stein in founding the *Archiv für Geschichte der Philosophie,* an early neo–Kantian journal. In 1895, the *Archiv* merged with the *Philosophische Monatshefte* to become the *Archiv für systematische Philosophie.* This merger reflected the shift from historical to specialized theoretical interests toward the end of the century, a symptom of then triumphant neo–Kantianism.

70. Diels, p. 42.

71. Ibid., p. 43.

72. Zeller, *Vorträge* 2: 480.

73. Ibid., 2: 481.

74. Ibid., 2: 485.

75. *Critique of Pure Reason,* trans. J. D. Mieklejohn (London, 1956), p. 25.

76. Aliotta, *The Idealistic Reaction against Science.*

77. *Vorträge* 2: 490.

78. *Vorträge* 2: 492, 500–2.

79. Ibid., 2: 505.

80. "Ueber das Kantische Moralprincip und den Gegensatz formaler und materialer Moralprincipien," *Vorträge* 3: 156–88; "Ueber Begriff und Begründung der sittlichen Gesetz," *Vorträge* 3: 189–225.

81. Ibid., 3: 156–57.

82. Ibid., 3: 165.

83. Ibid., 3: 173.

84. Ibid., 3: 177.

85. Ibid., 3: 187. Zeller struggled between a rational formal ethical philosophy and one based on empirical psychology. See, for example, ibid., 3: 222.

86. Ibid., 3: 188.

87. Ibid., 3: 182.

88. It has been argued that from 1871 to 1890, German power was used with a sense of responsibility and restraint. If this thesis is correct—and Bismarck's undeniable understanding of limits after the Franco–Prussian War seems to bear it out—then the standard criticism of liberals like Zeller for supporting Bismarck's policies loses some of its force. And it should not be forgotten that the Western democracies also had their liberal imperialists. On Bismarck's sense of proportion, see Gordon Craig, *From Bismarck to Adenauer. Aspects of German Statecraft*. rev. ed. (New York, Evanston, and London: Harper Torchbooks, 1965), pp. 1–20.

89. "Nationalität und Humanitat," *Vorträge* 2: 433 ff.

90. Ibid., 2: 435.

91. Ibid., 2: 440–41.

92. Ibid., 2: 444.

93. "Die Politik in ihrem Verhältnis zum Recht," *Vorträge* 2: 385–86.

94. "Das Recht der Nationalität und die freie Selbstbestimmung der Völker," ibid., 2: 393–432.

95. Ibid., 2: 419.

96. Ibid., 2: 409.

97. Ibid., 2: 419–20.

98. Ibid., 2: 431.

99. Lübbe, *Politische Philosophie*, p. 188.

100. The Kant Gesellschaft edition is *Kant und die Epigonen: Eine kritische Abhandlung* (Berlin, 1912), with a brief biography of Liebmann appended. On the influence of Liebmann's essay on early neo–Kantianism, see Vorländer, *Geschichte der Philosophie* 2: 418; Wilhelm Windelband, *A History of Philosophy* 2: 633–42; Meyer, *Abendländischen Weltanschauung* 5: 114.

101. *Die Epigonen*, p. 244.

102. Ibid., p. 226.

103. Vischer was a pre–March liberal who sat in the Frankfurt parliament. He espoused a secular religion of humanity which would find embodiment in the state. Politically, he was a democrat. Meinecke characterizes him as an impractical, somewhat utopian intellectual in politics, in " Drei Generationen deutscher Gelehrtenpolitik, "*Staat und Persönlichkeit* (Berlin, 1933), pp. 139–46.

104. *Vier Monate vor Paris, 1870–1871*.

105. *Die Epigonen*, p. 4.

106. Ibid., p. 5.

107. Ibid., p. 25.

108. Ibid., p. 41.

109. Ibid., p. 65 ff.

110. Ibid., p. 68.

111. Ibid., p. 99. Liebmann had great respect for Fichte and admonished Schopenhauer for having called him a windbag.

112. Ibid., p. 104.

113. Ibid., p. 108.

114. Ibid., p. 136.

115. Ibid., p. 157.

116. Ibid., p. 203.

117. Ibid., p. 206.

118. See Liebmann, *Ueber den objectiven Anblick; Zur Analyse der Wirklichkeit* (Strassburg, 1880); *Klimax der Theorien; Gedanken und Thatsachen.* See also A. Meyer, *Ueber Liebmanns Erkenntnis Lehre und ihr Verhältnis zur Kantischen Philosophie;* R. Eucken, "Worte der Erinnerung an Otto Liebmann," *Kant–Studien* 17 (1912): 1–3.

119. *The Encyclopedia of Philosophy,* s.v. "Neo–Kantianism."

120. Although Windelband became Liebmann's most intimate friend, Liebmann continued to seek the support and advice of Fischer. Some of his letters to the latter are found in the manuscript section of the Heidelberg Universitätsbibliothek, under Heid. 395, i6. The six letters are dated: 26.1.1882; 8.2.1882; 20.3.1882; 2.1.1885; 21.7.1894; 18.3.1897. The first three pertain to Liebmann's imminent move to Jena.

Chapter 4

1. Lübbe, *Politische Philosophie,* p. 96.

2. *Anton Dohrn,* 2d ed. (Stuttgart and Tübingen, 1948), quoted by Georg Eckert in *F. A. Lange, Briefe und Leitartikel,* p. 11.

3. Windelband, *History of Philosophy* 2: 642; Vorländer, *Geschichte* 2: 419 ff.; Meyer, *Abendländischen Weltanschauung* 5: 118 ff.; Ziegler, *Die geistigen und sozialen Strömungen,* p. 353.

4. Otto Adolf Ellissen, *Friedrich Albert Lange,* is the only biography of Lange. See also ADB, s.v. "Lange, Friedrich Albert"; and Eckert, *F. A. Lange, Briefe und Leitartikel,* for journalistic and political activities of the 1860s. Received too late for this study, but useful and indicative of renewed interest in Lange is Joachim H. Knoll and Julius H. Schoeps, eds., *Friedrich Albert Lange: Leben und Werk,* Duisburger Forschungen 21 (Duisburg, 1975).

5. Ellissen, pp. 1–2.

6. ADB 17: 624. Lange's father was the author of a reply to D. F. Strauss, *Das Leben Jesu nach den Evangelien* (Heidelberg, 1846–47). His orthodox religious views convinced the authorities in Zurich that he was an ideal alternative to Strauss.

7. See E. N. Anderson, *Social and Political Conflict in Prussia,* pp. 304–14.

8. Windelband, *History of Philosophy* 2: 569n, says that realist is a misnomer for Herbart: "Not only the main series of development from Reinhold, Schelling, Krause, Schleiermacher, and Hegel is idealistic, but also the series which is usually opposed to this, Herbart and Schopenhauer, insofar . . . as by idealism is understood the dissolution or resolution of experience in the process of consciousness."

9. Ellissen, p. 28–30.

10. On the reduction of religion to anthropology and mythology, see Franklin L. Baumer, *Religion and the Rise of Scepticism* (New York: Harcourt, Brace, and Company, 1960), pp. 148–62.

11. Ellissen, p. 48.

12. Ibid., p. 57.

13. Ibid., p. 62.

14. Ibid., p. 63.

15. Ibid., p. 77.

16. ADB 17: 628.

17. Ellissen, p. 89.

18. See ADB, s.v. "Ueberweg, Friedrich."

19. Ellissen, p. 104.

20. Ibid., p. 106.

21. Ziegler, p. 354.

22. Ellissen, pp. 106–7.

23. See Ziekursch, *Politische Geschichte* 1: 15 ff.; Anderson, *Social and Political Conflict in Prussia*, pp. 25–26. The professed aim of the New Era cabinet was to "permeate Prussia with the spirit of German idealism" (Ziekursch 1: 17). Minister–without–portfolio Rudolf von Auerswald and his brother Alfred had been leaders of the East Prussian liberal movement from the 1840s. They had inherited the East Prussian tradition of liberal idealism from the administrator Theodor von Schön, a disciple of Kant.

24. Ellissen, p. 108.

25. Ibid.

26. Ziekursch 1: 47.

27. Ellissen, p. 113.

28. Ibid., p. 126.

29. ADB 17: 624–30; Ellissen, pp. 131–32.

30. Franz Mehring, *Die Deutsche Sozialdemokratie,* pp. 246–56; Morgan, *The German Social Democrats*; Carl Landauer, *European Socialism* 1: 105 ff.

31. Ellissen, p. 167.

32. The Swiss democrats were campaigning for constitutional reform, wider suffrage, and an extension of civil liberties. The bourgeois opposition party was led by Alfred Escher, builder of the St. Gottard tunnel. Lange was involved in the passage of a new basic law for the canton of Zurich, which incorporated the democratic program. Ellissen, pp. 184–86.

33. Lübbe, p. 96. Lübbe sees Lange as having gone beyond the bourgeois liberal theory of the state, but there was no single liberal philosophy, as has been pointed out by Theodor Schieder, "Das Verhältnis von politischer und gesellschaftlicher Verfassung und die Krise des bürgerlichen Liberalismus," *Historische Zeitschrift* 177 (1954): 58–59.

34. Lange's work reflects the influence of English social thought; see also his book on Mill: *J. S. Mills Ansichten über die sociale Frage*.

35. Ellissen, p. 128.

36. Ibid., p. 133.

37. Rolf Weber, *Kleinbürgerliche Demokraten in der deutschen Einheitsbewegung,* p. 174.

38. *Arbeiterfrage, pp. 355–57*.

39. Weber, p. 172; Eckert, *F. A. Lange,* pp. 11–15, and his *Friedrich Albert Lange und die Sozialdemokratie in Duisburg,* Duisburger Forschungen 8 (Duisburg, 1965).

40. Ellissen, p. 169.

41. Ibid., p. 163.

42. Ibid., p. 137.

43. *Arbeiterfrage,* pp. 11–13.

44. Ibid., pp. 30n, 67, 152–54, 249, 251.

45. Ibid., pp. 170–71.

46. Ibid., p. 250.

47. Lübbe, pp. 98–99.

48. *Arbeiterfrage,* pp. 284–85; Ellissen, p. 141.

49. *Arbeiterfrage,* pp. 273–74.

50. Ibid., p. 265.

51. Weber, *Kleinbürgerliche Demokraten,* p. 173.

52. Ellissen, p. 146.

53. Ibid., p. 150. Ellissen wants to portray Lange as a patriotic German.

54. Ibid., pp. 195–96.

55. Lübbe, p. 25.

56. See Guido de Ruggiero, *The History of European Liberalism*, pp. 265–71.

57. See Brentano, *Die Arbeitergilden der Gegenwart*, 2 vols. (Leipzig, 1871–72), and *Mein Leben im Kampf um die soziale Entwicklung Deutschlands* (Jena, 1931); James J. Sheehan, *The Career of Lujo Brentano* (Chicago: University of Chicago Press, 1966). Brentano, like Lange, was an admirer of British labor organizations.

58. Weber, pp. 176 ff., 200–4.

59. Bertrand Russell, introduction to *The History of Materialism*, by Lange trans. E. E. Thomas, p. vi.

60. *Geschichte des Materialismus und Kritik seiner Bedeutung*, 10th ed., p. v–vi.

61. *Geschichte des Materialismus*, 1st ed. p. viii. Hereafter cited as *Materialismus*.

62. Ibid., p. 279.

63. Ueberweg *Grundriss der Geschichte der neueren Philosophie* 4: 421.

64. *Materialismus*, p. 283.

65. Ibid., p. 286.

66. Ibid., p. 287. Lütgert, *Die Religion* 3: 241 ff, also argues that materialism was an outgrowth of Hegel's monism, and contends that "Kant was completely forgotten," p. 248.

67. *Materialismus*, p. 294; *Die Arbeiterfrage*, pp. 259–61.

68. *Materialismus*, p. 295.

69. Ibid., p. 296.

70. Ibid., p. 304.

71. Ibid., p. 305.

72. Ibid., p. 312. Lange thought that Lotze had not outdone the materialists and jeered him as "joint manufacturer of the genuine Göttinger soul-substance with the title of a speculating Struwelpeter." Quoted by Kuntz, p. 19.

73. *Arbeiterfrage*, p. 259.

74. Vorländer, *Geschichte* 2: 241.

75. Ibid.; *Materialismus*, pp. 268–69.

76. *Materialismus*, pp. 241–42.

77. Ibid., p. 269.

78. Ibid., pp. 241, 541.

79. Ibid., p. 536.

80. Ibid., p. 512.

81. Ibid., p. 274.

82. Bernstein, *Evolutionary Socialism*, p. 224. For the Lange revival of the 1890s, see Nicholas Berdayev, "Friedrich Albert Lange und die kritische Philosophie in ihren Beziehungen zum Sozialismus," *Die Neue Zeit* 18 (1899–1900): 132–40; 164–74; 196–207.

83. Marianne Weber, *Max Weber: Ein Lebensbild*, p. 77.

84. *The Great Philosophers*, 1: 329.

Chapter 5

1. Fritz Heinemann, *Neue Wege der Philosophie*, p. 63.

2. Lübbe, *Politische Philosophie*, pp. 112 ff.; Keck, "Kant and Socialism."

3. George Mosse, *Germans and Jews*, p. 3.

4. Ibid., p. 7.

5. G. A. Kelly, *Idealism, Politics and History*, pp. 146–59.

6. Mosse, pp. 7, 169–70.

7. Ibid., p. 169.

8. Ibid., pp. 171–229.

9. Henri Dussort, *L'École de Marbourg*, pp. 63–64.

10. Keck, pp. 111–28.

11. Dussort, p. 67. DBJ Supplementary volume (1917–1919), 2: 230; *Neue Deutsche Biographie*, s.v. "Frankel"; ADB, s.v. "Frankel"; *The Jewish Encyclopedia*, s.v. "Frankel, Zacharias."

12. See Cohen, "Zur Kontroverse zwischen Trendelenburg und Kuno Fischer," *Zeitschrift für Völkerpsychologie und Sprachwissenschaft* 7 (1871): 249–71. Hereafter cited as ZVS.

13. Cohen, "Die platonische Ideenlehre psychologisch entwickelt," ZVS 4 (1866): 403–64; "Methodologische Vorstellungen von Gott und Seele," ZVS 5 (1868): 396–494; 6 (1869): 113–31.

14. DBJ Supplementary volume 2: 321; Dussort, p. 58.

15. Dussort, pp. 45–47.

16. Cohen, *Platons Ideenlehre und die Mathematik*.

17. See his *Religion und Sittlichkeit* (1907); *Der Begriff der Religion* (1915); and *Die Religion der Vernunft aus den Quellen des Judentums* (1919). See also Eva Jospe, "Hermann Cohen's Judaism: A Reassessment," *Judaism* 25 (Fall, 1976): 461–73.

18. NDB 3: 313. Dimitry Gawronsky, "Ernst Cassirer: His Life and Work," in P. A. Schilpp, ed., *The Philosophy of Ernst Cassirer*, pp. 3–37.

19. *Kants Theorie der Erfahrung*, p. 1.

20. Meyer, *Abendländischen Weltanschauung* 5: 119. The advanced idealism of this position represents a later phase of Cohen's thought. See, for example, his *Logik der reinen Erkenntnis* (1902), pp. 48–50.

21. Meyer, 5: 119.

22. Heinrich Levy, *Die Hegel-Renaissance*, p. 31.

23. *Theorie der Erfahrung*, p. 87. *Logik der reinen Erkenntnis*, pp. 15–17.

24. Heinemann, *Neue Wege der Philosophie*, p. 64.

25. Dussort, p. 107.

26. See Vorländer, *Kant und Marx*, and his "Eine Sozialphilosophie auf Kantischer Grundlage," *Kant-Studien* 1 (1897): 197–217. A thorough recent study is Keck, "Kant ånd Socialism."

27. In 1890, the SPD drew more than 1.3 million votes, surpassing all but the Catholic Center. But because of malapportionment, the SPD sent only thirty-five deputies to the Reichstag. In 1912, the SPD received 4.5 million votes and, owing to the electoral alliance with the Progressives, sent 110 deputies to the Reichstag. For electoral statistics, see Koppel Pinson, *Modern Germany*, pp. 572–73.

28. Rosenberg, *Imperial Germany*, pp. 56–57. Scheidemann later had to resign his office for refusing to pay formal court to the emperor. This incident reveals how much the SPD had become reconciled to the Reich in practice but how diligently its leaders avoided any symbolic recognition of that fact by refusing to join in purely ceremonial functions.

29. *Ethik des reinen Willens*, p. 320.

30. Franz Lindheimer, *Hermann Cohen*, p. 86.

31. Ibid., p. 94.

32. *Ethik*, p. 318.

33. Ibid., p. 315.

34. Ibid., p. 319; *Logik,* pp. 310, 338.
35. *Ethik,* pp. 319–20.
36. Ibid., p. 321.
37. *Logik,* pp. 147, 172.
38. Lübbe, p. 115.
39. *Ethik,* pp. 63–64.
40. Ibid., p. 80.
41. Lübbe, p. 105.
42. See his *Ueber das Eigentümliche des deutschen Geistes* (1914).
43. Keck, pp. 364–84. The term *Ideas of 1914* was popularized by Rudolf Kjellén, *Die Ideen von 1914: Eine weltgeschichtliche Perspektive* (Leipzig, 1915). See also Klaus Schwabe, "Zur politischen Haltung der deutschen Professoren im ersten Weltkrieg," *Historische Zeitschrift* 193 (1961): 609–34; Ringer, *Decline of the Mandarins,* pp. 180–200; Iggers, *German Conception of History.*
44. Keck, pp. 383–84.
45. Lübbe, p. 105.
46. *Ethik,* pp. 34, 254–55.
47. Ibid., p. 255.
48. *Das allgemeine, gleiche und direkte Wahlrecht,* in *Schriften zur Philosophie und Zeitgeschichte* 2: 331–34.
49. Lübbe, p. 108.
50. Cohen, Introduction to *Geschichte des Materialismus,* by Lange, p. vi.
51. Ibid.; *Kants Begründung der Ethik,* pp. 272–73.
52. Lübbe, p. 110.
53. Cohen had several distinguished students. Ernst Cassirer, the most eminent product of the Marburg school, published his *Das Erkenntnisproblem in der Philosophie und Wissenschaft der neueren Zeit* in 1906, when the influence of Marburg philosophy was reaching its peak. His prewar work was almost entirely in epistemology, with the major phase of his career coming after the war, the approximate end of this study. Cassirer's position on the significant political and philosophical issues of neo-Kantianism will be considered in chapter 7. Another important pupil whose works are now seldom read was Franz Staudinger, who concentrated on ethical problems in *Das Sittengesetz. Untersuchungen über die Grundlagen der Freiheit und Sittlichkeit* (1887); *Ethik und Politik* (1899); *Die Wirtschaftlichen Grundlagen der Moral* (1906). On Staudinger, see Keck, pp. 231–35. Staudinger was also the chief neo-Kantian respondent to Nietzsche in his *Anti-Zarathustra, Sprüche der Freiheit: Wider Nietzsche und anderer Herrenmoral* (1904). Karl Vorländer was the historian and generalist of the movement. Another important Marburger was August Stadler, who wrote *Kants Teleologie*(1874); *Die Grundzüge der reinen Erkenntnistheorie in die kantische Philosophie* (1876); *Kants Theorie der Materie* (1883); *Logik* (1912); and *Die Grundbegriffe der Erkenntnistheorie* (1913). Stadler was personally recommended to Cohen by Lange.
54. Heinemann, pp. 83–85, describes Cohen's philosophy as the swan song of the middle class, the final apologia for the cultural manifest destiny of the bourgeoisie. But Cohen did not attribute Germany's cultural achievements to any particular class, nor did he assign any future ethical or cultural mission to the middle class. He defended the culture generally associated with the German academics in art, music, and science, but politically he was a democrat with strong socialistic tendencies in the field of economic policies. He did not harbor the bourgeois fear and liberal apprehension that the rise of the masses would produce mediocrity and spoil *Kultur.* Heinemann's criticism ignores

Cohen's opposition to privilege in wealth, property, and education. Cohen did uphold the state—not necessarily the historic German state of the late nineteenth century—but the future state of laws and political equality.

55. Lübbe, p. 113.

56. Levy, *Die Hegel-Renaissance*, p. 33.

57. Ibid., pp. 33-37.

58. "Bernhard C. L. Natorp," *Der Grosse Brockhaus*, 13: 1932; *Die Religion in Geschichte und Gegenwart. Handwörterbuch für Theologie und Religionswissenschaft*, 3d ed., 4: 1322; F. Trost, "Paul Natorp," *Lebensbilder aus Kurhessen und Waldeck*, 6: 233-249.

59. Ernst Cassirer, "Paul Natorp," *Kant-Studien*, 30 (1925): 276-77.

60. Heinemann, p. 66.

61. Vorländer, *Geschichte* 2: 429.

62. H. Leisegang, *Deutsche Philosophie im XX. Jahrhundert*, p. 39.

63. Levy, p. 37.

64. Natorp, *Philosophie, Ihr Problem, und Ihre Probleme*, p. 91.

65. Ibid., p. 96; and his "Individualität und Gemeinschaft," *Philosophie und Pädagogik*, pp. 157-59.

66. *Philosophie, Ihr Problem*, pp.76-77.

67. Cassirer, "Paul Natorp," p. 291; H. Levy, "Paul Natorps praktische Philosophie," *Kant-Studien* 31 (1926): 311-30. These lectures were published as *Vorlesungen über praktische Philosophie* (1925).

68. Cassirer, "Paul Natorp," p. 291.

69. Vorländer, *Geschichte* 2: 430.

70. *Sozialpädagogik: Theorie der Willenserziehung auf der Grundlage der Gemeinschaft*, p. 68.

71. Ibid., p. 69.

72. Ibid., p. 71; and his *Religion innerhalb der Grenzen der Humanität*, p. 62.

73. *Sozialpädagogik*, pp. 76-77.

74. Ibid., pp. 79-80; and his *Philosophie und Pädagogik*, pp. 119 ff.

75. Leisegang, *Deutsche Philosophie*, p. 42.

76. Lübbe, *Politische Philosophie*, pp. 188-89.

77. Cassirer, "Paul Natorp," p. 279.

78. This article appeared in the *Philosophische Monatshefte* 23 (1887): pp. 257 ff. On Natorp's influence, see Cassirer, "Paul Natorp," pp. 282-83.

79. Cassirer, "Paul Natorp," p. 285; Passmore, *Hundred Years of Philosophy*, p. 188; Husserl, *Logische Untersuchungen*, 4th ed., 2 vols. (Halle, 1928), 1: 359, 379-80. Werner Brock, *An Introduction to German Philosophy*, pp. 15-16; M. Farber, *The Foundations of Phenomenology: Edmund Husserl's Quest for a Rigorous Philosophy* (Cambridge, Mass.: Harvard University Press, 1943), pp. 5-7, 201-02.

80. On Stammler's reputation abroad, see Isaac Husik's introduction to Stammler, *The Theory of Justice*, and the appendices by François Geney and J. C. H. Wu, which list international writings on Stammler to that date.

81. G. Radbruch, *Rechtsphilosophie*, 3d ed. (1932), p. 24, quoted in C.J. Friedrich, *The Philosophy of Law in Historical Perspective*, p. 160.

82. *Wer ist Wer?* (1909) s.v. "Stammler, Rudolf"; *Meyers Grosses Konversationslexicon*, s.v. "Stammler, Rudolf."

83. *Die Gerechtigkeit in der Geschichte*, in *Rechtsphilosophische Abhandlungen und Vorträge*, 2: 48-49.

84. *Wirtschaft und Recht nach der materialistischen Geschichtsauffassung*, pp. 331-32.

85. Friedrich, *Philosophy of Law*, p. 159.

86. Ibid., pp. 158–59.

87. *Wirtschaft und Recht.*, pp. 551–52; *Theory of Justice*, pp. 152–53; Isaac Breuer, "Der Rechtsbegriff auf Grundlage der Stammlerschen Sozialphilosophie," *Kant-Studien*, nos. 27, 25–29 (1912): 60–61.

88. *Theory of Justice*, p. 153; *Die Lehre von dem richtigen Rechte*, pp. 171–73.

89. *Theory of Justice*, p. 153.

90. *Die Lehre von dem richtigen Recht*, pp. 196–97.

91. *Die materialistische Geschichtsauffassung*, pp. 23, 56–57; *Wirtschaft und Recht*, pp. 23–24.

92. "R. Stammlers 'Ueberwindung' der materialistischen Geschichtsauffassung," *Archiv für Sozialwissenschaft und Sozialpolitik* 24 (1907): 94–120. Stammler made his rebuttal in the third edition of *Wirtschaft und Recht* (1914), pp. 670–86. Weber replied in "Nachtrag zu dem Aufsatz über R. Stammlers 'Ueberwindung' der materialistischen Geschichtsauffassung", in *Gesammelte Aufsätze zur Wissenschaftslehre*, pp. 556–79.

93. Lübbe, p. 187.

94. Friedrich, *Philosophy of Law*, p. 160.

95. *Theory of Justice*, p. 76.

96. Ibid., p. 87.

97. Ibid., p. 90.

98. Ibid., p. 92.

99. Rupert Emerson, *State and Sovereignty in Modern Germany*, pp. 162–63.

100. Erich Kaufmann, *Kritik der neukantischen Rechtsphilosophie*, p. 11.

101. Ibid., pp. 88–89.

102. Emerson, *State and Sovereignty*, p. 161.

103. Ibid., pp. 164–65.

104. *Wirtschaft und Recht*, p. 554.

105. *Der Krieg und das Recht*, in *Vorträge* 2: 42.

106. *Die Gerechtigkeit in der Geschichte*, p. 47.

107. Ibid., p. 54.

108. Lübbe, p. 121.

109. Stammler included in his *Wirtschaft und Recht*, pp. 621–33, a bibliography of publications dealing with neo-Kantianism, revisionism, and the controversy with the orthodox Marxists.

Chapter 6

1. Quoted in his *Präludien: Aufsätze und Reden zur Einleitung in die Philosophie*, p. iv. On Kantianism in the universities, see Ringer, *Decline of the Mandarins*, p. 91.

2. *Kant's Weltanschauung*, p. 2.

3. Ibid., p. vii.

4. Ibid. The Marburg and Baden schools were both transcendental in their interpretation of Kant's apriorism. Windelband, for example, was just as opposed to psychologism as Cohen: "*A priori* is, with Kant, not psychological, but a purely epistemological mark; it means not a chronological priority to experience, but a *universality and necessity of validity in principles of reason which really transcends all experience and is not capable of being proved by any experience*. . . . No one who does not make this clear to himself has any hope of understanding Kant," *History of Philosophy* 2: 534; author's italics.

5. Ringer, pp. 120–21, cites Rickert's *Ueber idealistische Politik als Wissenschaft*, special issue of *Die Akademie* (Erlangen, n.d.).

6. Ringer, p. 121.

7. Ralf Dahrendorf, *Society and Democracy in Germany*, p. 29, proposes these liberal criteria, and the lack thereof in Germany.

8. Although Dahrendorf tries to improve on the conventional and imprecise notion of "Western liberalism" as the model for measuring Germany, his "sociological theory of democracy" (ibid.) contains criteria of a patently Anglo-American character. He has therefore not entirely avoided the fallacy of applying exogenous standards to Germany.

9. On some of the epistemological issues between the two schools, see Paul Natorp, "Kant und die Marburger Schule," *Kant-Studien* 17 (1912): 193–222.

10. H. Stuart Hughes, *Consciousness and Society*, p. 191.

11. Ringer, p. 121.

12. Iggers, *German Conception of History*, p. 151.

13. DBJ, supplementary vol. 1 (1914–15): 182–85.

14. *Die Geschichte der neureren Philosophie in ihrem Zusammenhange mit der allgemeinen Kultur und den besonderen Wissenschaften;* first published in 1878.

15. *Geschichte der alten Philosophie*, 2d ed. (1894); *Geschichte der abendländischen Philosophie im Altertum*, 4th ed. (1923).

16. Pp. 7–8.

17. For example, his *Einleitung in die Philosophie*, p. 11.

18. *Präludien*, p. vi.

19. Ibid., pp. 262 ff.

20. Ibid., pp. 251–57.

21. Maurice Picard, *Values, Immediate and Contributory, and Their Interrelation*, p. 146.

22. *Präludien*, p. 263.

23. Ibid., p. 278. "Freedom is the consciousness of norms as determining powers over the activity of thought and the decisions of will."

24. Meyer, *Abendländischen Weltanschauung* 5: 128–29.

25. *Präludien*, p. 279.

26. In *Präludien*, 3d ed., 2 vols. (1907), 1: 355–80. Hereafter cited as *Präludien* (1907).

27. See Alfred Stern, *The Philosophy of History and the Problem of Values*, p. 118; Iggers, pp. 147–52; Ringer, pp. 324–26.

28. In *Gesammelte Schriften*, vol. 1.

29. Hajo Holborn, "Dilthey and the Critique of Historical Reason," *Journal of the History of Ideas* 11 (1950): 98–104.

30. R. G. Collingwood, *The Idea of History*, p. 108. See also Iggers, pp. 134–44, who says that Dilthey, unlike the neo-Kantians with whom he had much in common, doubted the possibility of a rational approach to cultural studies (p. 134); and Ringer, pp. 317–23. A critical view of Dilthey's influence on the quest for values and on the allegedly fatal value-relativism of the Weimar period is found in Wolfram Bauer, *Wertrelativismus und Wertbestimmheit im Kampf um die Weimarer Demokratie*, pp. 37–39.

31. "Dilthey and the Critique of Historical Reason," p. 108.

32. *Präludien* (1907), 1: 361–63.

33. Ibid., p. 364.

34. Holborn, "Dilthey and the Critique of Historical Reason," p. 94. The description of Rickert is in Hermann Glockner, *Heidelberger Bilderbuch, Erinnerungen von Hermann Glockner*, pp. 2–17.

35. See A. Faust, "Heinrich Rickert," *Deutsche Vierteljahrsschrift für Literaturwissenschaft und Geistesgeschichte* 11 (1933): 329–40, and his "Heinrich Rickert Nachruf," *Kant-Studien* 41 (1936): 207–20.

36. On the rumored Stosch-Rickert ministry, see Frederick B. M. Hollyday, "Bismarck and the Legend of the Gladstone Ministry," in *Power, Public Opinion and Diplomacy,* ed. L.P. Wallace, W. C. Askew, pp. 92–109.

37. Ibid., pp. 108–9.

38. Faust, "Heinrich Rickert," pp. 329–32.

39. Marianne Weber, *Max Weber,* pp. 166, 235.

40. Hollyday, pp. 106–7.

41. On Hugenburg, see Alan Bullock, *Hitler: A Study in Tyranny* new rev. ed. (New York: Harper Torchbooks, 1962), pp. 147–50, 246–47.

42. Faust, "Heinrich Rickert Nachruf," p. 216.

43. Faust, "Heinrich Rickert," p. 215. On Rickert's psychological problem, see Friedrich Meinecke, *Strassburg, Freiburg, Berlin, 1901–1919,* pp. 93–94.

44. The Rickert *Nachlass,* consisting mainly of lecture notes, is in the manuscript section of the Heidelberg Universitätsbibliothek under Heid. H. S. 2740. The gradual alteration of his notes from the early 1900s to the 1930s reveals a close interest in not only concurrent developments in philosophy but social and cultural matters as well. They deal mainly with his effort to avoid the extremes of intellectualism, on one hand, and vitalistic *Lebensphilosophie,* on the other. In any case, his classroom lectures suggest a mind of wider interests than his formal publications on historical logic would indicate. He liked to assert the primacy of theoretical reason in philosophy, but not for the totality of life (which would be intellectualism), and to reiterate his belief that only through scientific knowledge can anything be accomplished. See, for example, Heid. H. S. 2740/20.

45. *Die Philosophie des Lebens* (1921); *Kant als Philosoph der modernen Kultur* (1924); *Die Heidelberger Tradition in der deutschen Philosophie* (1931); *Goethes Faust* (1937). In his postwar lectures Rickert gave a spirited defense of Kant against charges of "coldness" made by Friedrich Paulsen and others, and stressed the continuity in Kant's work from the precritical through the critical period. Kant was not only a great philosopher but a great man, a "hero in his own way." He also defended Kant's act of obeisance to the king of Prussia. See Heid. H. S. 2740/31. Referring to the year of the Kant Jubilee (1924), he suggested that the complaint made by Furtwängler during the Beethovenfest of 1927—that the youth of today were far from the world of Beethoven—applied equally to their remoteness from Kant. "They wanted to make a film about Kant . . . but who knows anything about Kant today?" Heid. H. S. 2740/13. He wrote this and included it in his lecture in 1933! In the same series of lectures he pointed out that although the meaning of *national socialism* in Fichte must be seen as something different from the present phenomenon, Fichte was nonetheless its most important forerunner and thus deserves consideration. There is no hint of disapproval in his notes. Heid. H. S. 2740/44. Hans Kohn, *The Mind of Germany* (New York: Charles Scribner's Sons, 1960), p. 19, says that Rickert was not a National Socialist although he had said in the mid-1930s that ethical scruples would have to yield to the demands of the day.

46. Jaspers, *The Great Philosophers* 1: 277.

47. Aliotta, *The Idealistic Reaction against Science,* p. 204.

48. *Der Gegenstand,* p. 64; my emphasis.

49. Ibid., pp. 61–67.

50. Windelband, *Lehrbuch der Geschichte der Philosophie,* pp. 173–74, quoted by Ralph Barton Perry, *General Theory of Value* (New York: Longmans, Green and Company, 1926), p. 100.

51. *Der Gegenstand,* p. 66.

52. Teggart, *Theory and Process of History,* p. 66.

53. Rickert, "Urteil und Urteilen," *Logos* 3 (1912): 230–51.
54. Aliotta, p. 205.
55. *Der Gegenstand*, p. vi.
56. See Windelband's essay, "Was ist Philosophie?" *Präludien*, pp. 1–58.
57. Aliotta, p. 206.
58. *Die Grenzen der naturwissenschaftlichen Begriffsbildung* (1902), p. 252.
59. Ibid., pp. 250–51.
60. Ibid., p. iv.
61. "Zur Theorie der naturwissenschaftlichen Begriffsbildung," *Vierteljahrsschrift für wissenschaftlichen Philosophie* 18 (1894): 277–319.
62. Ibid., pp. 278–80.
63. Rickert, *Kulturwissenschaft und Naturwissenschaft* (1921), p. 35.
64. "Zur Theorie," p. 309.
65. *Idea of History*, p. 169.
66. *Der Historismus und seine Problem, Gesammelte Schriften*, 3: 120.
67. *Science and History: A Critique of Positivist Epistemology*, trans. George Reisman (Princeton: D. Van Nostrand, 1962), p. 1. Unfortunately this is Rickert's only major work yet translated into English.
68. For this criticism see Ernst Nagel, "The Logic of Historical Analysis," *The Scientific Monthly* 74 (1952): 162–69, reprinted in Hans Meyerhoff, *The Philosophy of History in Our Time* (New York: Doubleday Anchor, 1959), pp. 203–16. Rickert made clear that his "generalizing-individualizing" categories were extreme cases used to make clear his formal distinction between the two methods. See his *Science and History*, p. 5.
69. *Science and History*, p. 5.
70. Ibid., p. 19.
71. Ibid.; see also Rickert, "Geschichtsphilosophie," in W. Windelband, ed., *Die Philosophie im Beginn des zwanzigsten Jahrhunderts*, pp. 353–55.
72. *Science and History*, pp. 18–19.
73. Ibid., p. 19.
74. Ibid., p. 22. A convenient summary of Rickert's value theory is in his "Vom System der Werte," *Logos* 4 (1913): 295–327, in which he argues for an "open system" of values.
75. *Science and History*, p. 22.
76. Ibid., p. 25.
77. *Kulturwissenschaft und Naturwissenschaft*, pp. 157–58.
78. "Geschichtsphilosophie," p. 366.
79. Troeltsch, "Ueber den Begriff einer historischen Dialectik. Windelband, Rickert und Hegel," *Historische Zeitschrift* 109 (1919): 384.
80. Maurice Mandelbaum, *The Problem of Historical Knowledge*, pp. 89–91. Mandelbaum sees Rickert as a normative, anti-historicist, but others have argued that Rickert's dualism, and that of neo-Kantianism in general, lead to value relativism, hence historicism, by separating universal values from historical realities. This inspires the belief that "it is not possible to ground value judgments in a universally accepted doctrine of human nature," George Lichtheim, *The Concept of Ideology and Other Essays* (New York: Vintage Books, 1967), p. 32. He continues, "With Dilthey and Weber, the subjectivism already inherent in the Neo-Kantian interpretation of the categories as empty forms imposed upon an unknown and unknowable material leads away from the notion of truth as a universal." A similar viewpoint is found in the following: Arnold Brecht, *Political Theory*, pp. 215–20; Iggers, *German Conception of History*, pp. 152–59; Ringer, *Decline of the Mandarins*, pp. 334–36; W. Bauer, *Wertrelativismus*, pp. 26–28, who relies greatly on Brecht but extends

his critique to the legal philosophers of Weimar. J. H. Hallowell, *The Decline of Liberalism as an Ideology*, p. 69, sees positivism as the culprit in the separation of Ought from Is because of its rejection of everything beyond observable phenomena. But Kant encouraged this development with his own restriction of cognitive knowledge to the phenomenal world (p. 67). Leonard Krieger, Leo Strauss, and others who blame Kantian dualism for the death of natural law, follow the same line of argument. Surely in Rickert's case, the aim was the very opposite, as Iggers acknowledges (p. 158). It is important in Rickert's work to recognize the difference between expressed intentions and possible implications, otherwise, the real aim of his theory will be misunderstood. On Iggers' treatment of neo-Kantianism see Thomas E. Willey, "Liberal Historians and the German Professoriat: A Consideration of Some Recent Books on German Thought," *Central European History* 9 (June, 1976): 185–97.

81. *Idea of History*, pp. 165–81.

82. Ibid., p. 169.

83. Ibid.

84. Stern, pp. 121–37.

85. Ibid., p. 122.

86. *Kulturwissenschaft und Naturwissenschaft* (1912), p. 93; Stern, pp. 122–23.

87. Stern, pp. 133–34.

88. *Die Probleme der Geschichtsphilosophie*, p. 119.

89. Stern, p. 134.

90. Stern acknowledges that Rickert's values are postulates but he adds, "A postulate guarantees neither the reality nor the validity of the thing or idea postulated" (p. 135). He is right insofar as a postulate cannot establish *reality* but merely asserts an alleged moral necessity. The first part of his comment goes awry because the very purpose of a Kantian postulate is to establish the truth of values lying beyond the sensible world of things.

91. Quoted by Friedrich Engel-Janosi, *The Growth of German Historicism* (Baltimore: Johns Hopkins University Press, 1944), p. 6.

Chapter 7

1. "Kantgesellschaft. Mitgliederverzeichnis für das Jahr 1911," *Kant-Studien* 17 (1912): 173–87. Two decades earlier a German writer surveyed the philosophical scene and confessed that the watchword was still "back to Kant," but the question was—which Kant? The slogan, originally the theme of a common response to scientism and shallow materialism, had by then become an "apple of discord." Friedrich Jodl, "German Philosophy in the XIX Century," *The Monist* 1 (1890–91): 264–65. By the end of the century neo-Kantianism had become a catchall for anyone taking any aspect of Kant for his point of departure, regardless of his eventual destination. I have, therefore, concentrated on the two major branches, Marburg and Baden, both of which went well beyond Kant but still remained closer to the original Kantian projects in epistemology and moral philosophy, respectively.

2. Hans Vaihinger, "Zur Einführung," *Kant-Studien* 1 (1897): 8.

3. Hannah Arendt, *Eichmann in Jerusalem: A Report on the Banality of Evil* (New York: Viking Press, 1963), pp. 135–37.

4. *Consciousness and Society*, p. 309.

5. Meinecke, *Strassburg, Freiburg, Berlin*, p. 159.

6. *Social Teachings of the Christian Churches*, 1: 24.

7. Ibid., p. 25.

8. *Historismus,* pp. 119–22, 150–58, 207, 227–39, 311, 418, 559–65, 569, 577, 628, 661, 680. The many references to Rickert suggest that one of Troeltsch's main aims here was to examine Rickert's answer to the problem of *Historismus.*

9. "Ernst Troeltsch und das Problem des Historismus," *Schaffender Spiegel,* p. 214.

10. *Historismus,* p. 156.

11. Ibid., p. 150.

12. Ibid., p. 154.

13. Ibid., p. 156.

14. "Das stoisch-christliche Naturrecht und das moderne profane Naturrecht," *Historische Zeitschrift* 106 (1911): 264–81.

15. *Schaffender Spiegel,* p. 216.

16. *Deutscher Geist und Westeuropa,* pp. 31–58.

17. Ibid., p. 32.

18. Ibid., pp. 48–49.

19. Ibid., pp. 51–52. See also Robert Pois, *Friedrich Meinecke and German Politics in the Twentieth Century,* pp. 8, 9, 20; Iggers, *German Conception of History,* pp. 174–95; and Ringer, *Decline of the Mandarins,* pp. 341–49.

20. The idea of a Germanic middle Europe is traced in Henry Cord Meyer, *Mitteleuropa in German Thought and Action, 1815–1945* (The Hague: Nijhoff, 1955).

21. See Theodor Heuss, *Friedrich Naumann, der Mann, das Werk, die Zeit,* 2d ed. (Stuttgart: R. Wunderlich, 1949) and W.O. Shanahan, "Friedrich Naumann: A Mirror of Wilhelmian Germany," *Review of Politics* 13 (1951): 267–301.

22. *Deutscher Geist und Westeuropa,* pp. 50–51.

23. "The Ideas of Natural Law and Humanity in World Politics," in Gierke, *Natural Law,* pp. 201.

24. Ibid., p. 217.

25. Ibid., p. 218.

26. *Historismus,* p. 452.

27. Ibid., p. 212; and Meinecke, *Schaffender Spiegel,* p. 225.

28. *Schaffender Spiegel,* p. 226.

29. Marianne Weber, *Max Weber,* p. 235.

30. Ibid., p. 296. "Rickert habe ich aus. Er ist *sehr* gut, zum grossen Teil finde ich darin das, was ich selbst, wenn auch in logisch nicht bearbeiteter, Form gedacht habe. Gegen die Terminologie habe ich Bedenken."

31. Ibid., p. 353; "Roscher und Knies und die logischen Probleme der historischen Nationalökonomie," in *Gesammelte Aufsätze zur Wissenschaftslehre,* pp. 1–146.

32. "Roscher und Knies," pp. 3–4n2.

33. Ibid., p. 7n1.

34. Ibid., p. 27n1.

35. "Objectivity in Social Science and Social Policy," in his *Max Weber on the Methodology of the Social Sciences,* pp. 50–113.

36. Ibid., p. vii: "When Weber wrote Objectivity in Social Science and Social Policy (1904) he was still under the influence of Rickert."

37. Ibid., p. 50.

38. Ibid., p. 79.

39. "The Meaning of 'Ethical Neutrality' in Sociology and Economics," ibid., pp. 1–49.

40. "Objectivity in Social Science," p. 98.

41. Ibid., p. 101.

42. "Critical Studies in the Logic of the Cultural Sciences," ibid., p. 135n18.

43. "Ethical Neutrality," ibid., pp. 1–49.
44. Ibid., p. 1.
45. Ibid., p. 11.
46. Ibid., pp. 21–22.
47. Ibid., p. 47.
48. *Ueber das Eigentümliche des deutschen Geistes*, pp. 34–35.
49. Mommsen, *Max Weber und die deutsche Politik 1890–1920*, pp. 114, 121. Ringer, *Decline of the Mandarins*, pp. 200–13, counts Weber along with Naumann and others as part of the "politics of accomodation," that is, democracy and social reform for the purpose of imperial power.
50. Mommsen, *Max Weber*, p. 126.
51. Ibid., p. 122, from a letter to Michels.
52. Quoted by Mommsen, ibid., p. 137.
53. Simon, *Germany: A Brief History* (New York: Random House, 1966), p. 335.
54. See Bruce B. Frye, "A Letter from Max Weber," *Journal of Modern History* 39 (1967): 119.
55. "Politics as a Vocation," in H. Gerth, C. W. Mills, *From Max Weber: Essays in Sociology*, pp. 128–29.
56. Ibid., pp. 125–26.
57. Friedrich Sell, *Die Tragödie*, p. 310. See also Carlo Antoni, *From History to Sociology*, pp. 119–84.
58. 6th ed. (1922), p. 11.
59. *Die Deutsche Freiheit*, p. 22.
60. "Kausalitäten und Werte in der Geschichte," *Staat und Persönlichkeit*, p. 50.
61. *Die Deutsche Freiheit*, p. 25.
62. *Weltbürgertum*, pp. 9–10.
63. *Die Deutsche Freiheit*, p. 24.
64. Ibid., pp. 33–34, and *Strassburg, Freiburg, Berlin*, p. 123.
65. *Die Deutsche Freiheit*, pp. 34–35. Throughout his study, Pois, *Friedrich Meinecke and German Politics* stresses Meinecke's attachment to Naumann's prewar democratic imperialism as well as his dislike of party politics and Western parliamentary methods. Pois believes that Meinecke's conservatism made it impossible for him to recognize the true nature of National Socialism and the politicization of mass culture. See especially, pp. 34–84.
66. *Machiavellism: The Doctrine of Raison d'Etat and Its Place in Modern History*.
67. *Das Leben des Generalfeldmarschalls von Boyen*.
68. *The German Catastrophe*, pp. 118–21. Pois, p. 130, believes that Meinecke's return to aesthetic cosmopolitanism was archaic and perhaps not even genuine. It reflected his fundamental failure to recognize that Nazi ideology was an outgrowth of German *Kultur*. His polarizing of culture and power kept him from seeing the causal connections between the two. Pois differs sharply from previous commentators who have accepted Meinecke's postwar return to European values as authentic, for example, Richard Sterling, *Ethics in a World of Power*, Walther Hofer, *Geschichtsschreibung und Weltanschauung*, H. Stuart Hughes, *Consciousness and Society*. Pois also refuses to follow previous scholarship which distinguishes Meinecke's political views from the radical neo-conservatives of Weimar. He believes that in Meinecke's interwar attitude, we can see the "spectral traces" of Germany's radical right (p. 38). He thereby parts company with such historians as Von Klemperer and Sontheimer who portray Meinecke as an enemy of neo-conservatism and Nazism and as a good republican. See Klemens von Klemperer, *Germany's New Conserva-*

tism, pp. 92–96; Kurt Sontheimer, *Antidemokratisches Denken in der Weimarer Republic,* pp. 30, 39, 143, 145, 169, 213, 374, 393.

69. *The German Catastrophe,* pp. 111–12. Another essay indicative of Meinecke's postwar conversion to a European viewpoint is his "Ranke und Burckhardt," in *Aphorismen und Skizzen zur Geschichte,* 2d ed. (n.d.): 143–80.

70. Ibid., p. 115.

71. *Weltbürgertum,* pp. 10–11.

72. Ibid., p. 29.

73. Ibid., p. 20n2.

74. *Schaffender Spiegel,* p. 213.

75. *Strassburg, Freiburg, Berlin,* pp. 93–94.

76. "Kausalitäten und Werte in der Geschichte," p. 35n1, which has been translated by J. H. Franklin, in Fritz Stern, ed., *The Varieties of History,* pp. 267–88.

77. "Kausalitäten und Werte," p. 34.

78. Ibid.

79. Ibid.

80. Ibid., p. 35n1.

81. Meinecke, *Werke,* 3: 2.

82. On Meinecke's analysis of Rickert's value theory, see Hofer, *Geschichtsschreibung und Weltanschauung,* pp. 232–34, 287–89.

83. Sterling, *Ethics in a World of Power,* p. 5. See also Iggers, *German Conception of History,* pp. 174–228, on Troeltsch and Meinecke; Ringer, *Decline of the Mandarins,* 130–33, on Meinecke's politics.

84. For example, Meinecke, "Nationalismus und Nationale Idee," *Werke* 2: 83–95.

85. *Myth of the State* (1946).

86. *Freiheit und Form* p. xiii.

87. Ibid., p. x.

88. Simmel, *Die Problem der Geschichtsphilosophie. Eine erkenntnistheoretische Studie* (Leipzig, 1892). Here Simmel was very close to Rickert, but he gradually moved toward a metaphysics of life akin to the *Lebensphilosophie* Rickert criticized after the war. Some of his correspondence with Rickert has been published in Kurt Gassen, Michael Landmann, *Buch des Denkes an Georg Simmel: Briefe, Erinnerungen, Bibliographie* (Berlin: Duncker & Humblot, 1958). Simmel has not been included in this study as a neo-Kantian despite his proximity to Rickert and influence on Weber. He was a brilliant gadfly, whose interests extended from historical logic to the somewhat exotic topics of "shame" and "coquetry," rather than a systematic philosopher. See Rudolph H. Weingartner, *Experience and Culture. The Philosophy of Georg Simmel* (Middletown, Conn.: Wesleyan University Press, 1960); and a publication characteristic of his departure from neo-Kantian epistemological concerns *Lebensanschauung, Vier Metaphysische Kapitel* (Munich, Leipzig: Duncker & Humblot, 1922). In the first essay he articulates a view of the connection between past, present, and the expression of Life somewhere between Dilthey and Collingwood. His search for unity and transcendance turned him toward metaphysics, as explained by Willy Moog, *Die deutsche Philosophie des zwangzigstens Jahrhunderts,* pp. 77–89.

89. Gawronsky, "Ernst Cassirer," in P. Schilpp, ed., *The Philosophy of Ernst Cassirer,* p. 6.

90. Ibid., p. 17.

91. Ibid., p. 25.

92. *Die Philosophie der symbolischen Formen* (1923). In his *Substance and Function* (1910), Cassirer's task had been to examine the validity of Kantian precepts in relation to modern science, and to show that the "scientists themselves had come to recognize the func-

tional and symbolic role of theory," as opposed to the realistic and substantialistic conceptualizations of the past. He saw this trend as a vindication of neo-Kantian critical epistemology. Seymour W. Itzkoff, *Ernst Cassirer,* p. 65. "The final distillation arrived at by men such as Duhem, Hertz, and Poincaré was consistent with the so-called critical teachings of Kant." p. 67. Peter Gay, "The Social History of Ideas. Ernst Cassirer and After," in Kurt H. Wolff, Barrington Moore, Jr., *The Critical Spirit. Essays in Honor of Herbert Marcuse* (Boston: Beacon Press, 1967), explores the importance of Cassirer's substance-function distinction for the understanding of intellectual history, pp. 106–21.

93. Hajo Holborn, "Ernst Cassirer," in Schilpp, *Philosophy of Ernst Cassirer,* p. 44.

94. Heinrich Levy, *Die Hegel-Renaissance,* p. 43, and Fritz Kaufmann, "Cassirer, Neo-Kantianism and Phenomenology," in Schilpp, *Philosophy of Ernst Cassirer,* maintain that Cassirer was close to absolute idealism in making symbolic forms the manifestations of spirit. But for Cassirer, these forms more closely resemble Kantian categories of experience than expressions of absolute spirit.

95. *Essay on Man,* p. 186.

96. *European Socialism* 1: 250.

97. *The Dilemma of Democratic Socialism,* p. 142. George Lichtheim takes the neo-Kantian aspect of the revisionist debate more seriously than Gay: "The ideological cleavage helped to cement the political alignments . . . .Thus the expulsion of K. Eisner and his colleagues from . . . [Vorwärts] in 1905 was as much connected with Eisner's attachment to Kantian ethics as with his lack of enthusiasm for the idea of political strikes on the Russian model," *Marxism. A Historical and Critical Study,* pp. 294–95. On the "democratic" liberals of the 1890s and after, and their receptivity to the idea of cooperating with social democracy, see Beverly Heckart, *From Bassermann to Bebel. The Grand Bloc's Quest for Reform in the Kaiserreich, 1900–1914* (New Haven, London: Yale University Press, 1974); Konstanze Wegner, *Theodor Barth und die Freisinnige Vereinigung,* Tübinger Studien zur Geschichte und Politik (Tübingen: J. C. B. Mohr Paul Siebeck, 1968); Thomas E. Willey, "The 'Back to Kant Movement' and German Politics," *Indiana Academy of the Social Sciences, Proceedings* 2 (1967): 131–43; Peter Gilg, *Die Erneuerung des demokratischen Denkens im wilhelminischen Deutschland: Eine ideengeschichtliche Studie zur Wende vom 19. zum 20. Jahrhundert* (Wiesbaden: F. Steiner, 1963). On the question of working-class integration into national life, see Gunther Roth, *The Social Democrats in Imperial Germany: A Study in Working-Class Isolation and National Integration* (Totowa, N.J.: Bedminster Press, 1963). For a Marxian critique of both the bourgeois idealists and "vulgar Marxists" of the Second International, see Karl Korsch, *Marxisme et Philosophie,* trans. Claude Orsoni (Paris: Les Éditions de Minuit, 1964).

98. W. Kinkel, "Karl Vorländer zum Gedächtnis," *Kant-Studien* 34 (1929): 1–6; Keck, "Kant and Socialism," pp. 217–90, on Vorländer's relations with neo-Kantianism, revisionism, and German socialism.

99. *Immanuel Kant: Der Mann und das Werk* 2: 374; quoted in Kinkel, "Karl Vorländer," p. 3.

100. "Das realistische und ideologische Moment in Sozialismus," *Die Neue Zeit* 16 (1898): 264. Vorländer describes Bernstein's discovery of Kant in *Kant und Marx,* pp. 180–81.

101. Vorländer, *Kant und Marx,* p. 179. Bernstein, "Zur Würdigung F. A. Langes," *Die Neue Zeit* 10 (1892): 68–78, 101–9, 132–41. See also Keck, pp. 259–60.

102. "Das realistische und ideologische Moment," p. 225.

103. Vorländer, *Kant und Marx,* pp. 158–60; on Schmidt and Woltmann, Keck, pp. 260–65.

104. Gay, *Dilemma of Democratic Socialism*, p. 144.

105. "Das realistische und ideologische Moment," p. 264.

106. Gay, *Dilemma*, p. 146; Bernstein, *Evolutionary Socialism*, p. 200.

107. Quoted by Gay, *Dilemma*, p. 150.

108. Ibid., p. 147.

109. In *Die Neue Zeit* 15 (1897): 1–3.

110. Baron, *Plekhanov*, p. 167.

111. Ibid., pp. 330–31.

112. Ibid., 167.

113. "Kurt Eisner," DBJ, Supplemental volume (1918–1920), pp. 368–71. On Eisner's background and later part in the Bavarian uprising, see Alan Mitchell, *Revolution in Bavaria, 1918–1919*.

114. Mitchell, *Revolution in Bavaria*, p. 41.

115. Ibid., p. 53. Carl Schorske, *German Social Democracy, 1905–1917*, p. 70, calls Eisner a revisionist. Vorländer, *Kant und Marx*, p. 187, places him to the left of the revisionists. His lack of faith in the final socialist victory through gradual reform, his belief that Marxism should be supplemented rather than replaced by Kantian idealism, and his emergence as a revolutionary leader seem to indicate that Mitchell and Vorländer correctly question the revisionist label.

116. Mitchell, *Revolution in Bavaria*, p. 52–53.

117. Quoted by Vorländer, *Kant und Marx*, p. 187. Eisner's principal writings are *Schuld und Sühne* (1919), *Treibende Kräfte* (1915), *Unterdrücktes aus dem Weltkrieg* (1919), *Der Zukunftstaat der Junker* (1904). Many of his essays and newspaper articles were published in his *Gesammelte Schriften*.

118. Vorländer, *Kant und Marx*, p. 187.

119. Ibid., p. 123.

120. Eisner's articles on this subject appeared in *Vorwärts* September 2 to 13, 1905, under the title "Debatten über Wenn und Aber." Kautsky replied with "Die Fortsetzung einer unmöglichen Diskussion," "Noch einmal die unmögliche Diskussion," and "Der mögliche Abschluss einer unmöglicher Diskussion," in *Die Neue Zeit* 23 (1905), nos. 48–51.

121. Vorländer, *Kant und Marx*, p. 220.

122. Ibid., p. 221.

123. *Die Neue Zeit* 18 (1899): 35.

124. Ibid., p. 2.

125. Ibid., p. 4.

Conclusion

1. In Patrick Gardiner, ed., *Theories of History*, trans. W. Hastie (Glencoe, Ill.: Free Press, 1949), p. 25.

2. "Rechtslehre," *Metaphysik der Sitten*, in *Immanuel Kants Werke* 7:120.

3. Marianne Weber, *Max Weber*, p. 611.

4. Holborn, "Ernst Cassirer," p. 41.

5. Quoted by Antoni, *History to Sociology*, p. 112.

6. Jaspers, *The Great Philosophers* 1: 379.

7. Bendix, *Max Weber, An Intellectual Portrait*, p. 9.

8. "What Is Enlightenment?" in *Kant's Critique of Practical Reason and Other Writings in Moral Philosophy*, p. 286.

Bibliography

Unpublished Papers

All listed unpublished material is in the Heidelberg University Library manuscript section:

Fischer, Kuno. Papiere. Heid. MS. 2600–2606.
Liebmann, Otto. Briefe an Kuno Fischer. Heid. MS. 395,16.
Rickert, Heinrich. Papiere. Heid. MS. 2740–2740/173.
Windelband, Wilhelm. Papiere. Heid. MS. 1670–1673.

Primary Sources

Cassirer, Ernst. *Das Erkenntnisproblem in der Philosophie und Wissenschaft der neueren Zeit.* 2 vols. Berlin: B. Cassirer, 1906.
———. *Essay on Man: An Introduction to a Philosophy of Human Culture.* New Haven: Yale University Press, 1944.
———. *Freiheit und Form.* Berlin: B. Cassirer, 1916.
———. "Hermann Cohen und die Erneuerung der Kantischen Philosophie." *Kant-Studien* 17 (1912): 252–73.
———. *Individuum und Kosmos in der Philosophie der Renaissance.* Leipzig: B. G. Teubner, 1927.
———. *The Myth of the State.* New Haven: Yale University Press, 1946.
———. "Paul Natorp." *Kant-Studien* 30 (1925): 273–98.
———. *Die Philosophie der symbolischen Formen.* Part 1. Berlin: B. Cassirer, 1923.
———. *The Philosophy of the Enlightenment.* Translated by Fritz C. A. Koelln and James P. Pettegrove. Boston: Beacon Press, 1958.
———. *Die Platonischen Renaissance in England und die Schule von Cambridge.* Leipzig: B. G. Teubner, 1932.
Cohen, Hermann. *Aesthetik des reinen Gefühls. System der Philosophie.* 2 vols. Berlin: B. Cassirer, 1912.
———. *Der Begriff der Religion.* Giessen: A. Töpelmann, 1915.
———. *Deutschtum und Judentum.* Giessen: Von deutscher Zukunft, 1915.

————. "Einleitung." *Geschichte des Materialismus,* by F. A. Lange, 10th ed. Leipzig: Friedrich Brandstetter, 1921.

————. *Ethik des reinen Willens.* 2d ed. Berlin: B. Cassirer, 1907.

————. "Friedrich Albert Lange: Nachruf." *Preussische Jahrbücher* 37 (1876): 353–86.

————. *Kants Begründung der Ethik.* Berlin: Ferdinand Dümmlers, 1887.

————. *Kants Theorie der Erfahrung.* Berlin: Dümmlers Verlagsbuchhandlung, 1871.

————. "Zur Kontroverse zwischen Trendelenburg und Kuno Fischer." *Zeitschrift für Völkerpsychologie und Sprachwissenschaft* 7 (1871): 249–71.

————. *Logik der reinen Erkenntnis.* Berlin: B. Cassirer, 1902.

————. "Mythologische Vorstellungen von Gott und Seele." *Zeitschrift für Völkerpsychologie und Sprachwissenschaft* 4 (1866): 396–434., and 5 (1867): 113–31.

————. "Die platonische Ideenlehre psychologisch entwickelt." *Zeitschrift für Völkerpsychologie und Sprachwissenschaft* 4 (1866): 403–64.

————. *Platons Ideenlehre und die Mathematik.* Marburg: Elwert, 1879.

————. *Die Religion der Vernunft aus den Quellen des Judentums* 2d ed. Frankfurt am Main: M. J. Kauffmann, 1929.

————. *Religion und Sittlichkeit.* Berlin: M. Poppelauer, 1907.

————. *Schriften zur Philosophie und Zeitgeschichte.* 2 vols. Berlin: Akademie-Verlag, 1928.

————. *Ueber das Eigentümliche des deutschen Geistes.* Berlin: Reuther and Reichard, 1914.

Eisner, Kurt. *Gesammelte Schriften.* 3 vols. Berlin: B. Cassirer, 1919.

————. *Schuld und Sühne.* Berlin: Neues Vaterland, 1919.

————. *Treibende Kräfte.* Berlin: Neues Vaterland, 1915.

————. *Unterdrücktes aus dem Weltkrieg.* Munich: G. Müller, 1919.

————. *Der Zukunftstaat: Der Junker Manteuffeleien gegen die Sozialdemokratie.* Berlin: T. Glock, 1904.

Fischer, Kuno. *Akademische Reden.* Stuttgart: Cotta, 1862.

————. *Anti-Trendelenburg.* Jena: Deistung, 1870.

————. *Die Apologie Meine Lehre.* Mannheim: n.p., 1854.

————. *Diotima. Die Idee des Schönen, philosophische Briefe.* Leipzig: R. Reclam, 1928.

————. *Franz Bacon von Verulam: Die Realphilosophie und ihr Zeitalter.* Leipzig: F. A. Brockhaus, 1856.

————. *Geschichte der neueren Philosophie.* 5th ed. 10 vols. Heidelberg: Carl Winter, 1912.

————. *Goethe-Schriften.* 3 vols. Heidelberg: C. Winter, 1890–1904.

————. *Das Interdict meiner Vorlesungen und die Anklage des Herrn Schenkel.* Mannheim: n.p., 1854.

————. *Kleine Schriften.* 2 vols. Heidelberg: C. Winter, 1892.

————. *Kritik der Kantischer Philosophie.* Munich: F. Bassermann, 1883.

———. *Lessing als Reformator der deutschen Literatur.* Stuttgart: Cotta, 1881.

———. *Der Philosoph des Pessimismus: Ein Charakterproblem.* Heidelberg: C. Winter, 1897.

———. *Schiller-Schriften.* 2 vols. Heidelberg: C. Winter, 1891–92.

———. *System der Logik und Metaphysik oder Wissenschaftslehre.* 2d ed. Heidelberg: C. Winter, 1889.

Lange, Friedrich Albert. *Die Arbeiterfrage: Ihre Bedeutung für Gegenwart und Zukunft.* 3d ed. Winterthur: Bleuler-Hausheer, 1875.

———. *Friedrich Albert Lange. Ueber Politik und Philosophie: Briefe und Leitartikel, 1862 bis 1875.* Edited by Georg Eckert. Duisburger Forschungen 10. Supplement. Duisburg: Walter Braun Verlag, 1968.

———. *Geschichte des Materialismus.* Iserlohn: J. Baedeker, 1866.

———. *The History of Materialism.* Translated by E. E. Thomas. 3d ed. London: Kegan Paul, 1925.

———. *J. S. Mills Ansichten über die sociale Frage.* Duisburg: Falk and Lange, 1866.

Liebmann, Otto. *Zur Analyse der Wirklichkeit.* Strassburg: Trübner, 1880.

———. *Gedanken und Tatsachen.* 3 vols. Strassburg: Trübner, 1899–1904.

———. *Kant und die Epigonen: Eine kritische Abhandlung.* Kant-Gesellschaft. Berlin: Reuther and Reichard, 1912.

———. *Klimax der Theorien.* Strassburg: Trübner, 1884.

———. *Ueber den objektiven Anblick.* Stuttgart: Teubner, 1869.

———. *Vier Monate vor Paris, 1870–1871. Belagerungstagebuch eines Kriegesfreiwilligen im Gardefusilierregiment.* 2d ed. Munich: C. H. Beck, 1896.

Lotze, Rudolf Hermann. *Geschichte der Aesthetik in Deutschland.* Munich: Cotta, 1868.

———. *Grundzüge der Aesthetik: Diktate aus den Vorlesungen.* 2d ed. Leipzig: S. Hirzel, 1888.

———. *Grundzüge der Psychologie: Diktate aus den Vorlesungen.* 2d ed. Leipzig: S. Hirzel, 1882.

———. *Logik.* Leipzig: S. Hirzel, 1883.

———. *Metaphysic.* Translated by Bernard Bosanquet. 2d ed. 2 vols. Oxford: Clarendon Press, 1887.

———. *Metaphysik: Drei Bücher der Ontologie, Kosmologie und Psychologie.* Leipzig: S. Hirzel, 1879.

———. *Microcosmus: An Essay Concerning Man and His Relation to the World.* Translated by E. Hamilton and E. Constance Jones. New York: Scribner and Welford, 1888.

———. *Mikrokosmus: Ideen zur Naturgeschichte und Geschichte der Menschheit.* 2d ed. 3 vols. Leipzig: S. Hirzel, 1872.

———. *Praktische Philosophie.* Leipzig: S. Hirzel, 1882.

———. *System der Philosophie.* 2 vols. Leipzig: S. Hirzel, 1874–79.

———. *Ueber den Begriff der Schönheit.* Göttingen: Vandenhoeck and Ruprecht, 1845.

————. *Ueber die Bedingungen der Kunstschönheit.* Göttingen: Vandenhoeck and Ruprecht, 1847.

Meinecke, Friedrich. *Die Deutsche Erhebung von 1914.* Berlin: Cotta, 1915.

————. "Die deutsche Freiheit." In *Die Deutsche Freiheit: Fünf Vorträge.* O. Harnach, O. Hintze, F. Meinecke, P. Sering, E. Troeltsch. Gotha: Friedrich Andreas Perthes, 1917.

————. *Erlebtes, 1862–1919.* Stuttgart: K. F. Koehler, 1964.

————. "Ernst Troeltsch und das Problem des Historismus." In *Schaffender Spiegel.* Stuttgart: K. F. Koehler, 1923.

————. *The German Catastrophe.* Translated by Sidney B. Fay. Boston: Beacon Press, 1963.

————. "Kausalitäten und Werte in der Geschichte." In *Staat und Persönlichkeit.* Berlin: E. S. Mittler, 1933.

————. *Das Leben des Generalfeldmarschalls von Boyen.* 2 vols. Stuttgart: Cotta, 1896–99.

————. *Machiavellism: The Doctrine of Raison d'État and Its Place in Modern History.* Translated by Douglas Scott. New Haven: Yale University Press, 1957.

————. *Strassburg, Freiburg, Berlin, 1901–1919: Erinnerungen.* Stuttgart: K. F. Koehler, 1949.

————. *Weltbürgertum und Nationalstaat.* 6th ed. Munich, Berlin: R. Oldenbourg, 1922.

————. *Werke.* 6 vols. Edited by Hans Herzfeld, Carl Hinrichs, and Walter Hofer. Munich: R. Oldenbourg, 1962–66.

Natorp, Paul. *Allgemeine Psychologie nach kritische Methode.* Freiburg: J. C. B. Mohr, 1888.

————. *Philosophie, Ihr Problem und Ihre Probleme: Einführung in den kritischen Idealismus.* Göttingen: Vandenhoeck and Ruprecht, 1911.

————. *Philosophie und Pädagogik.* Marburg: Elwert, 1909.

————. *Platons Ideenlehre: Eine Einführung in den Idealismus.* Leipzig: Felix Meiner, 1903.

————. "Recht und Sittlichkeit." *Kant-Studien* 18 (1913): 1–80.

————. *Religion innerhalb der Grenzen Humanität.* Tübingen: J. C. B. Mohr, 1908.

————. *Sozialpädagogik: Theorie der Willenserziehung auf der Grundlage der Gemeinschaft.* Stuttgart: Frommans Verlag, 1899.

————. *Der Tag des Deutschen: Vier Kriegsaufsätze.* Hagen: Otto Rippel, 1915.

————. *Vorlesungen über praktische Philosophie.* 2 vols. Erlangen: Verlag der philosophischen Akademie, 1925.

Rickert, Heinrich. "Vom Anfang der Philosophie." *Logos* 14 (1925): 121–63.

————. "Vom Begriff der Philosophie." *Logos* 1 (1910–11): 1–35.

————. "Das Eine, die Einheit, die Eins." *Logos* 2 (1911–12): 26–79.

————. "Die Erkenntnis der intelligibellen Welt und das Problem der Metaphysik." *Logos* 16 (1927): 162–204.

————. "Fichtes Atheismusstreit und die kantische Philosophie." *Kant-Studien* 4 (1900): 137–67.

———. *Der Gegenstand der Erkenntnis: Ein Beitrag zum Problem der philosophischen Transcendenz.* Freiburg: J. C. B. Mohr, 1892.

———. "Geschichtsphilosophie." In Wilhelm Windelband, ed. *Die Philosophie im Beginn des zwanzigsten Jahrhunderts.* Festschrift für Kuno Fischer. Heidelberg: C. Winter, 1907.

———. *Die Grenzen der naturwissenschaftlichen Begriffsbildung: Eine logische Einleitung in die historischen Wissenschaften.* Tübingen: J. C. B. Mohr, 1902.

———. *Die Heidelberger Tradition in der deutschen Philosophie.* Tübingen: J. C. B. Mohr, 1931.

———. *Kant als Philosoph der modernen Kultur.* Tübingen: J. C. B. Mohr, 1924.

———. *Kulturwissenschaft und Naturwissenschaft.* Tübingen: J. C. B. Mohr, 1921.

———. "Lebenswerte und Kulturwerte." *Logos* 2 (1911–12): 131–67.

———. "Max Weber und seine Stellung zur Wissenschaft." *Logos* 15 (1926): 222–61.

———. "Die Methode der Philosophie und das unmittelbare. Eine Problemstellung." *Logos* 12 (1923–24): 235–81.

———. "Objektwert und Subjektwert." *Logos* 4 (1913): 85–100.

———. *Die Philosophie des Lebens.* Tübingen: J. C. B. Mohr, 1921.

———. "Die philosophische Grundlagen von Fichtes Sozialismus." *Logos* 11 (1922–23): 148–81.

———. *Die Probleme der Geschichtsphilosophie.* Heidelberg: C. Winter, 1924.

———. *Science and History: A Critique of Positivist Epistemology.* Translated by George Reisman. Princeton: D. Van Nostrand, Inc., 1962.

———. *System der Philosophie.* Tübingen: J. C. B. Mohr, 1921.

———. "Vom System der Werte." *Logos* 4 (1913): 295–327.

———. "Zur Theorie der naturwissenschaftlichen Begriffsbildung." *Vierteljahrsschrift für wissenschaftlichen Philosophie* 18 (1894): 277–319.

———. "Thesen zum System der Philosophie." *Logos* 21 (1932): 97–103.

———. "Urteil und Urteilen." *Logos* 3 (1912): 230–51.

———. "Die Wetten in Goethes Faust." *Logos* 10 (1921–22): 123–62.

———. "Wissenschaftliche Philosophie und Weltanschauung." *Logos* 22 (1933): 37–99.

Stammler, Rudolf. *Die Lehre von dem richtigen Rechte.* Berlin: J. Guttentag, 1902.

———. *Die materialistische Geschichtsauffassung.* Gütersloh: E. Bartelsmann, 1921.

———. *Rechtsphilosophische Abhandlungen und Vorträge.* 2 vols. Charlottenburg: R. Heise, 1925.

———. *The Theory of Justice.* Translated by Isaac Husik. New York: Macmillan Company, 1925.

———. *Wirtschaft und Recht nach der materialistische Geschichtsauffassung.* 3d ed. Leipzig: Veit, 1914.

Troeltsch, Ernst. *Deutscher Geist und Westeuropa: Gesammelte kulturphilosophische Aufsätze und Reden.* Edited by Hans Baron. Tübingen: J. C. B. Mohr, 1925.

———. *Der Historismus und seine Probleme. Gesammelte Schriften.* 3 vols. Tübingen: J. C. B. Mohr, 1922, vol. 3.

———. "The Ideas of Natural Law and Humanity in World Politics." In O. Gierke. *Natural Law and the Theory of Society,* translated by Ernest Barker. Boston: Beacon Press, 1957.

———. *Spektator-Briefe: Aufsätze über die deutsche Revolution und die Weltpolitik, 1918–1922.* Edited by Hans Baron. Tübingen: J. C. B. Mohr, 1924.

———. "Das stoisch-christliche Naturrecht und das moderne profane Naturrecht." *Historische Zeitschrift* 106 (1911): 264–81.

———. "Ueber den Begriff einer historischen Dialectik, Windelband, Rickert und Hegel." *Historische Zeitschrift* 109 (1919): 373–426.

Vorländer, Karl. *Der Formalismus der Kantischen Ethik in seiner Notwendigkeit und Fruchtbarkeit.* Inaugural dissertation. Marburg, 1893.

———. *Geschichte der Philosophie.* 2 vols. Leipzig: Felix Meiner, 1911, vol. 2.

———. "Goethe und Kant." *Kant-Studien* 23 (1918–19): 221–32.

———. "Goethes Verhältnis zu Kant in seiner historischen Entwicklung." *Kant-Studien* 2 (1898): 161–212.

———. *Immanuel Kant: Der Mann und das Werk.* 2 vols. Leipzig: Felix Meiner, 1924.

———. "Kant und der Sozialismus." *Kant-Studien* 4 (1900): 361–412.

———. *Kant und Marx: Ein Beitrag zur Philosophie des Sozialismus.* Tübingen: J. C. B. Mohr, 1911.

———. "Eine Neubegründung der Ethik auf Kantischer Grundlage." *Kant-Studien* 23 (1918–19): 444–55.

———. "Die neukantische Bewegung in der Sozialismus." *Kant-Studien* 7 (1902): 23–85.

———. "Rudolf Stammlers Lehre von richtigem Recht." *Kant-Studien* 8 (1903): 329–35.

———. "Eine Sozialphilosophie auf kantischer Grundlage." *Kant-Studien* 1 (1897): 197–216.

Weber, Max. *From Max Weber: Essays in Sociology.* Translated and edited by H. H. Gerth and C. Wright Mills. New York: Oxford University Press, 1958.

———. *Gesammelte Aufsätze zur Wissenschaftslehre.* Tübingen: J. C. B. Mohr, 1922.

———. *Gesammelte politische Schriften.* 2d ed. Tübingen: J. C. B. Mohr, 1958.

———. *Max Weber on the Methodology of the Social Sciences.* Translated and edited by E. A. Shils and Henry Finch. Glencoe, Illinois: Free Press, 1949.

———. "Der Sinn der Wertfreiheit in der soziologischen und ökonomischen Wissenschaften." *Logos* 7 (1917–18): 40–89.

Windelband, Wilhelm. *Einleitung in der Philosophie.* Tübingen: J. C. B. Mohr, 1903.

———. *Geschichte der abendländischen Philosophie in Altertum.* 4th ed. Munich: Beck, 1923.

———. *Geschichte der alten Philosophie.* 2d ed. Munich: Beck, 1894.

———. *Die Geschichte der neueren Philosophie in ihrem zusammenhange mit der all-*

gemeinen Kultur und den besonderen Wissenschaften. 5th ed. 2 vols. Leipzig: Breitkopf and Härtel, 1911.

———. *Geschichte der Philosophie.* Freiburg: J.C.B. Mohr, 1892.

———. *A History of Philosophy.* Translated by James Tufts. 2 vols. New York: Harper and Brothers, 1958.

———. "Kulturphilosophie und transcendentale Idealismus." *Logos* 1 (1910–11): 186–97.

———. *Kuno Fischer: Gedächtnisrede bei der Trauerfeier der Universität in der Stadthalle zu Heidelberg.* Heidelberg: C. Winter, 1907.

———. *Lehrbuch der Geschichte der Philosophie.* 3d ed. Tübingen and Leipzig: J. C. B. Mohr, 1903.

———. "Noch hundert Jahren." *Kant-Studien* 9 (1904): 5–21.

———. "Otto Liebmanns Philosophie." *Kant-Studien* 15 (1910): iii–xi.

———. *Präludien: Aufsätze und Reden zur Einleitung in die Philosophie.* Tübingen and Leipzig: J. C. B. Mohr, 1903.

———. *Präludien.* 3d ed. 2 vols. Tübingen: J. C. B. Mohr, 1907.

Zeller, Eduard. *David Friedrich Strauss in seinem Leben und seinem Schriften.* Bonn: E. Strauss, 1874.

———. *Friedrich der Grosse als Philosoph.* Berlin: Weidmann'sche Verlag, 1886.

———. *Geschichte der deutschen Philosophie seit Leibniz.* 2d ed. Munich: R. Oldenbourg, 1875.

———. *Kleine Schriften.* 3 vols. Berlin: G. Reimers, 1910–11.

———. *Die Philosophie der Griechen in ihrer geschichtlichen Entwicklung.* 6 vols. Leipzig: O. R. Reisland, 1903–22.

———. *Platonische Studien.* Tübingen: T. Osiander, 1839.

———. *Staat und Kirche: Vorlesungen an der Universität zu Berlin.* Leipzig: Fues, 1893.

———. "Ueber die Freiheit des menschlichen Willens, das Böse und die moralische Weltordnung." *Theologische Jahrbücher* 5 (1846–47): 28–29, 191–258.

———. *Vorträge und Abhandlungen.* Second collection. 3 vols. Leipzig: Fues, 1887.

Secondary Works, Articles and Other Sources

Aliotta, A. *The Idealistic Reaction Against Science.* Translated by Agnes McCaskill. New York: Macmillan Company, 1914.

Anderson, Eugene N. *The Social and Political Crisis in Prussia, 1858–1864.* New York: Octagon Books, 1968.

Angel, Pierre. *Eduoard Bernstein et l'évolution de socialisme allemande.* Paris: Marcel Didier, 1961.

Antoni, Carlo. *From History to Sociology.* Translated by Hayden V. White. Detroit: Wayne State University Press, 1959.

Aron, Raymond. *La philosophie critique de l'histoire: Essai sur une theorie allemande de l'histoire.* Paris: Librairie Philosophique J. Vrin, 1950.

Baron, Samuel H. *Plekhanov. The Father of Russian Marxism.* Stanford: Stanford University Press, 1963.

Barth, Paul. *Die Philosophie der Geschichte als Soziologie.* 2d rev. ed. Leipzig: O. R. Reisland, 1915.

Bauch, Bruno. "Kuno Fischer." *Kant-Studien* 12 (1907): 269–72.

Bauer, Wolfram. *Wertrelativismus und Wertbestimmheit im Kampf um die Weimarer Demokratie.* Beiträge zur Politischen Wissenschaft 3. Berlin: Duncker und Humblot, 1968.

Bebel, August. *Aus Meinem Leben.* Berlin: J. H. W. Dietz, 1946.

Beck, Lewis White. "Neo-Kantianism." *The Encyclopedia of Philosophy* 5 (1967): 468–73.

Bendix, Reinard. *Max Weber, an Intellectual Portrait.* Garden City, N.Y.: Doubleday Anchor Books, 1962.

Berdayev, Nicholas. "Friedrich Albert Lange und die kritische Philosophie in ihren Beziehungen zum Sozialismus." *Die Neue Zeit* 18 (1899–1900): 132–40, 164–74, 196–207.

Bergsträsser, Ludwig. *Geschichte der politischen Parteien in Deutschland.* 11th ed. Munich: Günter Olzog Verlag, 1965.

Bochenski, I.M. *Contemporary European Philosophy.* Berkeley: University of California Press, 1956.

Böhm, Franz, "Die Philosophie Heinrich Rickerts." *Historische Zeitschrift* 128 (1933): 1–33.

Brecht, Arnold. *Political Theory: The Foundations of Twentieth-century Political Thought.* Princeton: Princeton University Press, 1959.

Broch, Werner, *An Introduction to Contemporary German Philosophy.* Cambridge: Cambridge University Press, 1935.

Chelius, Franz. *Lotzes Wertlehre.* Erlangen: Junge und Sohn, 1904.

Collingwood, R. G. *The Idea of History.* New York: Oxford Galaxy Books, 1957.

Copleston, Frederick. *A History of Philosophy.* 7 vols. Garden City, N.Y.: Doubleday Image Books, 1965, vol. 7, parts 1 and 2.

Dahrendorf, Ralf. *Society and Democracy in Germany.* Garden City, N.Y.: Doubleday Anchor Books, 1969.

Dampier, Sir William Cecil. *A History of Science and Its Relations with Philosophy and Religion.* 4th rev. ed. Cambridge: Cambridge University Press, 1948.

Diels, Hermann. *Gedächtnisrede auf Eduard Zeller.* Abhandlungen der königlich-preussischen Akademie der Wissenschaften, philosophische-historische Klasse. Berlin, 1908.

Dilthey, Wilhelm. *Einleitung in die Geisteswissenschaften. Gesammelte Schriften.* 12 vols. Leipzig: Teubner, 1914–65, vol. 1.

Dussort, Henri. *L'École de Marbourg.* Edited by Jules Vuillemin. Paris: Presses Universitaires de France, 1963.

Eastwood, A. "Lotze's Antithesis between Thought and Things." *Mind,* n.s. 1 (1897): 305–24, 470–88.

Ellissen, Otto Adolf. *Friedrich Albert Lange: Eine Lebensbeschreibung.* Leipzig: Julius Baedaker, 1894.

Emerson, Rupert. *State and Sovereignty in Modern Germany.* New Haven: Yale University Press, 1928.

Eucken, Rudolf, Bruno Bauch. "Worte der Erinnerung an Otto Liebmann." *Kant-Studien* 17 (1912): 1–3.

Falckenberg, R. *Fechner und Lotze.* Geschichte der Philosophie in Einzeldarstellungen. Munich: Ernst Reinhardt, 1925.

———. "Aus Hermann Lotzes Briefen an Theodor und Clara Fechner." *Zeitschrift für Philosophie und philosophische Kritik* 111 (1897): 177–90.

———. *Lotzes Leben.* Stuttgart: F. Frommann, 1901.

———. "Zwei Briefe von Hermann Lotze an R. Seydel und E. Arnoldt." In W. Windelband, B. Erdmann, and H. Rickert, eds. *Sigwart-Festschrift.* Tübingen: J. C. B. Mohr, 1900.

Faust, August. "Heinrich Rickert." *Deutsche Vierteljahrsschrift für Literaturwissenschaft und Geistesgeschichte* 11 (1933): 329–40.

———. "Heinrich Rickert Nachruf." *Kant-Studien* 41 (1936): 207–20.

Friedrich, Carl J. *The Philosophy of Law in Historical Perspective.* 2d ed. Chicago: University of Chicago Press, Phoenix Books, 1963.

Gay, Peter. *The Dilemma of Democratic Socialism. Eduard Bernstein's Challenge to Marx.* New York: Columbia University Press, 1953.

Glatzer, Nahum U. *Franz Rosenzweig, His Life and Thought.* New York: Schocken Books, 1961.

Glockner, Hermann. *Heidelberger Bilderbuch: Erinnerungen von Hermann Glockner.* Bonn: H. Bouvier, 1969.

Goldmann, Lucien. *Immanuel Kant.* Translated by Robert Black. London: New Left Books, 1971.

Görland, Albert. "Hermann Cohens systematische Arbeit im Dienste des kritischen Idealismus." *Kant-Studien* 15 (1912): 222–51.

Gregor, Mary J. *Laws of Freedom in Kant: A Study of Kant's Method of Applying the Categorical Imperative in the Metaphysik der Sitten.* Oxford: Basil Blackwell, 1963.

Hallowell, John H. *The Decline of Liberalism as an Ideology with Particular Reference to German Politico-Legal Thought.* London: Kegan Paul, Trench, Trubner and Co., 1946.

Hamerow, Theodore. *Restoration, Revolution, Reaction: Economics and Politics in Germany, 1815–1871.* Princeton: Princeton University Press, 1958.

———. *The Social Foundations of German Unification 1858–1871: Struggles and Accomplishments.* Princeton: Princeton University Press, 1972.

Heidegger, Hermann. *Die deutsche Sozialdemokratie und die nationale Staat, 1870–1920.* Göttingen: Musterschmidt, 1956.

Heinemann, Fritz. *Neue Wege der Philosophie: Geist, Leben, Existenz.* Leipzig: Quelle und Meyer, 1929.

Helmholtz, Hermann. "Erkenntniss Theorie," *Wissenschaftliche Abhandlungen.* 2 vols. Leipzig: J. A. Barth, 1883, vol. 2, pp. 591–663.

————. *Vorträge und Reder.* 4th ed. Braunschweig: F. Vieweg und Sohn, 1896.

Hendel, Charles W., ed. *The Philosophy of Kant in Our Modern World.* New York: Liberal Arts Press, 1957.

Hofer, Walther, *Geschichtsschreibung und Weltanschauung.* Munich: R. Oldenbourg, 1950.

Höffding, Harald. *History of Modern Philosophy.* Translated by B. E. Meyer. 2 vols. New York: Harper Torchbooks, 1958.

Holborn, Hajo. "Die deutsche Idealismus in sozialgeschichtlicher Beleuchtung." *Historische Zeitschrift* 174 (1952): 359–417.

————. "Dilthey and the Critique of Historical Reason." *Journal of the History of Ideas* 11 (1950): 93–118.

————. *A History of Modern Germany.* 3 vols. New York: Alfred A. Knopf, 1959–1969.

Hook, Sidney. *From Hegel to Marx.* London: Victor Gollancz, 1936.

Hughes, H. Stuart. *Consciousness and Society: The Re-orientation of European Social Thought, 1890–1930.* New York: Alfred A. Knopf, 1958.

Hutchings, Patrick AE. *Kant on Absolute Value.* London: George Allen and Unwin, Ltd., 1972.

Iggers, Georg G. *The German Conception of History: The National Tradition of Historical Thought from Herder to the Present.* Middletown, Connecticut: Wesleyan University Press, 1968.

Jodl, Friedrich. "German Philosophy in the XIX Century." *The Monist* 1 (1890–91): 263–77.

Jones, Henry. *A Critical Account of the Philosophy of Lotze.* New York: Macmillan Co., 1895.

Jospe, Eva. "Hermann Cohen's Judaism: A Reassessment." *Judaism* 25 (Fall 1976): 461–73.

Kant, Immanuel. *Immanuel Kants Werke.* Edited by E. Cassirer. 10 vols. Berlin: B. Cassirer, 1922.

————. *Critique of Pure Reason.* Translated by J. M. D. Meiklejohn. New York: E. P. Dutton and Co., 1934.

————. *Kant's Critique of Practical Reason and Other Writings in Moral Philosophy.* Translated by Lewis White Beck. Chicago: University of Chicago Press, 1949.

————. *Fundamental Principles of the Metaphysic of Morals.* Translated by Thomas K. Abbott. Indianapolis, New York: Bobbs-Merrill Company, 1949.

Kaufmann, Erich. *Kritik der neukantischen Rechtsphilosophie.* Tübingen: J. C. B. Mohr, 1921.

Keck, Timothy Raymond. "Kant and Socialism." Ph.D. dissertation, University of Wisconsin, 1975.

Kelly, George Armstrong. *Idealism, Politics and History: Sources of Hegelian Thought.* Cambridge: Cambridge University Press, 1969.

Kinkel, W. "Karl Vorländer zum Gedächtnis." *Kant-Studien* 34 (1929): 1–6.

Klemperer, Klemens von. *Germany's New Conservatism: Its History and Dilemma in the Twentieth Century.* Princeton: Princeton University Press, 1957.

Koppelmann, W. "Lotzes Stellung zu Kants Kriticismus." *Zeitschrift für Philosophie und Philosopische Kritik.* 88 (1886): 1–46.

Kraushaar, Otto. "What James' Philosophical Orientation Owed to Lotze." *Philosophical Review* 47 (1938): 517–26.

Krieger, Leonard. *The German Idea of Freedom.* Boston: Beacon Press, 1959.

―――. "Kant and the Crisis in Natural Law." *Journal of the History of Ideas* 26 (April-June 1965): 191–211.

Kroner, Richard. "Anschauen und Denken. Kritische Bemerkungen zu Rickerts heterothetischen Denkprinzip." *Logos* 13 (1924–25): 90–141.

―――. *Kant's Weltanschauung.* Translated by J. E. Smith. Chicago: University of Chicago Press, 1956.

Kuntz, Paul Grimley, ed. Introduction to *Lotze's System of Philosophy* by George Santayana. Bloomington and London: Indiana University Press, 1971.

Labadz, Leopold, ed. *Revisionism: Essays on the History of Marxist Ideas.* New York: Frederick A. Praeger, 1962.

Landauer, Carl. *European Socialism: A History of Ideas and Movements from the Industrial Revolution to Hitler's Seizure of Power.* 2 vols. Berkeley: University of California Press, 1959.

Lehmann, G. "Kant im Spätidealismus und die Anfänge der Neu-Kantischen Bewegung." *Zeitschrift für philosophische Forschung* 17 (1963): 438–57.

Leisegang, H. *Deutsche Philosophie im XX. Jahrhundert.* Breslau: Ferdinand Hirt, 1928.

Levy, Heinrich. *Die Hegel-Renaissance.* Charlottenburg: R. Heise, 1927.

―――. "Paul Natorps Praktische Philosophie." *Kant-Studien* 31 (1926): 311–30.

Lilge, Friedrich. *The Abuse of Learning.* New York: Macmillan Company, 1948.

Lindheimer, Franz. *Hermann Cohen. Beiträge zur Geschichte und Kritik der neukantischen Philosophie.* Berner Studien zur Philosophie und ihrer Geschichte, 1st series. Bern: Sturzenegger, 1900.

Lindsay, T. M. "Hermann Lotze." *Mind* 1 (1876): 363–81.

Lübbe, Hermann. *Politische Philosophie in Deutschland: Studien zu ihrer Geschichte.* Basel: Benno Schwabe, 1963.

Lütgert, Karl. *Die Religion des deutschen Idealismus.* 3 vols. Hütersloh: C. Bertelsmann, 1925.

Maerker, Peter, *Die Aesthetik der Südwestdeutschen Schule.* Bonn: Bouvier Verlag Herbert Grundmann, 1973.

Marks, Harry J. "The Sources of Reformism in the Social Democratic Party of Germany." *Journal of Modern History* 11 (1939): 334–56.

Masur, Gerhard. *Prophets of Yesterday: Studies in European Culture, 1890–1914.* New York: Harper Colophon Books, 1966.

Mandelbaum, Maurice. *The Problem of Historical Knowledge.* New York: Liveright Publications, 1938.

Mayer, Gustav. "Die Trennung der proletarischen von der bürgerlichen Demokratie in Deutschland (1863–1870)." *Archiv für Geschichte des Sozialismus und der Arbeiterbewegung* 2 (1911–1912): 1–68.

Mehring, Franz. "Aus der Frühzeit der deutscher Arbeiter Bewegung: F. A. Lange, J. B. von Schweitzer, W. Liebknecht und A. Bebel." *Archiv für die Geschichte des Sozialismus und der Arbeiterbewegung* 1 (1910–11): 101–33.

———. *Die Deutsche Sozialdemokratie.* 3d. ed. Bremen: Schunemanns, 1879.

Metzger, Wilhelm. *Gesellschaft, Recht und Staat in der Ethik des deutschen Idealismus.* Edited by Ernst Bergmann. Heidelberg: C. Winters Universitätsbuchhandlung, 1917.

Meyer, A. *Ueber Liebmanns Erkenntnis Lehre und ihr Verhältnis zur Kantischen Philosophie.* Inaugural dissertation. Jena, 1916.

Meyer, Hans. *Geschichte der abendländischen Weltanschauung.* 5 vols. Würzburg: Ferdinand Schoeningh, 1949.

Mitchell, Allan. *Revolution in Bavaria, 1918–1919.* Princeton: Princeton University Press, 1965.

Mommsen, Wolfgang. *Max Weber und die deutsche Politik, 1890–1925.* Tübingen: J. C. B. Mohr, 1959.

Moog, Willy. *Die deutsche Philosophie des zwanzigsten Jahrhunderts.* Stuttgart: Ferdinand Enke, 1922.

Mosse, George. *Germans and Jews. The Right, the Left, and the Search for a "Third Force" in Pre-Nazi Germany.* New York: Grosset and Dunlap, 1970.

Nagel, Ernst. "The Logic of Historical Analysis." *The Scientific Monthly* 74 (1952): 162–69.

O'Boyle, Lenore. "The Middle-Class in Western Europe, 1815–1848." *American Historical Review* 71 (1966): 826–46.

Palmer, Richard G. *Hermeneutics: Interpretation Theory in Schleiermacher, Dilthey, Heidegger, and Gadamer.* Evanston, Illinois: Northwestern University Press, 1969.

Passmore, John. *A Hundred Years of Philosophy.* London: Gerald Duckworth, 1957. Paperback edition: Penguin Books, 1969.

Pflanze, Otto. *Bismarck and the Development of Germany: The Period of Unification 1815–1871.* Princeton: Princeton University Press, 1963.

Picard, Maurice. *Values, Immediate and Contributory, and Their Interrelation.* New York: New York University Press, 1920.

Pois, Robert. *Friedrich Meinecke and German Politics in the Twentieth Century.* Berkeley and Los Angeles: University of California Press, 1972.

Rand, Calvin G. "Two Meanings of Historicism in the Writings of Dilthey, Troeltsch and Meinecke." *Journal of the History of Ideas* 25 (1964): 503–19.

Reiss, Hans, ed. Introduction to *Kant's Political Writings.* Cambridge: Cambridge University Press, 1971.

Ringer, Fritz K. *The Decline of the German Mandarins: The German Academic Community, 1890–1933.* Cambridge, Mass.: Harvard University Press, 1969.

Rohr, Donald G. *The Origins of Social Liberalism in Germany.* Chicago and London: The University of Chicago Press, 1963.

Rosenberg, Arthur. *Imperial Germany: The Birth of the German Republic.* Translated by Ian F. D. Morrow. Boston: Beacon Press, 1964.

Rotenstreich, Nathan. *Jewish Philosophy in Modern Times: From Mendelssohn to Rosenzweig.* New York: Holt, Rinehart and Winston, 1968.

Ruggiero, Guido de. *The History of European Liberalism.* Translated by R. G. Collingwood, Boston: Beacon Press, 1959.

Saage, Richard. *Eigentum, Staat und Gesellschaft bei Immanuel Kant.* Stuttgart, Berlin, Cologne, Mainz: Verlag W. Kohlhammer, 1973.

Schilpp, Paul. ed. *The Philosophy of Ernst Cassirer.* Evanston, Illinois: The Library of Living Philosophers, 1949.

Schiller, F. C. S. "Value." *Encyclopedia of Religion and Ethics* 12: 584–89.

Schnabel, Franz. *Deutsche Geschichte im neunzehnten Jahrhundert.* 3d ed. 4 vols. Freiburg im Breisgau: Verlag Herder, 1954.

Schorske, Carl E. *German Social Democracy 1905–1917: The Development of the Great Schism.* New York: John Wiley and Sons, Inc., 1965.

Schroeder, A. *Geschichtsphilosophie bei Lotze.* Leipzig: Friedrich A. Wilhelm, 1896.

Schwabe, Klaus. "Zur politischen Haltung der deutschen Professoren im ersten Weltkrieg." *Historische Zeitschrift* 193 (1961): 601–34.

Seeber, Gustav. *Zwischen Bebel und Bismarck: Zur Geschichte des Linksliberalismus in Deutschland 1871–1893.* Berlin: Akademie Verlag, 1965.

Sell, Friedrich C. *Die Tragödie des deutschen Liberalismus.* Stuttgart: Deutsche Verlags-Anstalt, 1958.

Shanahan, W. O. "Friedrich Naumann: A Mirror of Wilhelmian Germany." *Review of Politics* 13 (1951): 267–301.

Sontheimer, Kurt. *Antidemokratisches Denken in der Weimarer Republik: Die politischen Ideen des deutschen Nationalismus zwischen 1918 und 1933.* Munich: Nymphenburger, 1962.

Stern, Alfred. *The Philosophy of History and the Problem of Values.* The Hague: Mouton and Co., 1962.

Stein, Ludwig. *Philosophische Strömungen der Gegenwart.* Stuttgart: Ferdinand Enke, 1908.

Sterling, Richard W. *Ethics in a World of Power: The Political Ideas of Friedrich Meinecke.* Princeton: Princeton University Press, 1958.

Strauss, Leo. *Natural Right and History.* Chicago: University of Chicago Press, 1959.

Stumpf, Carl. "Zum Gedächnis Lotzes." *Kant-Studien* 22 (1918): 1–26.

Teggart, Frederick J. *Theory and Process of History.* Los Angeles: University of California Press, 1941.

Thomas, E. E. "Lotze's Relation to Idealism." *Mind* 24 (1915): 186–206, 367–85, 481–97.

Thomas, R. Hinton. *Liberalism, Nationalism and the German Intellectuals, 1822–1847.* Cambridge: W. Heffer and Sons, Ltd., 1951.

Trendelenburg, Adolf. *Kuno Fischer und sein Kant.* Leipzig: S. Hirzell, 1869.

Ueberweg, Friedrich. *Grundriss der Geschichte der Philosophie.* Edited by T. K. Oesterreich. 12th ed. 4 vols. Berlin: E. S. Mittler, 1912.

Vaihinger, Hans. "Zur Einführung." *Kant-Studien* 1 (1897): 1–8.

Vlachos, Georges. *La Pensée Politique de Kant: Metaphysique de l'ordre et dialectique du progrès.* Paris: Presses Universitaires, 1962.

Vuillemin, Jules. *L'Héritage Kantien et la révolution Copernicienne.* Paris: Presses Universitaires 1954.

Waltz, Kenneth N. "Kant, Liberalism, and War." *The American Political Science Review* 56 (June 1962): 331–40.

Weber, Marianne. *Max Weber: Ein Lebensbild.* Tübingen: J. C. B. Mohr, 1926.

Weber, Rolf. *Kleinbürgerliche Demokraten in der deutschen Einheitsbewegung, 1863–1866.* East Berlin: Rütten und Loening, 1962.

Wehler, Hans Ulrich. *Krisenherde des Kaiserreichs, 1871–1918.* Göttingen: Vandenhoeck and Ruprecht, 1970.

Weill, E.; Ruyssen, Th.; Villey, M.; Hassner, P.; Bobbio, N.; Beck, L. W.; Friedrich, C. J.; Polin, R. *La Philosophie Politique de Kant.* Annales de Philosophie Politique. Paris: Presses Universitaires 1962.

Wentscher, Max. *Hermann Lotze: Leben und Werke.* Heidelberg: C. Winter, 1913.

Whitney, G.D., and Bowers, David F. *The Heritage of Kant.* Princeton: Princeton University Press, 1939.

Willey, Thomas E. "The Back to Kant Movement and German Politics." *Proceedings. Indiana Academy of the Social Sciences* 2 (1967): 131–43.

Ziegler, Theobald. *Die geistigen und sozialen Strömungen des neunzehnten Jahrhunderts.* 14th ed. Berlin: Georg Bondi, 1911.

Ziekursch, Johannes. *Politische Geschichte des neuen deutschen Kaiserreichs.* 3 vols. Frankfurt am Main: Societäts-Drückerei, 1925.

Index

Thomas E. Willey, associate professor of history at McMaster University, received his B.A. degree from Butler University (1959) and his M.A. and Ph.D. degrees from Yale University (1965). He has published several articles in scholarly journals.

The manuscript was edited by Marguerite C. Wallace. The book was designed by Gary Gore.

The typeface for the text and display is Baskerville, designed by John Baskerville. The text is printed on S.D. Warren's "66" paper. The book is bound in Joanna Mills' Arrestox "A" linen over binder's boards. Printed in the United States of America.